My friend Caleb McAfee, has hit a home run with his book *Start Your Own Business*. This work is practical, specific, wise and filled with "how-to's." I am so appreciative of his work. This will help thousands do business in a positive, powerful and effective way.

—Dr. Ron Jenson, Chairman, Future Achievement International, author of *Make a Life, Not Just a Living*

Start Your Own Business is a thorough and detailed reference for the novice as well as the experienced business person. Most importantly, Caleb weaves a practical Biblical perspective on the day-to-day aspects of running a business. Think of *Start Your Own Business* as a hugh checklist for all the operational elements of a business you'll eventually need to know to succeed in business. Invest in this book, you'll earn dividends the first day you use it.

—Kevin W. McCarthy, author of *The On-Purpose Person* and *The On-Purpose Business*

What an important message you are delivering to those contemplating a calling in the business arena. Your material is clear, concise and compelling! Your suppositions are profound and I believe every Christian would be well served to study this material. Indeed, business is a calling and those who enter it, should do so with a sense of calling, not merely a desire to make more money. I want to commend you on the practical side of your teaching. It is up-to-date and highly relevant! If every Christian going into business were to first read your book and make a diligent effort to follow its no-nonsense approach to business, elevated by its Christian world view, there would be few, if any failures. May God bless you in your efforts to lift up the name of Jesus in the lives of Christian business people, who are learning to function with excellence in the marketplace and be a witness to the nations!

—Michael Q. Pink, CEO Strategic Resource Institute, author of *The Bible Incorporated Into Your Life, Job and Business*

Start Your Own Business is an excellent blending of the spiritual and the practical aspects of a Christian owned business. It deals with, in a comprehensive way, the legal and governmental factors a new business owner must consider as well as the daily management considerations such as planning, strategy and gauging results. Yet, in every step, it so successfully builds the basis for these decisions upon the wisdom and ethics of the Holy Bible. This is an excellent book by a man who practices what he teaches.

—Eugene Pleasant, CPA

Caleb McAfee's *Start Your Own Business* is a must for Christians who desire to excel in their business and professional lives. This book is written by a believer for believers. Every business principle is supported by Scripture. You can't go wrong with this book. It is truly a "bible" for anyone desiring to begin a business that will last.

—Dr. J. Don George, Pastor, Calvary Temple, Irving, Texas

To start and build a business of their own is the dream of countless people in the land of opportunity. Without the benefit of wise counsel from someone who has "been there, done that," that dream too often turns into a personal and financial nightmare. This practical step-by-step guide helps the would-be entrepreneur avoid the pitfalls and seize the opportunities and rewards of business ownership.

—Tom Norfleet, President/CEO Natural efx

Caleb walks his talk. I have never met a man who has the business genius with such spiritual commitment. He has given us the book that puts God's laws and principles together for our business success. Every business person needs to read it.

—Terry Daugherty, DDS

The information contained in Caleb McAfee's book, *Start Your Own Business,* is the finest, most practical, step-by-step instructions I have ever read. These are biblical principles and methods that I have used to build my business. I highly recommend this book to anyone who desires to build the Kingdom of God by building a successful business.

—John Mills, President/CEO Destiny Insurance Services, Inc.

Our small publishing company is almost seven years old and I not only used *Start Your Own Business* when we did our start up, but I have used it as a reference many times over the years. This book should be mandatory reading for anyone considering starting a business.

—Murray Fisher, Publisher, Longwood Communications

Start Your Own Business

A Step-by-Step Guide to Successfully Starting and Operating a Profitable Business Based Upon Biblical Principles

Caleb McAfee

*On*Course Communications • P.O. Box 153989 • Irving Texas 75015-3989

For information about keynote
addresses, seminars
and resource material by
Caleb McAfee
write or call:

Caleb McAfee
P. O. Box 153989
Irving, Texas 75015-3989
(972) 438 1234

***

Scriptures, unless otherwise noted, are from the New International Version. (Copyright 1973, 1978, 1984 International Bible Society. Used by permission of Zondervan Bible Publishers.) Other Scriptures noted as TLB are from The Living Bible, Paraphrased. (Wheaton, Tyndale House, 1971)

ACKNOWLEDGMENT

Profound thanks to Mary—my loving wife, my best friend and my capable business partner. Since our marriage in 1961 she has been a helpmeet in the strictest sense of the word. Through these years she has valiantly stood by my side through every business venture and continues to do so as a co-laborer with Him in this teaching ministry. Believe me when I say, this book would not exist without her.

Thank you Mary McAfee. What a awesome gift of God you are to me!

TABLE OF CONTENTS

TABLE OF CONTENTS

TABLE OF CONTENTS

TABLE OF CONTENTS

TABLE OF CONTENTS

TABLE OF CONTENTS

TABLE OF CONTENTS

TABLE OF CONTENTS

Table of Contents

PREFACE

For millennia the Bible has served as a source of inspiration to millions. People around the world turn to it for *spiritual* guidance. Today, thousands are discovering the Holy Scripture also deals with the *practical* issues of life— marriage, child rearing, physical health, investing and business success. *Start Your Own Business* is about how to start and/or operate a business based upon the timeless business principles taught in God's Word.

From biblical times to today Jewish people have taught their children the Holy Scriptures—the Torah, the Prophets and Proverbs. Consequently many grow up to become financiers, industrialists, wholesalers, retailers and business owners. Throughout history their successes have been legendary. But the Law, the Prophets and Proverbs is a part of the Christian's heritage too. It is time that Christians rediscover business from a biblical perspective and recognize what Jesus taught—that business can be an important way to build the kingdom of God on earth.

As you read this book I believe you will be amazed how much the Bible says about business practices, especially how much Jesus has to say about it. Learning these principles and governing your affairs by them puts powerful forces into motion that can guide you on the road to business success. Indeed these principles will be the governing foundation, but this book will also deal with the practical steps you must take to build upon that foundation.

David pointed out:

> Your words are a flashlight to light the path ahead of me and keep me from stumbling.
>
> Psalm 119:105 (TLB)

Notice how the above verse is set apart from the rest of the text. This is the way Scripture will be treated in this book. Do not race over these passages. Read each one attentively, stopping to reflect and meditate on it. You'll discover that the Scriptures offer the master key to business success that can open every door you need opened and keep you from failure.

Look at Jesus' incredible assertion:

> If you remain in me and my words remain
> in you, ask whatever you wish, and it will
> be given you.
>
> John 15:7

That promise almost unbelievable, isn't it? Once you learn God's ways and conduct your affairs accordingly, your future is virtually unlimited! You can ask what you will! But remember this incredible promise is specifically addressed to those who have His words remaining, abiding and living *in* them.

Let's now begin your step-by-step journey to successfully start and operate your profitable business by doing it GOD'S WAY.

CHAPTER 1 | BUSINESS AS A CALLING

What you will find in this book is not mere theory. If you will learn and apply the strategies you are about to read and if you will make these biblical principles of success the operating policies of your new or existing business, you will set into motion the powerful laws of success that will inevitably produce a bountiful harvest for you. I use the word "harvest" because the purpose of this book is to help you *grow* a business.

To grow a thriving business you must plant seed. Page by page you will be assisted in properly preparing the soil and selecting the right kinds of seed. You will be guided step-by-step in the planting process and finally you will learn how to reap and enjoy an abundant harvest.

> A man's harvest in life will depend entirely on what he sows.
>
> Galatians 6:7 (Phillips Translation)

Today far more Christians are employees than are self-employed. Many people pray for increase but frankly they leave God little room to answer that prayer. Modern day employment tends to foster dependency upon a job to provide daily bread, health care and retirement. It is easy to fall into a comfort zone of dependency that will barely provide the costs of existing on Planet Earth and provide little, if any, seed for increase.

When the Apostle Paul ministered in the churches he founded in the first century, he taught those early Christian believers the practical steps to self sufficiency. In a letter to one of those churches, Paul reminded them of the principles he had emphasized when he had been with them:

> Make it your ambition to...mind your own business and to work with your hands, just as we told you...so that you will not be dependent on anybody.
>
> I Thessalonians 4:11,12

In their attempt to protect labor, many trade unions have foisted upon management a formula for promotion based upon seniority. Pay increases are generally based upon how long a person has been employed, not necessarily upon productivity. Certainly God can do anything, but in order for him to bless a person in such a position, he would have to circumvent the whole corporate system. Besides, as an employee, income is usually remunerated based upon an hourly scale. There is a physical limit to the number of hours a person can work.

Wealth Through Business

Wealth is created primarily through business. Annually *Forbes Magazine* publishes a list of the richest Americans. In a recent list of the sixty-four individuals or families with a net worth of one billion dollars or more, there were only nine whose wealth came through inheritance. Among those who inherited their wealth are the Rockefellers, the Hunts and the G.P. Gettys.

Most of the others on the list started from scratch and built businesses. Men like Bill Gates, a Harvard dropout who with another college dropout, Paul G. Allen, co-founded Microsoft Corporation. Today both men are multi-billionaires, Gates being the richest man in America today.

Also on the list are Richard DeVos and Jay van Andel who started Amway Corporation in their basements after running a drive-in restaurant.

H. Ross Perot is on the list. He borrowed $1,000 to start his electronic information technology company, EDS. Also there are David Packard and Bill Hewlett. They used $538 to begin their computer company, Hewlett-Packard, in a garage.

Not one of those listed on the "Forbes 400" list made his enormous wealth working for someone else. Today God is raising up a new breed of financial leaders, empowering them to create wealth through business. This new breed sees wealth, not as an end to be sought after, but as a tool to do the work of God. They are "anointed" for business.

Inversion
of Wealth

Today more and more Christians are discovering the biblical teaching about the inversion of the wealth of the wicked to its rightful owners, the righteous, as taught in Proverbs 13:22. How is such an inversion to take place?

Many Christians are believing for it, confessing it daily, but they don't have a clue how it will be implemented. Surely they can't believe the bank's computer will mysteriously add a few zeros to their balance, can they?

Could it be that the transference of wealth will be accomplished through Christians being involved in business? Billions of dollars are currently in the hands of godless businesses, drug lords and corrupt organizations whose hidden agenda is to purge God from this planet. Today God is anointing men and women to go into business, plunder the wealth of the sinner and use the spoils for the kingdom of God and his righteousness.

I have attempted to write this book in such a way that it will meet you at the level of your faith. Some readers may be believing God for the level of independence a small retail business can provide. Others are going for Satan's jugular vein and are believing God for a multi-national business that will produce millions of dollars in revenue.

Remember, Jesus promised:

> Everything is possible for him who believes.
>
> Mark 9:23

Why Go Into Business?

Why should a Christian go into business? Surely not for the same reasons an unbeliever would. An unbeliever may go into business for purely selfish reasons such as to create financial independence or to attain power, status and recognition.

For the believer, the only valid reason to start a business is because you sincerely believe God is directing you to do so.

You must be convinced it is His will and that your business will exist for his glory and enable you to more effectively serve the Lord.

In the Holy Scripture, from the Old Testament patriarchs to the disciples Jesus chose, we find men of faith who were self-employed entrepreneurs.

Remember that the father of our faith, Abraham, was a prosperous rancher. Peter was a commercial fisherman. They were businessmen.

Called Into
Business

More and more Christian entrepreneurs claim to have a "calling" to be in business. A calling is not reserved for spiritual endeavors alone. How can you differentiate between the spiritual and secular anyway? It is not that one is spiritual and the other is not. Both are spiritual. God is raising up servants "ordained" to be in business. A business can be a powerful means of doing good and spreading the Word of God.

As profit is generated, God's work can be funded. A business can be an effective vehicle not only to meet your own needs and the needs of employees, stockholders, suppliers, landlords and even creditors, but a means of underwriting world evangelization.

Paul reasons:

> How can they [the world's masses] hear without someone preaching to them? And how can they preach unless they are sent?
>
> Romans 10:14,15

I once heard a man refer to a business as a "Christian business." Technically there is no such thing. I believe he meant to say that it was a business owned by a Christian and operated on biblical principles.

That is what this book is about—how you as a Christian can successfully start a business and profitably operate it on biblical principles and thereby achieve your destiny in Christ.

God's Purpose for Granting Wealth

Why is God calling men and women today into the business arena and teaching them how to prosper? Moses clearly reveals the purpose behind God giving a person the power or ability to create wealth.

> But remember the Lord your God, for it is he who gives you the ability to produce wealth, and so confirms his covenant, which he swore to your forefathers, as it is today.
>
> Deuteronomy 8:18

What covenant? What forefathers? The above verse refers back to Abraham and God's pronouncement to him in Genesis.

> I will make you into a great nation and I will bless you; I will make your name great, and you will be a blessing.
>
> Genesis 12:2

It's our covenant too. Through faith we can be a blessing. Paul reminds us:

> He redeemed us in order that the blessing given to Abraham might come to the Gentiles through Christ Jesus. If you belong to Christ, then you are Abraham's seed and heirs according to the promise.
>
> Galatians 3:14,29

Those who clearly recognize this biblical purpose are usually entrusted with more and more power and ability. This power and ability is to produce an ever-increasing cash flow to finance the spreading of the gospel around the world.

It is noteworthy that in Deuteronomy 8:18 (see previous page), God does not directly give wealth per se. Notice that he promises to give the *ability* or *capacity* to produce wealth.

As you read this book, expect God to begin enhancing your abilities, revealing creative solutions and marketing ideas that will produce wealth.

Many business failures are a result of lack of ideas and inspired solutions.

> The plans [ideas] of the diligent lead to profit.
>
> Proverbs 21:5

God is not trying to hide these ideas from you but to reveal them.

> I am the Lord your God you teacheth thee
> to profit, which leadeth thee by the way
> thou shouldest go.
>
>   Isaiah 48:17,18 (KJV)

Again, God does not give the profit per se. He promises to teach you *how* to profit. This harmonizes perfectly with a phrase in the well-known passage from the Book of Joshua.

> For then *thou* shalt make thy way
> prosperous...
>
>   Joshua 1:8 (KJV)

God Owns Everything

It is vital to recognize that we and everything we do and have belongs to God. The business he may be calling you to begin will be his. He must have check writing privileges. It must be for his glory. Look upon the business as a vehicle not only to fund the gospel but to represent Christ to the marketplace—to be a blessing.

It is a mistake to lose sight of the underlying purpose in business and producing wealth. Satan wants to divert your attention away from God's purpose.

The Psalmist warned:

> Though your riches increase do not set
> your heart on them.
>
>   Psalm 62:10

Remember what Jesus identified as the proper pursuit of our life.

> But seek first his kingdom and his righteousness and all these things will be added to you.
>
> Matthew 6:33

Jesus promised that if we make his kingdom and his "right way of doing things" the foremost pursuit of our lives, then, as a by-product, the very things the world pursues and seldom attains to any degree of satisfaction, will be given to us.

Every office should have a plaque that reads:

The Top Priority
is to Keep
the Top Priority
the Top Priority
© Caleb McAfee

Bob Edmiston's Example

Bob Edmiston is an inspiring example of a Christian businessman. He is a distributor for Suburu, Isuzu and Hyundai cars in Great Britain. Edmiston's multi-million-dollar company, International Motors Group, is actually a conglomerate of 13 diverse businesses primarily involving vehicles.

It is reported that in 1989 his company grossed over $260 million producing a $40 million profit. Any shareholder would be delighted with such performance, but there are no shareholders. He owns the company, or more correctly stated, the Lord owns the company.

He says. "I believe God is interested in my business as long as my business is his business." He says that in his company he relies on prayer and an inward confirmation by the Holy Spirit before making any major decision.

According to an article in *Charisma Magazine* (August, 1990), in 1989 he donated nearly $4 million to missionary outreach in Eastern Europe and the Third World. He helps support 43 evangelists in Poland and 100 missionaries in the Philippines. He has started nine churches in India.

Edmiston says, "Money is not sinful. The kingdom of God needs it desperately." At one time in his life he considered going into full-time ministry, but he decided not to. He says, "Making money is what I do best. But it must be made for God's glory, not mine." No doubt, he is called to be in business.

Auntie Anne's Soft Pretzels

The story of Anne Beiler, founder of Auntie Anne's Soft Pretzels, is one unique to American business. You can savor her famous hand-rolled soft pretzels in major shopping malls across America. Raised in an Amish-Mennonite family, her first taste of entrepreneurship came at age 12 when she baked pies and cakes for her family to sell at area farmers' markets. At age 19, Anne married Jonas Beiler, a Lancaster, Pennsylvania native, who shared her commitment to faith and community service. From this setting emerges her inspiring story of success.

She was always a hard worker. In July 1987, while working as a waitress in Pennsylvania on weekdays, Anne managed a Maryland snack food booth on weekends. This is where Anne learned to twist hand-rolled soft pretzels. Within less than a year, trusting totally in God, Anne purchased a similar booth, sight unseen in Downingtown, Pennyslvania. She sold pizza, ice cream and soft pretzels. But it was the pretzels her customers wanted. Soon the soft pretzels and hand-squeezed lemonade were her only products. After refining the pretzel recipe to her own taste and selling as many as she could make, "Auntie Anne's Soft Pretzels" was born.

The transition from making soft pretzels to selling pretzel franchises has been part of Anne's personal growth as a business woman. Soon Auntie Anne's Soft Pretzels emerged as one of America fastest growing franchises. Anne considers her business opportunity as a growing, changing gift from God. She believes that managing the expansion of the business continues to be God's work for her. Her foundation of belief has meant putting others first and always sharing what she can. Anne's philosophy can be summoned up in a statement she makes, "You give to get, to give again."

Give she does. She and her husband provide the major funding of the Family Information Center, a free counseling service for families and marriages. The Center has helped many individuals and families, including those from the local Amish and Mennonite community.

Anne says that success is defined not so much in monetary gain but rather peace of mind and heart. She is just one of the many, many Christians who have started businesses.

Covenant
Transport

Each story serves as a source of inspiration. Some entrepreneurs operate mega businesses employing hundreds—men like David Parker, founder of Covenant Transport trucking. His pastor says this man seeks God's face daily. Each Covenant Transport 18-wheeler truck you see on the Interstate highways sends a message of what faith in God can do.

Of course not all Christian business men and women operate giant corporations. Some may be led to leave the comfort of a job with its dependable albeit low income to pursue a single man or woman operation, such as becoming a manufacturer's representative, graphic artist or photographer.

Achieving
Good Success

Doing what God has called you to do is good success. Success or failure should not be measured by sales volume or the number of employees only, but by whether or not a person is doing what God has called and anointed him or her to do. I know many people who have left jobs that barely enabled them to make ends meet. Their new businesses enable them to meet their own needs and to be a blessing to others. Even though their gross revenues will probably never be measured in millions of dollars, they are truly successful.

Desire and
Obedience

Once you have determined God has called you to be in business, a prerequisite for success is a burning desire to fulfill that calling. If you do not have this burning desire and intense drive, you should seriously question whether you should attempt to start a business. To succeed as an entrepreneur, two elements are required:

1. Intense desire mingled with faith—

> What things soever ye desire, believe that ye receive them and ye shall have them.
>
> Mark 11:24 (KJV)

2. Obedience to the laws of success—

These laws find their source in the "business handbook," the Holy Bible. The promise in Isaiah is.

> If you are willing [see Number 1 on the previous page] and obedient, you will eat the best from the land.
>
> Isaiah 1:19

If your motive for going into business is just to eat the best of the land, you will probably fail.

Serving Others— The Road to Success

Success will come as you tailor your products or services to satisfy human needs. The famous sales motivator, Zig Ziglar, a devoted follower of Jesus, says it this way, "You can have anything in life you want if you will just help enough people get what they want."

Jesus told his disciples:

> Whoever wants to become great among you must be your servant.
>
> Mark 10:43

What do you want men to do for you? Do you want them to make you a profit? Jesus sums up the Law and the Prophets when he said:

> So in everything, do to others what you would have them do to you.
>
> Matthew 7:12

The previous Scripture is sometimes referred to as the Golden Rule. To produce the gold of this rule it should be understood as, "Do *for* others what you would have them do *for* you." To reap benefits, you must serve by providing benefits. Your new company's profit will be ultimately dependent upon how efficiently your customers or clients are served.

Many of today's successful enterprises have found their market niche by being sensitive to a need that was not being adequately filled or not being satisfied at all.

Give More Than Expected

Stated in the simplest terms, all it really takes to be a striking success in any viable business is to always have your customers' or clients' best interests at heart; treat them with respect. Always give a lagniappe (meaning you must always give generous measure). Give them more than they expect.

> Do nothing out of selfish ambition or vain conceit, but in humility consider others better than yourselves. Each of you should look not only to your own interests, but also to the interests of others.
>
> Philippians 2:3,4

As Jesus taught in his Sermon on the Mount, go the extra mile (Matthew 5:41).

People can make you rich or keep you broke, depending on the way you serve them. Make people your special concern.

There are no unimportant customers, because there are no unimportant people.

The cardinal rule to increasing business profits is to increase service and value to others.

NOTES

CHAPTER 2 | THE CHRISTIAN ENTREPRENEUR

We are presently experiencing an entrepreneurial boom. What John Naisbitt wrote in his book, *Megatrends* is true; "We are shifting from a managerial society to an entrepreneurial society." In 1950, 93,000 new businesses were created. In 1990, over 900,000 were created. In 1995, the total number of part-time, home-based businesses hit 24.3 million, an increase of 2.1 million people from the year before, according to Link Resources Corporation, a New York City-based research and consulting firm. In 1996, nearly 3 million new businesses were created. That's over 8,000 a day.

Many big businesses are downsizing. Fortune 500 companies alone have laid off over 5 million employees in the last ten years. But today, there are millions of small businesses, many of which are home-based, thriving in America generating billions of dollars in revenues.

Operating your own business is a part of the American dream. If Americans start millions of businesses annually, imagine how many more must think about going into business for themselves; it represents freedom and much more money than most can expect from working for someone else.

"Small Business" Defined

Before we get more deeply involved in this subject, the term "small business" should be defined. Today there are about 22.56 million firms operating in the United States. More than 90% of them qualify under the U.S. Small Business Administration's (SBA's) definition of a small business.

Whether a business qualifies as small in the eyes of this government agency depends on the particular industry in which the firm operates. Under the SBA's definition the following are small businesses:

- Manufacturers with up to 1,500 employees

- Wholesale establishments with up to 500 employees with annual sales of up to $25 million

- Retail firms with yearly sales of up to $13 million

- Service companies with annual revenues of not more than $14.5 million

This gives you a new understanding of the word "small," doesn't it? Personally, I do not like the phrase, "small business." The phrase itself not only suggests diminutiveness but also suggests insignificance. No matter what size its revenues or payroll, a business must never be small in the eyes of the person who starts it.

The prophet Zachariah said:

> Do not despise the small beginning, for the eyes of the Lord rejoice to see the work begin.
>
> Zachariah 4:10

Small businesses are not small when you consider that they are responsible for 40% of the gross national product (GNP). Over 60% of the national work force is employed by small businesses.

Every Business Was Once Small

With the exception of corporate spin-offs, just about all of today's corporate giants were once small businesses. Seeds are small but they have the potential of producing a large harvest. Even the largest living thing by volume on Planet Earth, the giant Sequoia tree, began as a single tiny seed.

Jesus said:

> The kingdom of heaven is like a mustard seed which a man took and planted in his field. Though it is the smallest of all your seeds, yet when it grows it is the largest of garden plants.
>
> Mark 4:30-32

Any one of today's tiny, part-time, home-based businesses has the potential of becoming tomorrow's giant corporate conglomerate. That's why the government favors small business and created the SBA to "encourage, assist and protect the interests of small businesses."

In this book, we will use the following more restrictive definition of small business than the one used by the SBA:

- It will generally mean an independently owned and operated business of 30 or fewer employees.

- It could be a part-time business operated out of your home.

- It will refer to a company started with comparatively limited initial capital outlay.

- It will be a venture that falls into one of the following four categories:

  (a) manufacturing
  (b) wholesaling
  (c) retailing
  (d) service

Creativity And Innovation

Inc. magazine says, "Small businesses and medium-sized businesses are growing as never before. They are the sector that is creating the new ideas, the new products, the new jobs and the profits that are fueling our economic recovery."

This may be due to the flexibility and nimbleness of a small business contrasted to the often rigid policies of large, self-preserving corporations. Also, it's due to the fact that no one is saying it can't be done.

While the traditional mass marketers such as Kmart are taking a beating, small specialty firms that sell stylish leisure clothing at affordable prices, have zoomed ahead.

It is estimated that small businesses account for 24 times the production per dollar invested, as opposed to large businesses. To be a success, the small business operator must become creative and innovative.

Most successful entrepreneurs have a "can-do" attitude. In a sense the Christian can have an unfair advantage over an unbelieving entrepreneur—the anointing.

> I can do everything through him [Greek, *Christos*, meaning the anointed and his anointing] who gives me the strength.
>
> Philippians 4:11

However, as awesome as the anointing is, it will not make up for a lack of discipline. Most successful Christian entrepreneurs have discovered there is an inter-dependence between the anointing and discipline.

NOTES

CHAPTER 3 | *SHOULD YOU TAKE THE PLUNGE?*

"Should I go into business for myself?" This is a ponderous question only you can answer. Certainly, the rewards can be lucrative. But face it—sometimes just thinking about it is terrifying, isn't it?

Before going any further, consider what Jesus asked:

> Suppose one of you wants to build a tower. Will he not sit down and estimate the cost?
>
> Luke 14:28

There is a cost. You must pay a price for what you want in life and you must pay it up front. Sowing always precedes harvesting. The concept of any worthwhile achievement being easy will not appear in this book. As with everything worthwhile in life, the dividends you earn are in direct proportion to the contributions you make. Though starting a business is challenging and may even be terrifying, it can be the most rewarding step of your life.

Do It For The Right Reasons

Some Christians go into business for the wrong reasons, and as a consequence, many of them ultimately meet with failure and defeat. If a person is fiercely independent and goes into business to get out of the proverbial rat race and onto Easy Street, the motive is wrong.

Satan tempted Eve by persuading her to become her own boss. Even Christians can fall into that trap.

Jesus said:

> The one who received the seed that fell among the thorns is the man who hears the word, but the worries of this life and the deceitfulness of wealth choke it, making it unfruitful.
>
> Matthew 13:22

Faithfulness as another's employee is often a prerequisite for having your own business.

Jesus asked:

> If you have not been trustworthy with someone else's property, who will give you property of your own?
>
> Luke 16:12

You alone must determine if your desire to go into business is something God has placed in your heart or if it is a deceptive desire to be your own master, not taking orders from someone else. A consequence of taking joy in the Lord, is that God's will becomes your will.

The Psalmist David said:

> Delight yourself in the Lord and he will give you the desires of your heart.
>
> Psalm 37:4

**Being Employed
Has Benefits**

Before taking the plunge consider that working for someone else, in a nine-to-five job, is not all bad. Look at some of the advantages:

- It is much easier to control your budget if you know that every two weeks you are going to get a regular paycheck.

  Paul says:

  > Now when a man works, his wages are not credited to him as a gift, but as an obligation.
  >
  > Romans 4:4

- Your taxes are withheld for you.

- Often medical benefits are provided.

- There may be a profit-sharing plan you can participate in.

- Your employer may pay for educational expenses such as seminars and workshops.

- You can expect regular pay increases—at least a cost-of-living raise occasionally.

- You will generally work regular hours.

- When you are requested to work more than eight hours, you usually do so at overtime rates, unless you are in management.

- Your evenings and weekends may be free to enjoy with your family and friends in leisure activities.

- You usually get a paid vacation.

- The business always remains the ultimate responsibility of someone else.

Negative Aspects Of Self Employment

On the other hand, when you are in business for yourself:

- You may have to forget about the eight-hour workday and the carefree weekends, at least initially.

- You'll carry the whole responsibility on your shoulders.

- You'll have to fund any negative cash flow requirements. When you are in business for yourself, especially in the early months or even years, you probably will not be able to count on a regular income. Maybe no income! Instead of receiving money, you may be called upon to capitalize or fund your business.

- You will have to make all the decisions.

- You may have to perform chores you don't like.

- You will trade your single boss for a multiplicity of bosses—your customers or clients, your suppliers, your investors, your banker, your stockholders, etc.

But if you have the "calling," nothing I write will be able to dissuade you nor would I try.

The following are some evidences of a business calling:

- You have an unshakable inner sense that God has called you into business.

- You have an inner dissatisfaction about being an employee.

- You experience frustration when your ideas are ignored or if someone else takes credit for them.

- You have a general dissatisfaction about your job and an uneasy feeling that your future is in someone else's hands.

- You are convinced you can be a more effective servant of the Lord by being in business for yourself.

If you are willing to pay the price, the potential can be enormous. According to the IRS, 89% of individuals who earn over $50,000 a year are the owners of small businesses. Your income limit is directly related to what you *do* to earn it by providing products or services for customers.

It is the law of cause and effect. If you want to climb into the higher realms of income, usually there must first be some internal adjustments. You must believe the pathway is open to you, and believe there are no barriers such as heredity, race, gender or class restrictions. You must have an attitude of cheerful expectancy. You must have an unflappable "knowing" that success will be yours.

You will be leaving the paths of others who are content with the *status quo* to climb into the more rarefied realms of achievement and wealth. It will take time; it won't happen overnight. But think of it this way, the time will pass anyway, whether or not you pursue outstanding achievement.

Stop Thinking Ordinarily

The fact is, you are always moving in the direction of your dominant thoughts. You will ultimately become what you think about. Therefore, you must stop thinking in ordinary ways.

Ask yourself, "How can I provide enough service so that my rewards will add up to the financial goals God has put in my heart?"

The cutting away from the *status quo* has to begin in the mind and from the mind, find expression in the attitude. Many people are not willing to invest the hours and expend the energy it takes to successfully grow a business.

> A sluggard does not plant in season; so at harvest time he looks but finds nothing.
>
> Proverbs 20:4

Reasons for Business Failure

The Small Business Administration points out that only 15% of all small business operators and owners have attended a formal business school. Furthermore, 75% of small business operators have no previous business experience. It has been aptly said that education only costs once but ignorance costs over and over again.

According to Dunn & Bradstreet the major reason for small business failure is incompetence. It is not incompetence relating to the product or the service to be offered to the public. Usually the typical entrepreneur knows a great deal about his or her product—how to make donuts, how to lay concrete or design jewelry. The thing that typically leads to business demise is incompetence in the area of how to *run* a business.

Unfortunately, many who take the plunge into business don't invest the hours and effort needed to seek out the sources of information, wisdom and expertise required to develop competence.

> Buy the truth and do not sell it; get wisdom, discipline and understanding.
>
> Proverbs 23:23

Before taking the plunge consider the odds of failure. Many new businesses fail within their first six months of operation. Seventy-five percent of start-ups shut down within the first five years. These odds can be depressing. It makes you wonder how many businesses operating today will eventually fail or just give up trying? The great American dream often needlessly becomes the great American nightmare.

After you've read all these negative statistics, I hasten to add that your chances of success will be 93% to 95% if you can acquire the right knowledge and properly apply it.

> Make plans by seeking advice; if you wage war obtain guidance.
>
> Proverbs 20:18

Most businesses that fail are of the "fly-by-the-seat-of-their-pants" variety. These owners take unnecessary risks. They fail to plan. They just guess. They use the "crossed-finger theory" as their strategy. They don't learn by trial and error. Trial and "terror" is more indicative.

I suppose it would be possible to break the code of a combination lock by trial and error. But most would give up in despair long before random-choice luck would open the safe. How much easier if someone gives you the combination. You can get the combination numbers but it is not enough to just have the three numbers—you must have them in the right sequence.

Learn From Successful People

You can get counseling from retired executives for free. There is a division of the Small Business Administration called SCORE (Service Corporation of Retired Executives) that may be able to help you. It is staffed by over 12,000 volunteer, retired executives. SCORE also offers seminars in some areas of the country on the basics of business start-up. Check them out. Call 800-827-5722. Their internet homepage is: www://sba.gov.

If you don't have a burning desire, drive and dogged determination coupled with the persistence to seek out and learn the facts that lead to success in your given pursuit, you should seriously reconsider the advisability of going into business for yourself. The fact that you have invested in your future by acquiring this book demonstrates you may be willing to do what it takes to become a success.

In the early stages *you* are the business. You are its originator, energy and motivating force. The business's success depends entirely upon you. But just the proper attitude is not enough; nor is hard work. You must work hard, for sure, but work at the right things. You can work years and never discover the secrets that can make your business truly successful, or you can learn them quickly by following the methods used by other successful role models.

Are You A Risk Taker?

One of the first steps in evaluating whether you have what it takes to be in business for yourself is to determine if you are innately a risk taker. You must adopt a philosophy which accepts prudent risk as the price of opportunity and accepts the necessity of making errors as a part of the great learning process.

The deepest regrets come, not from recalling races we have run and lost, but from thinking about those contests in life that we have failed to enter. The "faint of heart" cling to the security of the salary that comes from a nine-to-five job.

The vast majority of business failures are not, as many would like to believe, the direct consequence of undercapitalization. To say that lack of cash flow is what causes business failure, is like saying that the chief reason for divorce is conflict—the key is to discover and deal with the source of the conflict.

In a new business, it is essential that the reason for lack of cash flow be ascertained and dealt with. For the most part, those business failures are the result of inexperience, poor management techniques and/or the lack of a well-thought-out business plan complete with written steps of action to reach preset goals.

To insure the survival of your new business, you must acquire a working knowledge of the basic principles of business, namely:

      (1) marketing
      (2) accounting
      (3) finances
      (4) taxes
      (5) "people skills" to deal with your public

Knowledge of these basics will greatly lessen the risks inherent in starting a small business.

Personal Qualifications

What are the personal qualifications needed to be a successful entrepreneur? They may be different than you think. If you have the qualities listed below, you will be more prone to overcome the immediate lack of plentiful start-up capital, inside connections, decades of experience and private backing.

Characteristics of the Successful Entrepreneur

1. A self-starter

2. Takes charge of things—a leader

3. Plans on paper before starting anything

4. Generally is an organized person

5. Gets along with and loves people

6. Enjoys helping people realize their potential

7. Stubborn—once the mind is made up is not easily dissuaded

8. Makes decisions quickly

9. Has a high energy level and takes health and vitality seriously

10. Disciplined; gets up early; exercises; will keep working as long as it takes to get a job done

11. Is not afraid of doing what most people dislike doing

12. Is "God-conscious" and looks to him for strength and guidance

13. Is self confident and remains optimistic in the face of challenges (what others call problems)

14. Has 'stick-to-itive-ness'; perseveres; follows through with a commitment

15. Is resourceful with an ability to handle things as they come up

16. Has a pronounced need to achieve

17. Is objective with an uncanny ability to see the whole picture

18. Has high self-esteem

19. Has a keen sense of humor and an ability to enjoy life

20. Is persuasive and believable

21. Is enthusiastic and puts 100% into everything he or she does

22. Maintains personal integrity at all costs

The Winning Attitude

The combination of these personal characteristics create what can be called the winning attitude. Such an attitude is a result of belief, motivation, imagination, action, enthusiasm and taking personal responsibility for his or her actions. Let's look at each of these essential qualities in greater depth.

Belief

In the book of Mark, Jesus made an incredible declaration:

> Everything is possible for him who
> believes.
>
> Mark 9:23

It is essential to have an unswerving faith in God's desire to bless you and to give you a bright future.

> "For I know the plans I have for you,"
> declares the Lord, "plans to prosper you
> and not harm you, plans to give you hope
> and a future."
>
> Jeremiah 29:11,12

It is also essential to believe in yourself and your God-given abilities and instincts. You shouldn't be proud of a gift (talent or ability) nor can you take credit for it, but you must take responsibility for it. To have this healthy belief in yourself will make you your own person without the need for someone else to tell you what to think. I define healthy self esteem as "seeing yourself as God sees you." He values you very highly!

A person who is always seeking external approval for his or her ideas and feelings will generally not overcome the obstacles of starting a business.

People who have what can be called a subjective "essence of belief" operating in their lives don't always flow with the crowd; they are not necessarily joiners. Often they must take the rejection that comes from being the lone dissenter in a group decision.

A person with the ability to stand alone does not always see rejection and criticism as a deterrent but as an incentive. Some would call this person stubborn but actually they have rock-solid willpower. The person who succeeds against all odds usually puts high demands on himself or herself. This person is accustomed to doing activities on his or her own.

This quality is quintessential if you are going to be your own boss. You will have to "boss yourself around." It's called self-discipline.

The Apostle Paul reminds Timothy:

> For God did not give us a spirit of timidity, but a spirit of power, of love and of self-discipline.
>
> 2 Timothy 1:7

Motivation

There is another quality that must be even stronger than your faith in yourself—motivation. Your motivation must be relentless. The successful entrepreneur has a deep-seated need, a craving that cannot be satisfied any other way. He or she has a calling to achieve, to create, to grow, to advance and to overcome.

The word motivation comes from the words "motive" and "action" or "movement." The motive must be a strong sense of direction (a goal) and the action must be an ability to always move in the direction of that goal. You chart your course by a goal and even if you do not reach it, you will be better as a result of setting it.

Inspired Imagination

There must be a keen inward witness of hearing God's voice. I call this "inspired imagination." It will empower you with an ability to take observations and information, twist it around, add to it and transform it into the next logical step. The step may not necessarily appear logical to others for some time.

> There is a way that seems right to a man, but in the end it leads to death.
>
> Proverbs 14:12

Successful entrepreneurs may have limited resources, but if they have inspired imagination, the limited resources won't be a problem for long. I've noticed that successful people don't dwell on the problems; their spirits are constantly postulating solutions. They have a certain level of curiosity even about areas in which they may not have had prior interest.

Seeing with the eyes of faith is a way to visualize how things can be different than they are now. To obtain solutions there must be a willingness to entertain seemingly improbable and impossible thoughts. People with highly developed faith are always searching for and finding fresh new ways to avoid the routine.

Action

The next essential quality is action. This is what separates the entrepreneur from the rest of mankind.

> Faith without works [corresponding action] is dead [ineffective].
>
> James 2:26

Unless you have the ability to act on your dreams and plans, they remain useless, idle daydreams. I've observed that most successful people make quick decisions, accepting the possibility that some of those decisions may be wrong. For example, at a restaurant, a successful person will probably take a short look at the menu and tell the waiter what he or she wants without much hesitation or deliberation. The quicker you are at decision-making, the easier it will be to deal with risk. A person can't just sit and think and have positive results. You must take action consistent with what you want.

> Whoever watches the wind will not plant;
> whoever looks at the clouds will not reap.
>
> Ecclesiastes 11:4

Enthusiasm

Next, those with the winning attitude will exhibit enthusiasm. The root from which the word enthusiasm is derived has the word God in it. It literally means to be filled with God (Greek: *Theos*). There is divine power in enthusiasm. It is easy to be enthusiastic once you recognize for Whom you are really working.

Paul told his workers:

> Whatever you do, work at it with all your heart [enthusiastically], as working for the Lord not for men.
>
> Colossians 3:23

Responsibility

And finally, those with the winning attitude take ultimate responsibility for their actions. Successful entrepreneurs know instinctively that they have no one to blame for a situation but themselves. They know no one is going to give them a hand gratuitously.

Paul says:

> Do not be deceived: God cannot be
> mocked. A man reaps what he sows.
>
> Galatians 6:7

From a human standpoint, success as a small business
operator is a "do-it-yourself" project. Your beliefs, thoughts,
decisions, conduct, theology, behavior and seeds planted or
not planted have created who you are, what you have or do
not have.

If the above qualities mirror you and your determination,
then you probably have the winning attitude. Take the leap.
You have what it takes to overcome the lack of experience
and money.

For this select, favored few, there is nothing as fulfilling or
rewarding as being in business. It should never be just the
financial potential to create substantial wealth that drives
you. To the Christian entrepreneur, money itself should not
be the predominant driving force.

What should drive high-achieving Christian entrepreneurs
is a sense of destiny and a powerful yearning to fulfill God's
plan for their lives. To the Christian who is called to do so,
being in business should be looked upon as the ultimate
means to maximize his or her potential as God's servant.

Being an entrepreneur affords the opportunity to develop
God-given creative ideas and make a worthwhile contribution to the kingdom of God as you fulfill your destiny.

Doing What
You Enjoy

Oh yes, it also allows you to stop "working." You read it right. One of my definitions of work is having to do something a person doesn't really want to do. Most business people I know put in long hours, not because they *have* to, but because they *want* to. It's enjoyable. They lose track of time. Work is fun and fun is work.

Each day is an exciting and fulfilling experience because you are doing what you enjoy most and because you feel you are in the center of God's will.

Resolve once and for all that you are called by God to be in business for yourself and that anything less is totally unacceptable, unthinkable and wholly out of the question.

If you're ready for the high adventure of entrepreneurship, WELCOME. Read on!

NOTES

CHAPTER 4 | THE FEMALE ENTREPRENEUR

As never before, females are becoming a part of the entre-preneurial boom, although from antiquity there have been women in business. In the Gospel of Luke we read of two women who financially supported Jesus and his staff. From what Luke wrote, we can reasonably conclude these women had private means, most likely from their own businesses.

> Joanna the wife of Cuza, the manager of Herod's household; Susanna; and many others. These women were helping to support them out of their own means.
>
> Luke 8:3

In the Book of Acts, Luke also mentioned a businesswoman who was a merchant of clothing.

> ...and a certain woman named Lydia, a dealer in purple cloth...
>
> Acts 16:14

Another New Testament example of a women in business was Dorcas. Read about her in Acts 9. Peter raised this manufacturer of garments from the dead.

In a few pages we will look at one of the most enterprising females of all time. The Holy Spirit prompted Solomon to include her story in the Book of Proverbs so she could serve as an inspiration and as a role model for women today.

Employment vs. Self-Employment

For a mother of small children, there is an enormous financial difference between being an employee and being self-employed. Taking into consideration the costs involved, such as child care and taxes, sometimes it does not make economic sense for some women to be employees. Let's look at the hard facts of the advisability or inadvisability of a woman working as an employee outside her home.

The form at the end of this chapter clearly demonstrates how a mother, earning close to minimum wage may be contributing very little help, if any, to the overall family finances considering the high cost of childcare, etc.

Even in cases where a woman earns substantially more than minimum wage, the effect of the additional income can push the family into another income tax bracket. For example, consider a family who is already in the 31 percent bracket (from $99,600-$151,750), the extra income the wife earns, say, $40,000, could bump them into the 36 percent bracket (from $151,750-$271,050). This means that much of the entire additional income generated by the working spouse will be taxed at 36 percent.

Furthermore, the more income a family makes, the less they will be allowed to take advantage of deductions such as medical expenses, casualty losses, rental losses, child care credit, IRA deductions, earned income credit and miscellaneous itemized deductions.

For a family in the maximum bracket (39.6 percent) living in a state with high state income tax rates, the additional income can be taxed as high as 50 percent or more. This can mean that her added income of $40,000 nets the family as little as $18,000-$20,000. If there is more than one child in child care, the picture looks even worse.

Benefits Of Self-Employment

The solution is for the wife to be a part of the family business or, if the husband is gainfully employed, to go into business for herself. The home-based business may allow her to spend more quality time with her children, even teaching them at home if she desires. At the same time, it can afford a possibility for unlimited income, potentially more than she would have had as an employee.

In addition to the lifestyle flexibility and income potential, she can now arrange for many of the same benefits traditional employees enjoy and get tax deductions for them too—such as retirement. If she works for her husband's small business, he can arrange a medical reimbursement program that will allow her to pay her family's health bill and fully deduct the expense.

Review Chapters 13 and 14 to understand more fully the powerful tax breaks her business can provide—automobile expense, travel and entertainment, being able to deduct up to $18,500 a year for office equipment like computers, answering machines, printers, fax modems, etc.

With tax breaks like these, even if she does not make as much as she would have had she been an employee, she may come out ahead.

And remember, we have dealt with just the figures. We have not factored in the psychological benefits of being self-employed or the aspects of unlimited income potential.

In the past some women were bound by sexist traditions that relegated their entrepreneurial ventures to professions such as making crafts, sewing, child care or maid services.

Today there are female business owners quite successful at writing, photography, graphic arts, mail order, export/import, sales training, financial planning, real estate developing—the list is endless, all operated successfully as a home based business.

The Proverbs 31 Woman

The Book of Proverbs ends with a graphic description of an exemplary self-employed wife. In Solomon's day, such a woman was rare. She ventured beyond the more traditional ideas of her day regarding women in business. As you read her story in the last chapter of Proverbs, look at the enormous contribution her home-based businesses produced for her and her family.

Follow as we examine several passages from her story. You will observe she was a very industrious woman and operated what we would call today a conglomerate of small businesses.

> A wife of noble character who can find?
> She is worth far more than rubies. Her
> husband has full confidence in her and
> lacks nothing of value. She brings him
> good, not harm, all the days of her life.
>
> Proverbs 31:10-12

Her first business is in the area of milling of wool and flax. She discovers she has an eye for value. She searches long and far for sources of raw materials she can buy wholesale to produce fabric for resale.

> She selects wool and flax and works with
> eager hands. She is like the merchant
> ships, bringing her food from afar. In her
> hand she holds the distaff and grasps the
> spindle with her fingers.
>
> Proverbs 31:13,14,19

Although she is involved in business, she takes steps to insure that her family is not neglected. She obviously is well adept at time management.

> She gets up while it is still dark; she pro-
> vides food for her family and portions for
> her servant girls.
>
> Proverbs 31:15

Out of the profits from her milling business she ventures into real estate and the agricultural business. Notice growth was underwritten internally, not from lenders or venture capitalists and that she puts her heart into her work.

> She considers a field and buys it; out of her earnings she plants a vineyard. She sets about her work vigorously; her arms are strong for her tasks.
>
> Proverbs 31:16,17

Unlike some business people today who don't know whether or not they are turning a profit, she keeps abreast of her progress. By spending time reviewing her profit and loss statements, she keeps a careful eye on the bottom line.

> She sees that her trading is profitable, and her lamp does not go out at night.
>
> Proverbs 31:18

One of the underlying secrets of her striking success is that she is a giver and a volunteer. By being careful to be generous and caring to the poor and needy she involves God in her finances. (See Proverbs 19:17.)

> She opens her arms to the poor and extends her hands to the needy.
>
> Proverbs 31:20

She prepares for the future. She does not have a "lack" mentality. Because of her diligent preparations she never fears whether or not her family is well cared for.

> When it snows, she has no fear for her household; for all of them are clothed in scarlet.
>
> Proverbs 31:21

Her home as well as her personal clothing reflect success. Notice that *after* the businesses are operating profitably, she directs some attention to home decorating. No doubt she is a strong contributing factor to the respect and honor her husband receives.

> She makes coverings for her bed; she is clothed in fine linen and purple. Her husband is respected at the city gate, where he takes his seat among the elders of the land.
>
> Proverbs 31:22,23

Her next venture is in the retail garment and wholesale sash business. Her decorum reflects a rare personal power and confidence that enables her to have no fear of the future. The word "laugh" suggests she has a sense of humor.

> She makes linen garments and sells them, and supplies the merchants with sashes. She is clothed with strength and dignity; she can laugh at the days to come.
>
> Proverbs 31:24,25

Now as an accomplished business person, incredibly she enters into yet another business—the seminar business.

> She speaks with wisdom, and faithful instruction is on her tongue.
>
> Proverbs 31:26

She's an attentive and wise manager of her businesses and household. She remains clearly focused on what is most productive and worthwhile. She is not aloof but stays energetically involved, planning and directing for future growth and expansion.

> She watches over the affairs of her household and does not eat the bread of idleness.
>
> Proverbs 31:27

Many would conclude that with so many business ventures her family would be neglected. Quite the contrary. She is loved and honored by her family.

> Her children arise and call her blessed; her husband also, and he praises her: "Many women do noble things, but you surpass them all." Charm is deceptive, and beauty is fleeting; but a woman who fears the LORD is to be praised.
>
> Proverbs 31:28-30

Now she can be rewarded for her many accomplishments. She deserves the praise because of her diligence. She has justifiably earned the accolades.

> Give her the reward she has earned, and let her works bring her praise at the city gate.
>
> Proverbs 31:31

What an outstanding role model! It must be that women are being inspired by this outstanding example because today women-owned businesses are booming. They are growing at twice the national rate of all U.S. firms.

According to The National Foundation for Women Business Owners:

- Women-owned businesses produce more than $1.6 trillion in annual sales.

- Women now own 36% of all U.S. firms.

- Businesses owned by women have a higher survival rate than the average U.S. business.

So, female reader, let Proverbs 31 be your inspiration and, if God beckons, take your rightful place in America's entre-preneurial revolution.

Working Mother—
Income and Expenses

Gross income per week (40 hrs. @ $6.00/hr.)		$240.00
Less: Tithe (10%)	$24.00	
Offerings (5%)	12.00	
Federal income tax (15%)	36.00	
Social Security tax (7.65%)	19.00	
Transportation (10 trips of 5 mi. @ 32½¢ per mile)	15.75	
Child care (1 child)	70.00	
Meals/coffee @ $6/day	30.00	
Convenience foods at home	20.25	
Extra clothing (including cleaning & cosmetics)	6.00	
Beauty shop	14.00	
Other ("I owe it to myself") items	5.00	
Total Expenses		$252.00
NET USABLE		($12.00)

TIME SPENT:

On the job	40 hours
Lunch	5 hours
Travel	5 hours
Hours away from home	50 hours

CHAPTER 5 | *CHOOSING AND NAMING THE BUSINESS*

Now we approach the challenge of choosing the right business. Before you read this, look over the list of businesses at the end of this chapter. Consider your God-given abilities, background and experience as you peruse the list.

Customers or clients will not do business with you simply because you are a nice guy. Your product or service must have superior qualities that will attract new and loyal customers or clients.

In your quest for the correct business, ask the following questions:

1. Are there shortcomings in an existing product or a service?

    The idea for your business doesn't have to be entirely new. There may be a product in common usage you can improve significantly. For example, a company's manufacturing tooling may not allow for a handle, etc. There may be a need for a short run of parts for a commonly used discontinued item. Always be looking for hidden opportunities. Can it be made smaller, foldable, lighter, thinner, faster, cheaper, disposable, reversible or with a better guarantee?

2. Why isn't there a ...?

How many times have you heard someone exclaim, "Someone needs to make a way to ..."? You may be able to turn a problem into an opportunity. One of the best ways to make money is to solve problems. A sign on the back of a cement truck gives good advice for a start-up business. It said, "Find a need and fill it!"

What Can You Be Enthusiastic About?

So what business is right for you? It will be beneficial if your experience and training can be put to direct use in the new business venture. What are your talents, aptitudes, hobbies and interests? You should choose a business idea that is exciting, fun and in harmony with your convictions, interests and abilities.

Your business should be something you can be enthusiastic and passionate about. It should be something you believe in and be a product or service you use or will use. Most of all, it should be something you can do in the name of the Lord since, after all, it will be the Lord's business.

> And whatever you do, whether in word or deed, do it all in the name of the Lord Jesus, giving thanks to God the Father through him.
>
> Colossians 3:17

Problems can present possibilities and opportunities. Tasks and chores others don't like to do such as cleaning homes, detailing vehicles or maintenance work, are opportunities you may be able to develop into a service-related business.

For potential start-up business ideas, read local and national newspapers such as *USA Today* and the *Wall Street Journal*. Search magazines such as *Inc., Entrepreneur, Venture, Success, Fortune, Business Week, Money* and *Kiplinger's Personal Finance*. Look for the announcement of new products. Perhaps a manufacturer needs a distributor in your area? You won't know until you ask. You may be able to negotiate exclusive rights for a period of time.

As you make contact with manufacturers, do so confidently expecting God to give you favor.

> For the Lord God is a sun and shield; the Lord bestows favor and honor; no good thing does he withhold from those whose walk is blameless.
>
> Psalm 84:11

The Anointing In Business

As you pursue the business of His choice, as a Christian, you have a decided edge over an unbeliever—the anointing. You are not in the pursuit of finding the right business alone. You have a partner. You are not limited to your own strengths and abilities. The appropriate response to any challenge must be like Paul's confession of faith:

> I can do everything through Him who gives me strength.
>
> Philippians 4:13

Because of the Holy Spirit you have every reason to feel empowered. Expect favor even above those persons, who in the natural, appear to be more qualified.

Solomon was right when he stated:

> The race is not to the swift or the battle to the strong, nor does food come to the wise or wealth to the brilliant or favor to the learned.
>
> Ecclesiastes 9:11

But for the Christian, Solomon was wrong when he concluded:

> But time and chance happen to them all.
>
> Ecclesiastes 9:11

For you, business success is not a matter of accidentally being at the right place at the right time.

> The steps of good men are directed by the Lord. He delights in each step they take.
>
> Psalm 37:23 (TLB)

Maybe God will direct you to go to the library. An afternoon invested in the library can bring a wealth of ideas. Look at trade magazines in your field of interest. Some larger libraries may have foreign trade journals. For example, you may locate a Korean company wishing to market their products in the U.S. Could you become their American representative? You won't know unless you ask.

If you are still in a quandary about which business is right for you, see if your public library has the book, *How to Pick the Right Small Business Opportunity* by Kenneth J. Albert (McGraw Hill). If your library does not have it, ask them to get it for you through their inter-library loan program.

Become an
Idea Scout

Many great ideas and trends start in California and Texas. A fact-finding vacation to one of these states to scout out new ideas could prove productive.

If you attend one of the popular small business shows given across America, be cautious of sweeping claims that may be made there. These shows are sometimes called "franchise shows." Many times the only profit goes to the promoter, and the participant in the "opportunity" often ends up with dashed hopes and a garage full of over-priced merchandise.

Remember Solomon's advice:

> A simple man believes anything but a prudent man gives thought to his steps.
>
> Proverbs 14:15

The *New English Bible* renders the above proverb as, "A clever man understands the need for proof."

Don't discount your own ideas. They may be inspired. Why do many people have so little respect for their own ideas anyway? Have you ever seen the announcement of a new idea and said to yourself, "I thought of that idea a long time ago"? Actually, ideas themselves are a dime a dozen but those who put them into action are priceless.

If you feel there is no market for the business you are skilled in, don't give up in despair. Read, listen and talk to the experts to determine where a need exists.

Consider enrolling at your local college in night classes in your selected field.

Once you settle on a business, it is wise to learn from the experts who have already succeeded in that field. Learn as much as you can about the market. Go on an all-out, fact-finding mission.

> Plans fail for lack of counsel, but with many advisers they succeed.
>
> Proverbs 15:22

Learn who your competitors are and what they are doing right. Remember you do not have to reinvent the wheel. You may only have to refine and improve it so it will be better and give more value for your customer's or client's dollar.

Because humans change slowly, improving an existing product or concept is much safer than trying to market a radically new one.

McDonalds started small with the simple hamburger stand but became great by developing ways to become more innovative. They learned to do it better, faster and cheaper and thus became a leader in their field.

Seek out seminars in your chosen field. A major reason for early business failure is because people don't do their homework. The needed research may take weeks, but it should be viewed as necessary groundwork to enhance your ultimate success potential. Talk to everyone you can find who has experience in your field. Ask! Ask! Ask!

Get Experience

Consider going to work for a period of time for a well-managed company in the field you wish to pursue. Maybe you could moonlight while keeping your current job. If you do use this strategy, serve the employer as a profitable servant. Of course, it would be dishonest to use an employer just to learn proprietary secrets.

Paul instructed Titus:

> Teach slaves [employees] to be subject to their masters [employers] in everything...not to steal from them...so that in every way they will make the teaching about God our saviour attractive.
>
> Titus 2:9,10

Better to delay your plans for the new business than to forge ahead prematurely and suffer costly mistakes.

Before you make the final choice of a business, you will need to know if your potential customers will like your product or service? This is a very important question to answer.

Do Your
Market Research

A story is told of a new company that created the world's best dog food. The entrepreneur researched all the nutritional requirements of a dog and created a food that would keep the animal in vibrant health and extend its life span.

In the company's first year of operation it did very poorly—so poorly that the officers sought the services of a renowned marketing expert. The expert agreed upon a sizeable retainer and set out to do his research. He fed the food to many breeds and sizes of dogs.

He finally presented his findings. The report was written on one sheet of paper—only one sentence. It read, "The reason you fell short of projections is because dogs do not like it."

If "dogs" do not like your product, it is better to discover it now, before you sink time and money into an ill-conceived idea.

Before finalizing your new business choice, you should do extensive market research. Sometimes I believe the reason people go recklessly into an ill-conceived business is not because they are too lazy to do the market research but because they fear that the research will expose the inadequacies of the plan. Some people do not want to hear the truth.

> A prudent man sees danger and takes refuge, but the simple keep going and suffer for it.
>
> Proverbs 22:3

Here are some steps to help determine the viability of your proposed venture:

1. Talk to your prospective customers.

Ask them if they would buy your product or use your service. This is called test marketing. If you are dealing with your friends, tell them to be brutally honest because you have a lot at stake. You may have to remind them of this proverb:

> Faithful are the wounds of a friend.
>
> Proverbs 27:6

2. Talk to prospective sales people.

If your product will require the services of outside sales people, ask prospective salespersons if they feel they can sell your product and what they think a customer or client will pay for it.

Many small business operators are surprised and disconcerted to discover that national discount chain stores can sometimes retail a product for less than the small business operator has to pay for it wholesale. They are rudely awakened to a fact known as the "economy of scale." Chain discount stores can buy products by the trainload at deep discounts.

Regrettably, most customers are disloyal, selfish and greedy. If they can buy a product or service cheaper elsewhere, they will. Most will not buy from you just because they like you.

3. Talk to people presently in your intended field.

Seek out people who are already in your selected business. Ask them, "If you weren't already in this business, would you go into it?" If the answer is no, shouldn't that tell you something?

4. Talk to your banker.

Even though you may not be seeking a loan, talk to a commercial banker. He or she looks at business plans daily and are familiar with the market.

5. Talk to the Lord.

Regardless of what your prospective customers, prospective sales people, the people in your intended field or bankers say, it is essential for you to clearly settle that it is God's will for you to make this step.

A person whose spirit is sensitive to God's leading can take comfort in this verse.

> In his heart a man plans his course, but the Lord determines his steps.
>
> Proverbs 16:9

Jesus delighted to always do the will of the Father and so should we.

> Then I said, "Here I am...I desire to do your will, O my God; your law is within my heart."
>
> Psalm 40:7,8

If, after following the steps listed on the previous pages, you determine that your desire to be in a certain business is not God's best for you, seek the grace to pray the same prayer Jesus prayed.

> Yet not as I will, but as you will.
>
> Matthew 26:39

Buying a Business Or a Franchise

An alternative to creating a business is to buy a franchise. For an up-front franchise fee plus royalties (a percentage of the gross revenues), the franchisor will sell you the right to use its company name. Some well-known examples of franchises are McDonalds, H&R Block, Midas Muffler and Auntie Anne's Soft Pretzels.

Buying a franchise combines the excitement that comes from starting a business with the safety net of the franchisor's proven system. In some cases, it may be a short-cut to success.

A franchise can give you instant recognition because you will be able to operate your business as though it is part of a large chain. Of course, in exchange for this, you will become standardized and may have to forfeit some of your freedom and innovative style.

For a list of 5,000+ franchises available worldwide, call 800-543-1038 to order the International Franchise Association's Franchise Opportunities Guide ($15 plus $6 shipping).

Before entering into a franchise agreement, I strongly suggest that you have your attorney review the contract and explain in layman's language what you are signing before you sign anything.

Solomon warns:

> It is a trap for a man to dedicate something rashly and only later to consider his vows.
>
> Proverbs 20:25

Investigate the franchise thoroughly. It is much easier to get into a situation than it is to get out. Seek answers to the following:

- What is the financial strength of the franchisor?

- Does the franchisor have a distinctive trademark?

- Will I have an exclusive territory?

- How will my territory be defined?

- Are the marketing and operational systems well defined and documented?

- What kind of training can I expect to receive?

- Will I receive on-going support in the future?

- Will the franchisor allow me to voice my opinions regarding the business?

- Do I have a sufficient amount of capital set aside to start and operate the business?

Write and ask the International Franchise Association about the company. Their address is:

International Franchise Association
1350 New York Avenue, N.W., Suite 900
Washington, D.C.   800-543-1038

Ask the franchisor for a copy of its Uniform Offering Circular (UFOC). This circular is required by federal law to disclose twenty-two categories of basic information ranging from corporate financial results to the franchise agreement.

After you've read everything the franchise company supplies you, do some independent investigating. Call and visit ten or more franchisees (the UFOC lists them). Ask them the following questions:

- How long have you been a part of this franchise?

- Have you been satisfied with the support you have received from the franchisor?

- What advice would you give someone considering this franchise?

- Would you buy the franchise again?

- How much did you make the first year?

- How much did it really cost to get started?

- Has the franchisor fulfilled their part of the contract?

The Small Business Administration publishes material to help you evaluate a franchise. For the SBA office nearest you, dial 800-ASK-SBA or download from the SBA on-line: http:\\www.sba.gov. *Free.*

Also contact Council of Better Business Bureaus at 703-276-0100 for a copy of *Facts on Selecting a Franchise* or write:

Better Business Bureaus
4200 Wilson Blvd. Suite 800
Arlington, VA 22203

Is Your Business Franchisable?

While on the subject of franchises, if your non-franchise business experiences great success, think big! Don't overlook the prospects of your becoming a franchisor. If, after an appropriate period of time, your company is making a healthy profit, your business may be a viable candidate for franchise expansion.

Many entrepreneurs with a business that would work in similar markets in other parts of the country have earned millions of dollars by franchising their concepts.

As a franchisor, success will depend upon your ability to convince the prospective franchisee you have overcome the many hurdles and pitfalls of starting and successfully running the business. You must also convince the prospective franchisee that your franchise fee and royalties will cost him or her less than the expensive mistakes of learning the hard way—by trial and error.

Your outcome will depend upon your ability to reproduce your success by teaching someone else how your business works and your ability in management and motivational skills.

Even though the business may be profitable for you, the question is, is the business affordable and potentially profitable for a franchisee after the initial investment, the franchise fee and payment of an on-going royalty? Sometimes these additional fees make the difference between profit and loss for a business.

To franchise, your business must be easily systematized to the extent that the procedures and policies can be placed in an operations manual. The manual must be written clearly so a franchisee can follow the procedures and obtain the same results as you have had. Before franchising your business, ask yourself the following questions:

- Is there a point of difference between my business and my competitors'?

- Will my business "translate" to other areas of the country or other market situations?

- Does my business have sufficient history to enable me to reasonably project its long-range potential for success?

- Have I been in business long enough to prove my concept is able to thrive not only in good times, but also survive downturns in the market?

If you are going to be a franchisor, packaging is of the utmost importance. Your company-owned unit should have achieved a unique and desirable image. Any promotional literature must appear professional in every detail.

Many successful franchisors didn't set out to be in the franchising business. Their main goal was to run their own businesses successfully. The idea of franchising occurred to them only as interested parties started asking if they could buy a franchise.

To learn more about franchising, call 800-734-2235 or write:

U.S. Department of Commerce
Herbert Hoover Building
14th St. & Constitution Avenue, N.W.
Washington D.C. 20230

Internet: \\www.doc.gov

Two trade associations that can send you information are:

International Franchise Association
1350 New York Avenue, N.W., Suite 900
Washington, D.C.
800-543-1038

American Franchisee Association
2730 Wilshire Boulevard, Suite 400
Santa Monica, CA 90403
312-431-0545

Buying an Existing Business

There may be some advantages to buying an existing business. A going business may produce a profit much faster than a new one. The business may have goodwill and a loyal customer base. It also may have good employees. Furthermore, the seller may finance the business at more desirable terms than a bank.

But often the disadvantages outweigh the advantages. You may inherit ill will, incompetent employees, obsolete inventory, an uncooperative landlord or a lease with unattractive terms and conditions. However you may be able to turn these disadvantages into a price advantage when negotiating the purchase.

If a business is on the market, especially one offered by a business broker, be cynical. Investigate why it is on the market. Accept nothing but audited financial statements, and even then, keep looking for the fatal flaw. The reason often given why a business is offered for sale is because the owner wishes to retire. If the business is successful, why won't the employees buy it? Good businesses that are sold are rarely offered publicly.

Yet there may be some wonderful opportunities available out there. There may be a real change in the owner's life— a divorce, burnout, partnership breakup, etc. If you do find such an opportunity, you must move quickly.

Just because the existing owner is experiencing problems doesn't mean you will. Do you see a solvable problem? Do you see something the owner does not see? If the problem is solvable and the price is right, it may be an outstanding opportunity.

Before buying an existing business, go to the library or a bookstore and get these three books:

The Complete Guide to Buying and Selling a Business
      by Arnold S. Goldstein

How to Buy a Small Business
      by M. J. Mangold.

How to Buy a Good Business with Little or None of Your Own Money
      by Lionel Haines.

Have a qualified attorney and an accountant give their approval to the documents before buying any business.

Choosing a Name

Now that you have chosen the right business, it is time to choose a company name. Get the whole family involved in the selection process. You may be surprised how creative your children can be.

It is best to have a name that clearly communicates to your

customers what the company does, makes or sells. It shouldn't be a tongue twister but should flow phonetically.

Maybe you should avoid the temptation to have your personal name as part of the company name. Consider what could happen—your company could grow and be bought by new owners who wouldn't operate it with the same spirit of integrity you do, or heaven forbid, what would it mean to your name if the business should fail and/or go bankrupt?

> A good name is more desirable than great riches; to be esteemed is better than silver or gold.
>
> Proverbs 22:1

Using an Assumed Name

When you use any name other than your own, you operate with what is legally known as a fictitious name. It is sometimes called an "assumed name" or a "dba" (doing business as). You are required by law to record whatever assumed name you choose at your county clerk's office.

You can record this yourself. Ask the clerk to let you see the alphabetized listing of fictitious names. Some counties have this list on computer or microfilm. Others have it recorded in large log books. If your search reveals that no one else has reserved your selected name, you may file it by paying a nominal fee. This authorizes you to use the chosen name in that particular county. You will need to file separately in each county in which you do business.

A fictitious name must be renewed periodically, usually every five years, and in some counties every ten years. Ask your county official. If you fail to renew, someone else can file for your name and you will be unable to operate under that name anymore.

Using a Corporate Name

To obtain a corporate name requires you or your attorney to check with the Secretary of State's office in your particular state to determine if any other corporation is using your selected name or one that is confusingly similar. In some states you can call the Secretary of State's office yourself to determine name availability.

If a review of the records reveals that your selected name, either the assumed name or the corporate name, is taken, before you give up with a broken heart, check with the registered owner of the name. It could be that the previous business might have failed or for one reason or another, is no longer using the name. The owner may be willing to let you have it.

For existing assumed names, the county clerk's office can tell you how to go about getting it re-registered to you. For corporations, the Secretary of State's office can help.

Prior to allowing you to open a business bank account using an assumed name, banks will usually require that you supply them with a copy of the assumed name certificate or the certificate of incorporation granting you the use of a particular name.

Registering a Name Nationally

If you anticipate becoming regional or national in scope,

your chosen name should be registered as a trademark or as a service mark. A name or symbol such as Coke® or Ivory® is trademarked. If your intent is to operate a small home-based company, such national registration is probably unnecessary in the beginning.

You can now register a trademark with only the intent to use it. Previously, the mark had to have been in use before it could be registered. Seek out the services of a professional for such registrations. Many law firms provide this service or you can use a search firm like Thomson & Thomson of North Quincy, Massachusetts. Call them at 800-692-8833 for more information about their services and their costs for searching and registering a trademark.

For a brief introduction defining trademarks and their functions, request:

> *Basic Facts about Trademarks*
> U.S. Government Printing Office
> Washington, D.C. 20402
> 202-512-0132
> $4.25. Request booklet 003-004-00682-0.
>
> Internet http://www.access.gpo.gov/su_docs

State and Local Sales Tax

Nearly all states have a sales tax on most products and some rendered services. You will be required to collect the tax and remit it to your State Treasurer. If your state has a sales tax you must apply to your State Comptroller for a Sales Tax Permit for each place of business. Your particular state may call this a Seller's Permit, a Resale Number or a Resale Certificate.

Some businesses may require a permit or license at the state level. Most businesses will also need a city license and/or county license which can be applied for through the city or county clerk's office. Certain types of businesses such as restaurants are required to obtain special permits from local health authorities, fire and police departments.

For most small businesses you will not be required to obtain federal licenses unless you are engaged in interstate commerce, common carrier transportation, radio and television, manufacture of drugs, preparation of meat products or investment counseling. Contact the Federal Trade Commission at 202-326-3650 in Washington D.C. 20580 to obtain a listing of which businesses require federal licenses.

Internet: //www.ftc.gov.

List of Possible Businesses

- A -
Accountant
Aerobics instructor
Advertising specialist
Air charter service
Agent/manager
Alterations
Aluminum recycling
Animal breeder—cats, dogs, etc.
Animal husbandry
Antique dealer
Appliance repair
Appraiser—antiques
Aquarium maintenance
Art dealer
Arts and crafts
Attendant—newborn baby
Auctioneer
Auto body repair
Auto dealer—buy, sell
Auto detailing
Auto mechanic

- B -
Baby-sitting service
Bait shop
Baseball card trader
Beauty parlor
Belts and scarves design
Beekeeper—sell honey
Birdbath—design and/or manufacture
Boat mechanic
Bodyguard
Bookkeeping
Bookbinding

Bookstore
Bridal consultant

- C -
Cake making
Calligraphy
Candy maker
Candle maker
Car rental
Care of elderly and sick
Career counselor
Caricature artist
Carpet cleaning, dyeing, repair
Catering service
Charter boat service
Child care
Children's wear—design
Chimney sweep
Christmas decorations—design and/or sell
Clown—parties
Comforters—design and make
Consulting
Contractor/remodeling
Cookie maker
Computer—
    Instruction
    Programming
    Repair
    Sales
Copy service
Cosmetology
Court reporting
Custom racquet covers—design and/or manufacture

- D -
Dart boards—design and/or manufacture
Day care center
Decorative files—boxes & folders
Delivery service
Desktop publishing
Dietician
Dog obedience training
Doll maker
Dry cleaning

- E -
Electrolysis
Electronic repair
Embroidery
Exercise instructor
Espresso bar

- F -
Fashion designer
Freelance artist
Freelance writer
Fund raiser
Furniture designer/refinisher

- G -
Ghost writing
Gold leafing—frames, etc.
Graphic designer of books, brochures, calendars, etc.
Greenhouse design
Grow fruits, vegetables, flowers, herbs, spices

List of Possible Businesses

- H -
Handbags—design
Hats—design and/or
    manufacture
Health care
House sitting
Hydroponics

- I -
Income tax preparation
Install fences
Install insulation
Insurance sales
Interior designer

- J -
Janitorial
Jewelry box design
Junk dealer

- L -
Landscape design
Laundry—pickup and
    delivery
Lawn maintenance
Leatherwork
Lettering—doors, windows
Lettering—house numbers
    curbs
Luggage tag maker

- M -
Maid service
Mail order
Make-up specialist
Manicures—go to people
Manufacture—
    Beds for pets

Bird feeders
Bird houses
Dried flower
    arrangements
Hammocks
Jewelry
Kites
Lamps
Lawn furniture
Magazine racks
Napkin holders
Puppets
Sweat bands
Sweaters—pets
Manufacturer's rep
Manufacturing
Massage therapy
Messenger service
Miniature doll houses
Mobile hairdresser
Mobile mechanic
Mobile pet grooming
Mobiles—kids rooms
Model
Motorcycle repair
Moving business
Multi-level marketing
Musician

- N -
Nanny service
Needlepoint
Newsletter publishing
Nursery
Nutritionist

- P -
Packaging service
Painter
Paper hanging
Paper route
Pedicures—go to the
    people
Personal trainer
Personalized labels—
    clothing
Pet boarding—keep
    animals
Pet grooming
Photography
Piano tuner
Place mats
Plaques
Plant maintenance—home
    or office
Plasterer
Plumbing
Pool maintenance
Prepare food & deliver it
Printing
Proofreading
Property management
    (may require license)
Public relations
Publishing

- Q -
Quilts

- R -
Raise chickens, eggs
Real estate
    development/sales
Recording—speeches,
    weddings

List of Possible Businesses

Recycling
Repair gutters
Repair stereos, televisions, typewriters
Restaurant
Retailing
Re-upholstery
Roommate service—put people together for a fee
Rubber stamp-design and/or manufacture
Recreational vehicle specialist

- S -
Sailboat leasing
Sales training
Sewing
Screen printing
Sculptor
Sharpening tools
Shoe repair
Sign painter
Singer
Singing messages
Slip cover maker
Small business consultant
Sound recording
Stained glass
Stationery design
Stuffed animals
Swings

- T -
Tape duplication

Taxi service
Taxidermy
Teaching:
    Accounting
    Appliance repair
    Art
    Automobile repair
    Ballet
    Baking
    Cabinet making
    Computer skills
    Continuing ed courses
    Culinary arts
    Desktop publishing
    Drawing
    Electricity
    Electronics
    English
    First aid
    Flower arranging
    Flower drying
    Foreign language
    Golf
    Graphic design
    Guitar
    Guns and gun safety
    Horseback riding
    Jewelry design
    Judo
    Karate
    Knitting
    Mathematics
    Modeling
    Modern dance
    Nutrition

    Office skills
    Oil painting
    Photography
    Piano
    Plastering
    Plumbing
    Public speaking
    Real estate
    Remedial reading
    Racquetball
    Salesmanship
    Tennis
    Typing
    Voice
    Water Colors
    Weaving
    Woodworking
Towels—embroidery
Transportation
Tree—maintenance
Tutoring

- V -
Vending machines
Video taping—business, weddings, insurance claims

- W -
Wallpaper hanger
Welding/soldering
Wholesaling
Window cleaning/glazing
Woodworking
Word processing
Writer

CHAPTER 6 | *MULTILEVEL MARKETING*

RECOMMENDATION

Read this chapter even if you have no interest in multilevel marketing. It contains strategies that apply to every area of business.

One way to start and operate a small business requiring very little start-up capital is to become an independent contractor with a reputable multilevel marketing company (MLM). Some companies prefer the words "network marketing" instead of multilevel marketing. In this chapter I will refer to this method of marketing as simply MLM.

For decades many products have been marketed through MLM and, if current trends continue, more and more will be marketed by independent representatives of these companies. Today there are many great MLM companies, some moving billions of dollars of merchandise each year through this system of distribution.

MLM's
Rocky History

MLM is riddled with a spurious history. But the industry has come a long way from its tempestuous beginning. Much of its bad reputation is from those early days when so-called pyramid schemes abounded.

You, like others, may be someone who in the past had a bad experience with MLM. In this chapter you will discover some of the needless reasons why people fail and how you can avoid being a part of the dismal fallout.

It is important that you not allow a past failure to negatively influence present opportunities. When did your bad experience occur? Was it years ago? That was probably a different environment, a different marketing plan, with a different company offering different products or services.

My friend, Tom Norfleet, a leading MLM consultant from Dallas, Texas points out, "Something else is different now too. YOU. You've probably grown and matured spiritually and intellectually. Yet many are allowing the burden of a past failure to negatively influence them from getting involved in something they are ideally talented to do."

MLM's Bright Future

MLM is here to stay. Years ago the government may have been its foe. Now the government, recognizing they can't kill the MLM industry has begun to regulate it. What was once looked upon as specious by many has today gained widespread acceptance and respectability.

Nearly all products are sold with what, in essence, is a multilevel profit distribution plan. The manufacturer sells at a profit to a wholesaler. The wholesaler marks it up and sells to a distributor. Likewise the distributor sells to a retailer who, in turn, marks the product up and sells to the ultimate consumer.

Usually MLM refers to retailing products or services to others, typically your friends and neighbors, and earning a commission on these sales. What makes it multilevel is that you can sponsor or recruit others into the business. As these recruits sell to others, you will get a commission or, as the industry calls it, an override, on their efforts plus overrides on their recruits' recruits, down several levels or generations, depending upon the marketing plan. This sales force is generally referred to as a downline.

Dividing the Good From the Bad

Care should be exercised in the selection of the MLM company you will represent. Even though you may have only a nominal cash investment, if you fail, you run the risk of loss because you will be making an investment of your most valuable assets—your irreplaceable time and your contacts.

The following questions can help you determine if MLM is right for you:

- **Is it a good company?**

    It should be a company with some operating history, ideally a minimum of two years. Having said this, a start-up company, though more risky, may offer an excellent ground-floor opportunity. Regardless of the company's age, it should be well funded and professionally and competently managed by people of integrity.

- **Do you have a good sponsor?**

    Of almost equal importance to the selection of

the company itself is the selection of a sponsor. If your sponsor is weak or new to the business, what about his or her sponsor or his or her sponsor's sponsor? These people are generally called the upline. They have a vested interest in you; consequently, they should be able to cover for the inexperience of your sponsor and help train you.

- **Is the product a part of a growing industry?**

  Have you heard this old saying, "The rising tide lifts all ships"? It doesn't have to be an exploding industry, but it should be a growing industry. If it is a declining industry much energy will be needlessly expended going against the flow.

- **Is the timing correct?**

  You should look for an idea whose time has come. The idea should be on the cutting edge of technology and general popularity. If most of your personal contacts have already been exposed to the product, your success will be greatly hampered.

- **Is it a good product or service?**

  It must supply a need and perform equal to the claims of the company's literature. Ideally it should be something superior to what can be purchased in conventional retail stores.

- **Is the product consumable?**

  If the product is something like vitamins that must be replenished each month, it is easier to create a durable income stream from repeat business than if the product is a once-in-a-lifetime purchase.

- **Is the product fairly priced?**

  One problem with some MLM programs is that they sometimes has such heavy commissions built into the overrides that the ultimate consumer of the product must pay more than the fair market value of similar products bought through conventional shopping. Clearly, in such cases, people will not buy the product if they are not participating in the business opportunity.

- **Is it something you enjoy?**

  It usually takes time to build an income stream. You may not be able to hit a home run right out of the batter's box. If representing the product or service is not something you enjoy, you may not be willing to invest the time and effort it takes to make it succeed. Will you be able to heed Solomon's advice? He wrote:

  > Whatever your hand finds to do, do it with all your might.
  >
  > Ecclesiastes 9:10

- **Is the marketing plan good?**

  The plan must be easy to understand and to explain. The company should have attractive literature that clearly explains it.

  The plan should be realistic. Some companies show marketing plans demonstrating the power of five representatives recruiting five or even ten recruiting ten and so forth. On paper, a veritable, though unrealistic, money-making machine emerges. Everyone entering an MLM business would make millions if everyone did what they were supposed to do. Regrettably they don't.

Sometimes out of greed, people ignore the above questions. They get involved with no intention of ever selling the over-priced products but only to recruit others to sell them. People who have a desire to get rich quick usually are looking for ways to make large amounts of money without commensurate labor.

Paul wrote:

> People who want to get rich fall into temptation and a trap and into many foolish and harmful desires that plunge men into ruin and destruction.
>
> I Timothy 6:9

With the weak marketing plans of some MLM companies, unless you have "chutzpah" and are a dynamic motivator with exemplary leadership skills, you probably will be disappointed in the production of other people.

MLM is not unlike any other entrepreneurial activity. An individual's success resides in his or her persistent action. With the right company many people have done outstandingly well in MLM.

If you can find the right company operated professionally by people of integrity, a company well researched and funded, a company offering a good compensation plan with a quality, fairly-priced product or service that adequately meets the needs of the ultimate user, with the Lord's approval, go for it—MLM can work for you.

The Church and MLM

If you are actively involved in a church, the challenge will be to maintain a proper detachment from your MLM business when it comes to church. This is not to say you cannot share a business opportunity with church friends. It is, however, inappropriate to use the church environment as a forum to prospect immediately before, during or after church services.

When this suggestion is ignored, sometimes church visitors are converged upon, not to welcome them or pray with them, but to try to recruit them into an MLM program before some other church member does.

Sometimes couples think they are being invited to someone's home for fellowship only to be forced to listen to a business opportunity presentation. Some feel used and become disillusioned with church altogether.

A pastor must exercise extreme caution in his or her involvement with MLM. It is easy for a pastor's influence to be eroded because the pastor tries to get the congregation involved in an MLM program. This is not to say that a pastor cannot be involved in an MLM program, but a pastor must make the ministerial calling the foremost pursuit.

As a cautionary note, steps should be taken to insure that in your quest to create a residual income you maintain proper priorities. Sometimes people get so deeply involved in their business that church interests wane. Maybe this is why Jesus refers to the "deceitfulness of wealth" (Matthew 13:18-23) because building a business has the potential to cause people to lose their focus.

> For the love of money is a root of all kinds of evil. Some people, eager for money, have wandered from the faith and pierced themselves with many griefs.
>
> I Timothy 6:10

As a believer, we are promised that if we make the kingdom of God and his righteousness (his right way of doing things) our foremost pursuit, then the things most people pursue and seldom attain will be ours.

Jesus said:

> Therefore I tell you, do not worry about your life, what you will eat or drink; or about your body, what you will wear...for the pagans run after these things, and your heavenly Father knows that you need them. But seek first his kingdom and his righteousness and all these things will be given to you as well.
>
> Matthew 6:25-34

MLM—A People Business

All business is people business, but none is more so than network marketing. You must have an excellent working knowledge of your products but to be truly successful at MLM you must concentrate on sharpening your leadership skills in influencing people. This business requires recruiting, sponsoring, training and lots of inspiring and motivating people.

Furthermore, people who fail at network marketing often do so because they operate it as a hobby. They don't operate it as a business. Seldom does someone succeed who just casually tries the business. To succeed, you must take the business seriously and be willing to invest part of your life (time) into it.

There is a difference between part-time and spare-time. Don't expect to build a great MLM business in your spare time. Rarely does a person reach lofty goals doing it in his or her spare time. To succeed at any worthwhile endeavor you must put in a disciplined effort and organize your life to *find* or *create* the time necessary.

The way our economy is structured, most people must work 40 hours per week for mere survival. The hours you put in over the basic 40 are generally what builds equity and wealth. Success may require a commitment to give up some TV and other timewasters. Most people who enter a MLM program retain their regular job. With perseverance some realize their goal of making it their primary business.

> Sow your seed in the morning, and at evening let not your hands be idle, for you do not know which will succeed, whether this or that, or whether both will do equally well.
>
> Ecclesiastes 11:6

Who Do You Know?

Assuming you have chosen a good company and are whole-heartedly committed to making your involvement a success, here's how to begin.

Make a list of people you know whom you believe will look favorably upon your business opportunity and take it seriously. I recommend you make a list of at least 50 names of motivated people. Your success is ultimately based on the quality of your sales force, so you will want to recruit the best.

Paul's advice to Timothy about how the church should grow also applies to business expansion.

> And the things you have heard me say in the presence of many witnesses entrust to reliable men who will also be qualified to teach others.
>
> II Timothy 2:2

It is only natural for you to share what you are excited about with your friends. The average person knows or is acquainted with over 200 people so the 50 names should be easy to assemble. Start with your neighbors, relatives and co-workers; they are more prone to allow you to present your program or product than a total stranger would be. Don't stop jogging your memory until you have at least 50 names. After your friends have been listed, concentrate on acquaintances.

Use the following questions to jog your memory:

Who do you know at work?

Who do you know from the branch office?

Who are your business colleagues?

Who are your competitors?

Who used to work at your old job?

Who are your exercise buddies?

Who sends you E-mail?

Who belongs to your computer user's group?

Who are the friends you chat with on the Internet?

Who do you know from church?

Who do you know from civic activities?

Who are your fellow hobby enthusiasts?

Who are your neighbors?

Who are your former neighbors?

Who are your relatives?

Who did you buy your house from?

Who sold you your car?

Who does your dry cleaning?

Who is your optician?

Who are your spouse's friends?

Who are your children's friends?

Do you know any firemen?

Who sells your groceries?

Who sold you your wedding ring?

Who repairs your jewelry?

Who repairs your shoes?

Who grooms your pet?

Who services your office equipment?

Who sells you office supplies?

Who is your painter?

Who is your travel agent?

Who was the best man at your wedding?

Who was the maid of honor at your wedding?

Who runs the local delicatessen?

Who just moved into your neighborhood?

Who is your veterinarian?

Who appraises real estate?

Who sold you storm doors or windows?

Who is the justice of the peace?

Who services your appliances?

Who does your plumbing?

Who upholstered your furniture?

Who sold you your piano? Who tunes it?

Who gives your children lessons— music, ballet, karate, etc. ?

Do you know any nurses?

Who is your doctor?

Who is your attorney?

Who are your bridge partners?

Who does your hair?

Who cleans your carpet?

Who was the bride and groom at the last three weddings you attended?

Who is active in the PTA?

Who fishes?

Who sells tackle?

Who are hunting buddies?

Who sells tires?

Who changes your oil?

Who is your florist?

Who is the local undertaker?

Do you know any police officers?

Who heads a civic club?

Who is your postman?

Who is your church staff?

Who is your Sunday School teacher?

Who is your druggist?

Who is your dentist?

Who is your banker?

Who repairs your TV?

Who takes photographs?

Who does home maintenance?

Who delivers newspapers?

Who does printing?

Who details cars?

Who is your stockbroker?

Who is your financial planner?

Who is your insurance salesperson?

Who mows your yard?

Who runs the health food store?

Who is on your Christmas card list?

Who are members of your bowling league?

Who attended your class reunion?

Who are your fraternity or sorority members?

Who is in your church directory?

Whose business cards are you keeping?

Who sends you birthday cards?

Who is your chiropractor?

Who is your child's orthodontist?

Think of the names you will get from these questions as your working capital. Almost any business can ultimately overcome poor management if it has adequate working capital to pay for its mistakes.

Think of your list of names just as you would the balance in your bank account. If all you ever do is make withdrawals, no matter how large the account, eventually it will be depleted. So replenish the names. Ask for referrals. Your recruits will supply different names. It can compound if you work it.

Making
Your First
Presentations

After you have assembled the names, make appointments with the ones who respect you and over whom you have some influence. In the beginning, it may be best if your sponsor can accompany you when you visit them.

Because you are more vulnerable at this juncture, it is usually advisable to use someone else's more mature and grounded belief to help begin the business and to establish your belief.

The enemy or savior of your MLM business resides in your belief system. Initially you have a high degree of enthusiasm. You are excited about the potential of this opportunity. Yet some of your friends may say, "You are doing what?" "Those schemes don't work." "It's illegal..."

It is easy to lose the tenuous hold on belief now because it is not well grounded from personal success in the program. For this reason, ask your sponsor to accompany you as you are being trained and established.

Later you will be training your recruits by accompanying them. By training your recruits to reproduce themselves two or three times and likewise to train their recruits to reproduce themselves two or three times, the power of multiplication goes to work to produce a formidable sales force.

The WIN-WIN
Formula

You and your recruit will be facing two foes:

- Call reluctance
- Sales resistance

When these two forces are combined, they create a serious adversary that must be faced and defeated if you are going to succeed in the MLM industry. The best attack is to change your mindset from the competitive mode.

It is self defeating to conclude that if you make the sale, you win and by inference, your prospect loses; or if you don't make the sale, by inference, your prospect wins and you lose.

The proper outlook should be the WIN-WIN formula. Here your perspective is, "If I make the sale we both win. If I don't make the sale, we both lose." Once this philosophy becomes a part of your belief system, success will more easily follow.

Sowing and
Reaping

Your harvest will be in direct proportion to the amount and quality of the seed you sow and where it is sown.

The principles taught by Jesus in the Parable of the Sower offer some useful insights to anyone involved in sales, especially MLM selling.

A farmer went out to sow his seed. As he was scattering the seed, some fell along the path, and the birds came and ate it up. Some fell on rocky places, where it did not have much soil. It sprang up quickly because the soil was shallow. But when the sun came up, the plants were scorched, and they withered because they had no root. Other seed fell among thorns, which grew up and choked the plants. Still other seed fell on good soil, where it produced a crop--a hundred, sixty or thirty times what was sown.

Matthew 13:3-9

In this parable, it is understood that the sower was aiming at the good soil. Sometimes he missed. But he knew if he kept sowing, the law of averages would work in his favor.

Since selling is like a numbers game, keep sowing. As in the parable, some of your seed will fall along the path and the birds will devour it. In this case the birds may be any negative influence like friends, family or circumstances. Some "bird" can say a discouraging word and that recruit will drop out.

Some of your recruits will be like the seed that landed on rocky soil. It will produce people who don't have what it takes to complete the project. When hard times come, their enthusiasm will wane and they will soon drop out.

Then there are the thorns. Oh yes, those thorns. The thorns are the alluring attractions that blind from view the important issues. Jesus interpreted the thorns as the deceitfulness of wealth. But as in the parable, if you keep sowing, some seed will fall in the right place and that seed will produce bountifully. The important lesson to learn from this parable is to keep sowing.

The late Rev. H.C. Noah, who for over 30 years pastored Oak Cliff Assembly of God in Dallas, Texas said, "The greatest ability is 'stick-ability'." How very true, especially in the MLM business. Unfortunately many drop out just before the harvest. In business, sometimes success comes to the one who can outlast the competitors.

Setting a
Good Example

It is one thing to *recruit* someone into your marketing organization but it is quite another thing to *sponsor* him or her. Training is inherent in the sponsoring process and the best way to train is by example.

Remember the Law of Genesis: "Everything reproduces after its own kind." Your business will be a reflection of you—your commitment, zeal and enthusiasm.

Most people will follow whatever example they have, good or bad. Consequently the more personal attention you give to the training of *your* new recruits, the more personal attention they are likely to give to *their* recruits.

Let your recruits know you intend to call them frequently for the next few weeks, not to annoy them but to assist and encourage them. It is important not to be pushy but to be available to help them to the extent they will let you.

Seeing Through
Other's Eyes

People are interested primarily in themselves. No matter how altruistic or unselfish people may be, they are more interested in themselves and their families' well-being than in yours. To succeed in any business, understand this maxim.

This is not to say people are not interested in the needs of others, but that interest is subordinate to their own needs. It is their own needs that motivate them to action. Customers or representatives don't care about you as much as they care about themselves.

Someone once said, "People don't care how much you know until they know how much you care." They really don't want to know about the features of your product or service. They want to know how these features will benefit them.

Right or wrong, since this is the case, an important key to success is to learn to put the interests of others ahead of your own and attempt to see things through other's eyes.

Paul told the Philippians:

> Do nothing out of selfish ambition or vain conceit, but in humility consider others better than yourselves. Each of you should look not only to your own interests, but also the interests of others.
>
> Philippians 2:3,4

Your prospect is not interested in how much money you will make if he or she joins your sales team. Your prospect wants to know how much he or she will make. Therefore, to be most effective, you should focus the emphasis on the benefits the other person will receive.

Love People—
Use Money

Leaders who produce outstanding results usually have a great sense of respect and appreciation for people. Losers love money and use people. Winners love people and use money.

To succeed follow these suggestions:

- Help your recruits succeed.

- Help them recruit and train a solid group of enthusiastic recruits.

- Help them make money.

- Help them to feel good about themselves and their involvement with you and the company.

- Motivate! Motivate! Motivate!

If you earnestly pursue your MLM business with passion and treat and motivate the folk you sponsor with genuine love and concern, your new organization will grow and flourish and so will you.

NOTES

CHAPTER 7 | LEGAL FORMS OF OWNERSHIP

Once you've decided what product or service your new business will represent, and settled on the name, the next step is to decide the legal form of ownership for your business. This chapter will help you select the form of ownership that will best meet your specific needs.

There are essentially three legal forms of ownership under which a business can be operated:

- The sole proprietorship

- The partnership

- The corporation

There is a new fourth legal form called a limited liability company (LLC) available in some states.

In the following descriptions of the forms of ownership we will reference stockholder and partnership interests, but always remember the two overriding principles of stewardship:

1. God owns everything. He is the ultimate stockholder.

2. God has deferred the management of what we possess into our hands.

A Sole Proprietorship

The sole proprietorship is the simplest structure of ownership and requires no legal documentation to make it valid. Hence, no attorneys are required to draft and record documents. I generally recommend that most new businesses be started as a sole proprietorship, especially if it will be a home-based business.

A sole proprietorship is what the name implies. It is generally defined as a business completely and directly owned and operated by one person. It does not necessarily mean it has to be a one person operation. The word "sole" refers to ownership. However, in many states, if married, the spouse is considered to have one-half undivided interest in the business.

A sole proprietorship can have employees just like any other form of ownership and if you do, you will be required to withhold taxes on them.

Self-Employment Tax

In a sole proprietorship, there are no payroll taxes to be withheld on yourself because technically you are not an employee. However, for tax purposes you will be considered "self-employed" and must pay a self-employment tax of 15.30% on the first $68,400 of the net income from your small business plus 2.90% Medicare hospital insurance on all additional monies above the $68,400.

For tax purposes, all the profits and losses are the owner's and are reported on the owner's personal tax return on Schedule C and carried to Form 1040. (See Chapters 13 and 14.)

The net income computed on Schedule C is then used on Schedule SE as the basis to compute self-employment tax. The figures on these forms ultimately end up on Form 1040. Get IRS Publication 533, *Self-Employment Tax*, for more information.

Advantages: ***SOLE PROPRIETORSHIP***	1. Ease of formation 2. Sole ownership of profits 3. Control and decision making comes from one owner 4. Changes in day-to-day management decisions can be made quickly 5. Minimal governmental control 6. No double taxation
Disadvantages:	1. Unlimited liability which extends to all the owner's assets (This can be lessened by obtaining proper insurance coverage.) 2. Unstable business life (The business may be crippled or terminated upon the illness or death of owner.) 3. Usually less available capital 4. Perhaps a limited viewpoint and experience (one person's)

As a sole proprietorship, you may shift funds in and out of the business account and withdraw funds without incurring tax consequences. You cannot do this under other forms of ownership.

You can also deduct from your gross income 45% in 1998 and 1999 of amounts paid for health insurance for yourself, your spouse and dependents. This deduction is limited to income derived from the business for which the insurance plan was established. The health insurance deduction will be increased to 50% in 2000 and 2001, 60% in 2002, 80% in 2003 through 2005, 90% in 2006 and 100% in 2007 and thereafter.

For my first few years as an entrepreneur, I chose the sole proprietorship. In this form of ownership, I took full responsibility for my own success or failure.

One of the problems of the sole proprietorship may be lack of capital. A common solution is to bring in a partner or partners to contribute the needed funds. However, before you do that, it is usually wise to first seek alternate forms of raising capital. Give God an opportunity.

> For the eyes of the Lord run to and fro throughout the whole earth, to show himself strong in the behalf of them whose heart is perfect toward him
>
> II Chronicles 16:9

God is diligently searching for those who will not compromise. Few people ever give the Lord enough time to provide needed capital and show himself strong on their behalf.

Partnerships

A partnership is defined as an association of two or more individuals operating as co-owners of a business for profit. The partnership is not considered a legal entity separate from the partners themselves. Instead, each partner shares equal liability.

There are examples in Scripture of men joining efforts to accomplish a common cause or goal. Consider Paul and Apollos. Each had different responsibilities and each was rewarded according to his contribution.

Paul wrote:

> I planted the seed, Apollos watered it, but God made it grow...the man who plants and the man who waters have one purpose, and each will be rewarded according to his own labor.
>
> I Corinthians 3:6,8

In the final analysis, God himself must be the managing partner. However we must always bear in mind that he will only bless mans' efforts. We must supply the natural; he, the supernatural.

Two or more joined together can be greater than the sum of their parts. This is called synergism. As an example of synergism, consider God's conditional promise to the Children of Israel.

> If you follow my decrees and are careful to obey my commands, five of you will chase a hundred, and a hundred of you will chase ten thousand.
>
> Leviticus 26:3,8

A partnership can begin with a simple handshake. The law does not require a formal, written document. However, it is highly advisable to have a competent attorney prepare a written agreement spelling out the duties of the partners and their obligations to each other.

The partnership must register in the county or counties where the business will be located. You may have to file a "dba" (doing business as) document or an assumed name certificate at your county clerk's office.

Advantages:	1. Ease of formation (Legal expenses and formalities, while greater than with a sole proprietorship, are few compared to the requirements for incorporation.)
	2. Direct rewards (Partners are motivated to apply their best abilities because of direct sharing of the profits.)
	3. Growth and performance facilitated (In a partnership it is often possible to obtain more capital and a better range of skills than in a sole proprietorship.)
PARTNERSHIP	4. Flexibility (There is more flexibility in decision making than with a corporation but less than with a sole proprietorship.)
	5. Relative freedom from governmental control
Disadvantages:	1. Unlimited liability of all partners in a general partnership (In the case of a limited partnership, only the general partner would have such liability.)
	2. Unstable life For example, what happens on elimination or death of a partner? (Many provisions such as this need to be covered in detail in a written partnership agreement.)
	3. Relative difficulty in obtaining large sums of capital
	4. A business can be bound by the acts of a single partner
	5. Difficulty of selling partnership interest

Make sure your partner(s) has something to offer you and that you, in turn, have something to offer him or her. For example, you may have the expertise and time and your partner may have the resources and contacts.

CAUTION! Know your partner—don't be unequally yoked together. Be sure your partner has the same objectives and life philosophy as you. Also be aware that each partner has personal liability for the total debts of the partnership. Just because you have, as an example, a 20% undivided interest in the partnership doesn't mean that you cannot be held responsible for 100% of the partnership debts.

Don't let your intense desire to get start-up capital tempt you to compromise and choose the wrong partner. A potential partner may be congenial when he or she wants to be involved in your new business undertaking, but when pressures come and if sales do not reach expectation, a dark side of the character of the investor may emerge. By then, it's too late. You are already legally bound.

It may be wise to use your own limited capital and grow more slowly rather than to be answerable to partners, a board of directors, stockholders or a lender. This is a decision you must make.

Once your business is a success, it will be a success as a result of your anointed effort, activity, ingenuity and expertise. It may be disquieting to have to share the rewards, the money, the management and the fame with an investor, a partner or stockholders. Think about this before you follow conventional wisdom.

Obviously a believer should not violate the Scripture below that clearly forbids the linking of a believer with an unbeliever in any common task or undertaking.

> Do not be yoked together with unbelievers. For what do righteousness and wickedness have in common? Or what fellowship can light have with darkness … what does a believer have in common with an unbeliever … therefore be separate," says the Lord.
>
> II Corinthians 6:14-17

Surprisingly, we are told to not even associate with a believer who is a greedy person. Paul said:

> You must not associate with anyone who calls himself a brother…but is greedy.
>
> I Corinthians 5:11

Even if the potential partner is a believer, do you really know about his or her character? Use careful discernment because outward appearances may hide a character flaw.

I once asked a friend for a personal reference on one of his acquaintances. He refused saying, "I do not know that individual." I replied, "That's not so. You've known him for years. Don't you play golf with him regularly?" My friend replied, "That's true, but I've had no money dealings with him." The true character of a person rises to the surface when money is involved.

Remember, God may discipline his children when they violate his ways. The book of Proverbs lists greediness, ignorance, stinginess, stubbornness, laziness, gluttony, craftiness and the covering of sins as actions that bring on poverty.

Here's a sobering thought: if your partner, although a believer, has any of the above characteristics, he or she is subject to the Lord's chastening. As his or her partner, could you become an innocent victim when your partner is chastened by the Lord? Think about that before you indiscriminately take in a partner just because he or she can contribute dollars.

Just as in a sole proprietorship, the owner-proprietor is not considered an employee for tax purposes. Likewise in a partnership, a partner is not considered an employee for income tax and payroll tax purposes. However, a partner can be paid a management fee.

The partnership itself must file an informational tax return, Form 1065, but the partnership pays no income tax because the earnings (income or loss) flow directly to the individual partners to the extent of their ownership in the partnership.

There is a special form of partnership known as a limited partnership. It is called limited because it provides for limited liability. This kind of arrangement permits a quasi-corporate entity to exist.

In a limited partnership, one or more individuals make an investment in the business and are given part ownership in return. They are known as limited partners. They cannot participate in the operation of the business.

The business or partnership will be managed by you as the general partner. The limited partners earn a share of the company's profit or loss without the danger of being held liable for business debts. You as the general partner bear all the liability.

I will not discuss this legal form of ownership in any detail except to say that in a limited partnership there must be at least one general partner who assumes the liability and manages the partnership affairs and at least one limited partner who generally has liability only to the extent of his or her investment and has no management functions whatsoever.

In most states, the limited partnership agreement must be filed with the Secretary of State. Seek out a competent partnership attorney if you should elect this form of ownership.

Again, a loud note of caution! Get God's approval before

entering into any partnership. Don't let your emotions obfuscate or cloud sound judgment. If you do choose this form of ownership, don't do it with a mere verbal understanding and a handshake. I often see verbal partnerships where relatives are involved. Get a competent attorney to draw a partnership agreement, clearly spelling out every eventuality, such as:

- duties of each partner

- a "buy-sell" clause in the event of disagreement

- what happens at the death, bankruptcy, or mental incompetency of a partner, etc.

If you must be in a partnership, hold at least 51% of the ownership if at all possible. A "silent partner" is the best partner you can have.

"C" Corporations

A "C" corporation is an artificial legal entity, separate from its stockholders, officers and employees. Although there are exceptions, for many new businesses, a corporate form of ownership is not advisable. You can always incorporate at a later date if it becomes beneficial.

The biggest advantage of the corporation is that the debts of the corporation do not expose the officers or shareholders to liability unless they have personally guaranteed the obligation. One debt which does flow through the corporate veil to the individuals is unpaid taxes, including federal, state and payroll.

The corporation has a perpetual existence and does not "die" upon the death of the stockholder. It can, of course, cease to exist by the consent of the owners or by failure to pay the state franchise tax which is due and payable annually.

CORPORATION *Advantages:*	1. Limitations of the stockholder's liability 2. Ownership is readily transferable 3. Separate legal existence 4. Stability (In case of death or illness of owner, the entity continues to exist.) 5. Delegated authority 6. Ability of corporation to draw on the expertise and skills of more than one person
Disadvantages:	1. Activities are limited by the charter and various laws 2. Potential for manipulation and exploitation by minority stockholders 3. Extensive governmental regulations and reporting 4. Less incentive for managers who don't share in the profits 5. Expense of forming and maintaining a corporation 6. Double taxation

The corporation exists as a legal "person" and as such it pays taxes at a corporate rate. A major reason for it is to limit the personal liability of the owners (stockholders) from debts and liabilities. However, this advantage is thwarted by the refusal of most lenders to lend to a new corporation without a personal guarantee from the officers for repayment. Despite this, the limited liability of a corporation can still be an important protection from lawsuits, judgments and any amounts owed to suppliers who do not require such personal guarantees.

In most states you can incorporate without the assistance of an attorney by personally making application to the Secretary of State and filing the articles of incorporation for their approval. However, in most cases, the fee the attorney may charge to do it for you is probably money well spent.

Not only is it costly to incorporate, but it is also costly and time consuming to maintain the corporation. Before incorporating consider the costs—recurring franchise taxes, corporate income taxes, costs of ongoing attorney's fees for keeping corporate minutes and accountant's fees for filing quarterly payroll returns and annual tax returns.

Corporate Income Tax Rates

The federal income tax rate for a corporation is as follows:

CORPORATE TAX RATES

Taxable Income	Tax Rate
Not over $50,000	15%
$50,000 - $75,000	$7,500 + 25% of the amount over $50,000
$75,000 - $100,000	$13,750 + 34% of the amount over $75,000
$100,000 - $335,000	$22,250 + 39% of the amount over $100,000
$335,000-$10,000,000	$113,900 + 34% of the amount over $335,000

Consider this drawback. Not only must the corporation itself pay taxes on its own taxable income based upon the corporate tax rates, but you as an individual, must also pay taxes on any profits or salaries you take out of the corporation as personal income. This results in an onerous double taxation which may be avoided by electing to have an "S" corporation instead of a "C" corporation. This is discussed later in this chapter.

If you incorporate or already have a corporation, do not overlook the following benefits available to you:

1. Lower tax rates

Since double taxation occurs only if the corporation pays out money as dividends, some small corporations elect to pay no dividends. Instead the lesser taxed profits are held as retained earnings to be invested in expansion. This tax strategy can backfire. A tax (in addition to the regular tax) called an Accumulated Earnings Tax is imposed at the rate of 39.6% on accumulated taxable income exceeding the $250,000 minimum accumulated earnings credit ($150,000 for some personal service corporations). See a tax attorney for details if you feel this could be a problem.

2. Fringe Benefits

a. Medical insurance

The corporation, except for an "S" corporation, may deduct the medical insurance premiums it pays and the employee is not required to include them as taxable income. In other words, your corporation may pay your medical and dental premiums as a non-taxable perk for you.

However, accident and health insurance premiums paid by an "S" corporation for a more-than-2%-shareholder employee are deductible by the corporation and are included in the shareholder's gross income.

For tax years beginning after 1997, a shareholder-employee may deduct 45 percent of the cost of the health insurance premiums paid on his behalf. This can be a substantive advantage because personally paid health insurance is deductible on Schedule A only if your medical expenses are more than 7.5% of your adjusted gross income which eliminates the deduction for most people.

b. Disability insurance

Disability insurance premiums are deductible by the corporation and are not taxable to the employee.

c. Life insurance

To the extent that the *group term life insurance* coverage does not exceed $50,000, the premiums are deductible to the corporation and not taxable to the employee. See an experienced insurance agent for details.

"S" Corporations

An "S" corporation combines most of the elements of a regular "C" corporation with one very important benefit available to the partnership. Like in a partnership, profits and losses of an "S" corporation flow directly to the individual shareholders. This is particularly attractive for businesses anticipating losses during the initial stages of operation.

When this happens, shareholders have the benefit of reporting their shares of the "S" corporation's loss on their individual tax returns and thus reduce their personal taxes. However, there are certain limitations on the amount of loss. See IRS Publication 589 for more information.

Limited Liability Company (LLC)

A promising new form of ownership known as a limited

liability company (LLC) permits a business to operate like a traditional partnership. At the same time, unlike a partnership, the LLC protects the owners from all personal liability for business debts.

It offers several advantages over "S" corporations such as an ability to offer several different classes of stock with different rights. There is no limit on the number of shareholders, corporations or partnerships that may participate in an LLC.

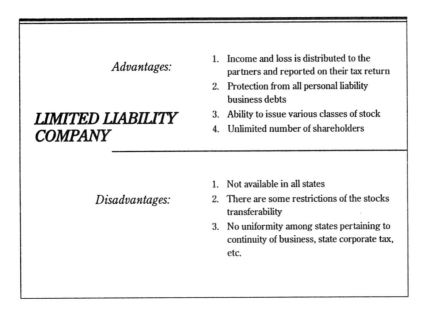

Advantages:	1. Income and loss is distributed to the partners and reported on their tax return
	2. Protection from all personal liability business debts
LIMITED LIABILITY COMPANY	3. Ability to issue various classes of stock
	4. Unlimited number of shareholders
Disadvantages:	1. Not available in all states
	2. There are some restrictions of the stocks transferability
	3. No uniformity among states pertaining to continuity of business, state corporate tax, etc.

At this time, not all states have statutes permitting this form of ownership. Look for others to follow.

Comparison Between Legal Forms of Ownership

	SOLE PROPRIETORSHIP	GENERAL PARTNERSHIP	LIMITED PARTNERSHIP	REGULAR CORPORATION	"S" CORPORATION
Simplicity in operation and formation	Simplest to establish and operate	Simple, informal but should have a formal agreement	More complex and expensive to establish. Requires written agreement, filing with State. Management by general partners only	Complicated and expensive	Same as regular corporation except profits and losses flow through to stockholders. Requires professional attention.
Liability for debts, taxes and other claims	Owner has unlimited personal liability	All partners have unlimited personal liability	General partners are personally liable; generally limited partners liable only to extent of their investment	Stockholders not generally liable for corporate debts unless personal guarantee. Officers may be liable for employee taxes if unpaid by corporation.	Stockholders not generally liable for corporate debts unless personal guarantee. Officers may be liable for employee taxes if unpaid by corporation.
Taxation	Income taxed to owner at individual tax rates	Income taxed to owner at individual tax rates	Income taxed to owner at individual tax rates	Income taxed at rates lower than those of individuals	Income taxed to owner at individual tax rates with some exceptions
Double taxation if profits Are withdrawn	No double taxation if profits are withdrawn from business	No double taxation if profits are withdrawn from business	No double taxation if profits are withdrawn from business	Yes, but not on salaries to owners who are employees of the corporation	No double taxation if profits are withdrawn from business, in general
Deduction of losses by owner	Yes	Yes	Yes, generally limited partners' deductions cannot exceed the amount of the investment	No, corporation must "carry over" losses to offset future profits	Yes, in general, but see a tax attorney for particulars
Social security and self-employment	Self-employment tax of 15.3% on first $68,400 plus 2.9% of all additional monies	Self-employment tax of 15.3% on first $68,400 plus 2.9% of all additional monies	Self-employment tax of 15.3% on first $68,400 plus 2.9% of all additional monies	Both employee of corporation & corporation pay 7.65% of first $68,400 plus both pay 1.45% each of all additional monies	Both employee of corporation & corporation pay 7.65% of first $68,400 plus both pay 1.45% each of all additional monies
Unemployment	Owner pays no unemployment tax on earnings	Owner pays no unemployment tax on earnings	Owner pays no unemployment tax on earnings	Yes, pays unemployment taxes	Yes, pays unemployment taxes
Retirement plans	Can have KEOGH retirement plan	Can have KEOGH retirement plan	Can have KEOGH retirement plan	Corporate retirement plans usually about same as KEOGHs at this time. Must be self-employed to have KEOGH	Corporate retirement plans usually about same as KEOGHs at this time. There are limitations
Insurance	45% in 1998 of health insurance costs can be deducted but can not exceed the net profit from business	45% in 1998 of health insurance costs can be deducted but cannot exceed the net profit from business	45% in 1998 of health insurance costs can be deducted but cannot exceed the net profit from business	Medical, disability and group term life ARE deductible with exceptions	Medical, disability and group term life ARE deductible with exceptions

CHAPTER 8 | DEVELOPING A BUSINESS PLAN

Thousands of years ago King Solomon penned these
words:

> Any enterprise is built by wise planning,
> becomes strong through common sense
> and profits wonderfully by keeping
> abreast of the facts.
>
> Proverbs 24: 3-4 (The Living Bible)

For the business operator, careful planning or as Solomon
calls it, "wise planning," is an essential key to insure profits
and continued business success.

God instructed the Prophet Habakkuk:

> Write the vision and make it plain.
>
> Habakkuk 2:2

The above verse from the book of Habakkuk is certainly
sound advice for anyone starting a business. By reducing
your business plans and goals to writing, you focus your
thinking. This will produce the single-mindedness necessary to put into motion powerful, inexplicable forces that

can bring to pass what is written on the page. If people could only recognize the awesome power of goal setting and wise planning, these actions would be given foremost attention.

Planning Tools

Let's look at some basic planning tools that can be vital to your business' progress and success. These important tools can help you become and remain cognizant of your true performance and help you identify the variables that can positively impact your financial success.

Forecasts

The first tool we'll examine is a forecast. A forecast enables you to look at your business' financial future. To create a forecast requires you to do what many people go to great lengths to avoid—think.

You will analyze the operations and ensuing cash flow that might result from various reasonable assumptions that can be expected to occur. You can analyze the anticipated effects of a change in a course of action. You can consider various "what if's" to determine the financial impact of unanticipated contingencies. Computerized spreadsheets can make it easy for you to illustrate your "what if's." The tool of forecasting will help you determine and prepare for the <u>future</u> <u>financial</u> <u>requirements</u> of your business.

Consider questions such as:

- What if I open a new office?

- What if I develop a web page?

- What if I hire two salespersons?

- What if I open a branch office?

- What if I add an 800 telephone line?

- What if I open a mail order division?

- What if I institute a direct mail program?

Early in the morning, perhaps with a steaming cup of fresh-ly brewed coffee, you could fill a yellow pad sheet with ideas to analyze in your projections.

A Budget

The second tool is a budget. Solomon said:

> A prudent man foresees the difficulties ahead and prepares for them; the simple-ton goes blindly on and suffers the conse-quences.
>
> Proverbs 22:3 (The Living Bible)

A budget is an essential tool to help you implement day-to-day decisions. Once in place, it can help you identify expenses that may get out of line. In any successful under-taking there must be a solid financial base. It is generally agreed that you are doing things right if you are producing a profit. Only a workable budget will help you produce that profit consistently.

A budget will help you identify specific areas that may not be cost effective. It may take some time to prepare, but once you have quantified the costs and expenses of the aspects of your proposed or existing business, the budget will become a powerful tool to help you stay on the right track to success and profitability.

Goals Keep
You on Course

Remember, in *Alice in Wonderland,* when Alice comes to the junction in the road and asks the Cheshire Cat for advice?

"Cheshire-Puss…would you tell me, please, which way I ought to go from here?"

Cheshire-Puss responded, "That depends a good deal on where you want to get to."

"I don't much care where," said Alice, to which Cheshire-Puss said, "Then it doesn't matter which way you go."

If your goal isn't clearly defined, it will lack justification for existence.

Goals Keep
You Focused

The Colorado River has cut narrow gorges through solid rock to form towering cliffs on each side. Like those cliffs, a well-formulated goal will keep you from diverting to non-productive activities that do not hasten you to the accomplishment of your goal.

Paul, the Apostle, knew how to keep his focus. His goal was to win the prize. He said:

> But one thing I do...I press on toward the goal to win the prize for which God has called me heavenward in Christ Jesus.
>
> Philippians 3:13,14

Goals not only define a desired destination or accomplishment, they actually propel you toward their attainment.

Solomon said:

> Where there is no vision, the people perish.
>
> Proverbs 29:18 (KJV)

The Hebrew word translated "perish" in the above passage is the same word used to describe the Children of Israel when they worshiped the golden calf. They had cast off all restraints.

You should set goals that will help keep your course straight and help channel your energy toward your desired destination.

> Let your eyes look straight ahead, fix your gaze directly before you. Make level paths for your feet and take only ways that are firm. Do not swerve to the right or the left.
>
> Proverbs 4:25-27

The first objective of your business should be for it to glorify God. This objective must transcend all other goals.

> But seek first his kingdom and his righteousness.
>
> Matthew 6:33

If you will heed the recommendations below, you will be

helped immeasurably in your new endeavor.

1.   Clearly identify *where* you have been called to go.

2.   Develop a plan showing *how* you will get there.

Goals Must Be in Writing

Whether you will have a one-person office or a staff of one hundred or more, you need a written master plan. Write a description clearly defining what you want your business to look like at a given point in the future, say in three or five years. Re-read what you have written, refine and expand it often. This will be your vision. It will help you stay on track and implement a plan of action to help make it a reality.

Your business goals should be so familiar to you that you can say them from memory in 50 words or less.

State Goals in the Present Tense

To be most effective your written set of goals should be stated in the present tense. Your goals should be so real that you can say them in the present tense as though they are a present reality. Faith can make them a reality and they will soon be manifested.

Jesus promised:

> Whatever you ask for in prayer, believe that you have received it and it will be yours.
>
> Mark 11:24

Your goals should definitely be quantifiable. This means they should be stated in dollars earned, units sold or other measurable terms. This will facilitate easy tracking and mid-course corrections.

Once the above steps are taken, you should have a clearer understanding of *where* you want to go. You will have clearly identified your goals for the new business, goals that are consistent with your faith and values.

Now you need to write a book detailing *how* to achieve the goals. Yes, you read it right! It will not be a book for publication. This book is to help you determine how you will take the seed, i.e., ideas and assets you have, and turn them into fulfilled goals.

It is best to write this book using a computer with a word processing program so you can edit it easily as your plan of action unfolds and becomes clearer. If you don't have a computer, get one! In the meantime buy a spiral-bound theme notebook and write it out by hand.

Organize your material in logical order even though your eyes may be the only ones to ever see it. Writing it in this manner enables your thinking to be more focused. Perfection is not your goal. You want an action plan that will guide you now and in the future. Business schools call this a "business plan."

Poor management is almost always a strong contributing

factor for business failure, and poor management is a result of lack of planning. Do your homework. Your book must not contain unrealistic assumptions.

Often a business plan is prepared solely to attract lenders or investors. Unfortunately, once the start-up is funded, the business plan is often put away, never to be looked at again. That is a mistake. The plan you will write is an operating plan. It must be frequently revised and updated to respond to changing markets and conditions. It will evolve as your business grows.

Write your business plan, even if yours will be a part-time, personally financed, home-based business. The time spent to create this plan will be an investment that will yield high dividends and make success far more likely.

Outline of a Business Plan

Below is a suggested outline. It is important that you be as detailed as possible. You would not think of starting to build a house without first drawing a blueprint. It is the same principle with your business. First you need a written business plan.

As you write, you will be researching the facts you will need to formulate a well-thought-out plan of action. The book you are writing will force you to think, analyze and develop a realistic plan.

Sit down at your computer and type, "Here is my plan to successfully open this new business and operate it profitably for the glory of God..."

I. My business —

    A. In a paragraph summarize what my business will be:

        What will I name the business?

        Why did I choose the name?

        How does the name convey what my business
            does or will do?

        How will the phone be answered?

        Will the business name be a part of my company
            logo?

    B. The nature of my business—example, wholesale,
        service or manufacturing

    C. My desired image

        Quality?

        Service?

        Discounts?

    D. Legal form of ownership

        Why did I choose this form?

    E. Discuss patents or other legal
        protections.

    F. In a brief statement state my business goal(s)

        Short-range goals (1-3 years)

        Long-range goals (4+ years)

    G. Will I join a trade organization?

        Which one(s)?

The Chamber of Commerce?

II. Location of business

   A. Describe the location

      If working at home, how am I going to isolate the office area from distractions?

   B. Why did I choose the location? (not because it is close to home)

      What is the traffic count?

      Parking facilities?

      Condition of the building?

      Public transportation?

   C. Lease terms and why?

III. Trade fixtures, and equipment and supplies

   A. What kind of computer and software will I need?

   B. Equipment required?

      Will trade fixtures and office equipment be purchased or leased?

      Can I get a discount?

      Can I get what I need by buying used equipment?

   C. What kind of telephone equipment will I need?

      Multiple lines?

      A toll-free number?

      A fax machine?

D. What supplies will I need?

Stationery?

Business cards?

Invoices?

Receipts?

Brochures?

IV. Funding the start-up expenses

A. How much will I need?

B. Where will I get the needed capital?

C. How much insurance will I need?

D. What tax liability will I have?

V. Outline all operational expenses

A. Show projected sales for next 5 years

B. Show projected expenses for next 5 years

C. Determine when break-even occurs

VI. The marketing plan

A. Who are my targeted customers or clients?

What are their characteristics?

Age?

Income?

Family status?

Tastes?

B. What share of the market do I plan to capture?

How?

C. Who is my competition?

How will I be distinctive?

How is my competition failing to exploit the potential market?

What is my competition doing right?

What is my competition doing wrong?

D. How did I arrive at my price schedule?

How does it compare to the competition?

E. What are my advertising plans?

Will I need a Yellow Page advertisement?

How will my potential customers or clients know I am in business?

What will my sign look like?

Will I need a web page?

F. Show a one-year promotional calendar.

G. What will be my credit policy?

Return merchandise policy?

H. What sales training do I need?

Show plan for acquiring the needed education

VII. Personnel

A. Show an organizational chart

Name key personnel including yourself, with a succinct job description plus educational background, experience and skills for each.

    B. Show a detailed compensation plan including fringe benefits.

    C. Will I have an employee retirement plan?

    D. Outline plans for employee training.

VIII. Inventory

    A. How much will be required?

    B. How will I manage the inventory?

    C. List the names of suppliers.

    D. List the names of clients or buyers.

    E. List the names of my mentors.

    F. Do I have a support group or a board of advisors?

IX.   Spiritual

    A. How do I know I am "called" to begin this business?

    B. How will I treat the Lord's tithe as the firstfruit?

    C. How will this business help me fulfill God's calling?

    D. How can I best reflect Christ in my business practices?

    E. How can I be involved in evangelism and discipleship as a business person?

This outline is to serve as a prompter. It is not exhaustive. Write on any other item you think of that is not included here. The more detailed you can be, the clearer your vision will become.

If the business plan will be used to raise start-up capital, it must be prepared in an acceptable form. Consider using a computerized template for building a business plan such as:

BizPlanBuilder
JIAN Tools For Sales, Inc.
800-346-5426

This program works on PCs and Apple Macintoshes. It works with your existing word processing and spreadsheet software. It does impressive 12-month budgets, a 5-year income statement, cash-flow projections, proforma balance sheets and break-even analysis. Your projections will flow automatically throughout all of your statements. With this program you can easily make "what-if" projections.

There are other business plan software packages available such as:

Plan Write
Business Resource Software, Inc.
800-423-1228

Plan Maker
Power Solutions for Business
800-955-3337

Business Plan Writer
Dynamic Pathway Co.
800-543-7788

Visit your public library for resources to help you develop the business plan. Some suggested books to look for:

How to Create a Successful Business Plan
by David E. Gumpert Publishing

The Successful Business Plan
by Rhonda M. Abrams,
Oasis Press

How to Write a Successful Business Plan
by Julie Brooks and Barry Stevens,
American Management Association

NOTES

CHAPTER 9 | *PRINCIPLE OF TITHING*

Are you aware that many men who founded some of today's great companies were godly men who were faithful tithers? Let's look at some of their inspiring stories.

Quaker Oats Company

Does the name Henry P. Crowell sound familiar to you? How about the company he founded—Quaker Oats? While yet a young man Crowell heard a sermon by Dwight L. Moody. He made a remarkable commitment to the Lord. He said, "I can't be a preacher, but I can be a good businessman." He prayed, "If you will let me make money, I will use it in your service." He bought a little run-down mill called Quaker Mill. Within ten years folk everywhere knew about Quaker Oats. Not only did he faithfully tithe but it is reported that he gave far beyond the tithe and funded the Lord's work for over forty years.

Colgate Palmolive Company

Who hasn't heard of the Colgate Palmolive Company? Do you know that a tither founded it? William Colgate left home when just a teenager. He felt that his father was too poor to keep him. With his only belongings tied in a bundle he met an old canal-boat captain. He confided to the captain that he was leaving home to lessen the financial burden on his parents. He explained to the old man that the only trade he knew was soap and candle making. The old captain knelt and prayed for the lad and then looked him in the eye and said, "Someone will soon be the leading soap maker in New York. It can be you. Be a good man, give your heart to Christ, pay the Lord all that belongs to him, make an honest soap, give a full pound and I'm certain you'll be a prosperous and rich man." Those words apparently made a strong impression on him.

He tithed from the first dollar he made as an employee. Soon he was made partner of the company he worked for and ultimately became the owner of the business. He, like Henry Crowell gave far beyond the tithe. It is reported that his giving grew from 20% to 30% to 40% to 50% and finally he was giving all his income. He gave millions to the Lord's work. Think about that.

John D Rockefeller, Sr

Some of today's well-know wealthy families initially gained their wealth when the patriarch of the family committed to tithing. Take the Rockefellers as an example. Listen to John D. Rockefeller, Sr.'s own words:

"Yes, I tithe, and I would like to tell you how it all came about. I had to begin work as a small boy to help support my mother. My first wages amounted to $1.50 per week. The first week after I went to work, I took the $1.50 home to my mother and she held the money in her lap and explained to me that she would be happy if I would give a tenth of it to the Lord. I did, and from that week until this day I have tithed every dollar God has entrusted to me. And I want to say, if I had not tithed the first dollar I made, I would not have tithed the first million dollars I made."

Today the heirs of many of these great industrialists may have wandered far from the principles that created such enormous wealth and influence. Many of their companies are now publicly held and the stockholders don't have a clue that they are still reaping a harvest of the righteous acts of their founders. To sustain such success and blessing there needs to be a rediscovering of the principle of putting God first and building a business as a way of seeking the kingdom of God.

R.G. LeTourneau

My father was particularly impressed by R.G. LeTourneau. LeTourneau was the creator and manufacturer of giant earth-moving machinery. As my dad would receive the offering at the church he pastored he was fond of referring to LeTourneau as a man who could not out give God. Before the end of his illustrious career this manufacturer would reverse the percentages and give God 90% and retain 10% for himself.

I remember that my parents received a regular publication from the charitable foundation LeTourneau started and funded with 90% of the stock of his corporation. Each month the publication would show pictures of the monster machines, some weighing as much as 200,000 pounds. And each newsletter always incorporated tithing because LeTourneau attributed his great success to it. Before his death in 1969 he had contributed millions and millions of dollars to the work of God worldwide.

Other Notable Tithers

We could go on and on and list names like J.L. Kraft of the Kraft Cheese Company, Wallace Johnson, the founder of Holiday Inns, or the founder of Welch's grape juice. Each of these godly businessmen was committed to tithing and I firmly believe that was the key to their outstanding success and legacy.

When the issue of tithing as applied to the small business is raised, many opinions abound. Often the small business operator is left in a dilemma. Should he or she tithe on gross revenues, net profits, salary taken or taxable gain? This chapter should help you answer this question.

Benefits of Tithing

God specifically promises that tithing will open the floodgates of heaven and provide an abundance of blessing.

Careful research of God's Word reveals there is not a single Scripture commanding obedience to the tithe or giving that does not, in the context, couple that command with a blessing to those who comply. The blessings are manifold. Prominent among the rewards of tithing listed in Malachi 3 is God's promise that he will rebuke whatever devours, devalues or destroys.

> "Bring the whole tithe into the storehouse, that there may be food in my house. Test me in this," says the Lord Almighty, "and see if I will not throw open the floodgates of heaven and pour out so much blessing that you will not have room enough for it. I will prevent pests from devouring your crops, and the vines in your field will not cast their fruit," says the Lord Almighty. "Then all the nations will call you blessed, yours will be a delightful land," says the Lord Almighty.
>
> Malachi 3:10-12

Before I address the more technical aspects of the tithe as it pertains to business income, let's look at a larger issue—the tither's attitude.

The attitude in which you tithe is of supreme importance, far more important than the amount of the tithe. In the ninth chapter of his second letter to the church at Corinth, Paul offers some clear-cut instructions regarding the proper heart attitude required when offering gifts to the Lord.

First, he points out that you must be *willing* to give.

> Not as one grudgingly given.
>
> 2 Corinthians 9:5

The truth is, you don't *have* to tithe; you *get* to. It is a privilege to involve heaven in your business affairs. Look upon it as an opportunity. How could you begrudge giving if you know what awesome things the gift can accomplish in your behalf?

Next, Paul points out that your gift should be regarded in the same way a farmer treats seed. He reminds them:

> Whoever sows sparingly will also reap sparingly and whoever sows generously will also reap generously.
>
> 2 Corinthians 9:6

After this gift-seed analogy, Paul's instruction is to give in the following ways based upon a heart decision:

- Not reluctantly
- Not under compulsion
- Cheerfully

> Each man should give what he decided in his heart to give, not reluctantly or under compulsion, for God loves a cheerful giver.
>
> 2 Corinthians 9:7

Now here is the amazing thing. If you follow his advice, the amount of your gift will not ultimately decrease your resources. Paul promises:

> And God is able to make all grace abound to you, so that in all things at all times, having all that you need, you will abound to every good work.
>
> 2 Corinthians 9:8

If you will commit to giving in this way, you will soon discover that God will commit to give you the very seed to plant and will continue to do so until you are reaping a bountiful harvest.

> Now he who supplies seed to the sower and bread for food will also supply and increase your store of seed and will enlarge the harvest of your righteousness. You will be made rich in every way so that you can be generous on every occasion.
>
> 2 Corinthians 9:10,11

Tithing on Gross Income

In Old Testament times Israel was engaged in an agrarian economy. From the scriptural account we specifically know that Abraham tithed of his gross.

> Then Melchizedek king of Salem brought out bread and wine. He was priest of God Most High, and he blessed Abram, saying: "Blessed be Abram by God Most High, Creator of heaven and earth. And blessed be God Most High, who delivered your enemies into your hand." Then Abram gave a tenth of everything.
>
> Genesis 14:18-20

Abraham trained his family to tithe. His grandson, Jacob, vowed to tithe of everything God gave him.

> Then Jacob made a vow, saying, "If God will be with me and will watch over me on this journey I am taking and will give me food to eat and clothes to wear so that I return safely to my father's house, then the Lord will be my God and this stone that I have set up as a pillar will be God's house and of all that you give me I will give you a tenth."
>
> Genesis 28:20-22

In those ancient days few people were employees as we use the word today. Most families were, in a sense, small business operators, just as most families in America as recently as the mid 1940s were engaged in some form of the agriculture business. In Bible times, these farmers and ranchers had no problem computing the tithe. If there was an increase of the herd, it was every tenth animal that constituted the tithe.

> The entire tithe of the herd and flock— every tenth animal that passes under the shepherd's rod—will be holy to the Lord. He must not pick out the good from the bad or make any substitutions.
>
> Leviticus 27:32,33

Tithing of the gross increase was not limited to the increase of livestock. It involved the first tenth of agricultural increase as well.

Concerning everything else the law reads:

> A tithe of everything from the land, whether grain from the soil or fruit from the trees, belongs to the Lord; it is holy to the Lord.
>
> Leviticus 27:30

Solomon revealed the outstanding benefits of tithing.

> Honor the Lord with your wealth, with the firstfruits of all your crops; then your barns will be filled to overflowing, and your vats will brim over with new wine.
>
> Proverbs 3:9,10

In the above verse, the word "crops" is the harvest. True, the family businesses of Bible times bare little resemblance to modern day businesses with non-family-member employees. But when those ancient farmers harvested a crop, it is reasonable to assume that they, like modern businesses, had expenses. They had the cost of supplies and livestock care, and yet the tithe was taken off the top. How could this be?

Some Christians seem to have a dual standard when it comes to the tithe on earned income compared to the tithe on business income. They understand the tithe must be paid on the gross earnings of wages, but somehow feel it would be impossible to tithe on the gross revenues of a business.

In the case of earned income the only costs to earn it is a person's labor. Therefore all sums received in exchange for the labor is increase and thus tithable. On the other hand, there may be hard costs involved in the production of business income for costs such as raw materials, rent, advertising and salaries. Technically your tithable increase is your net earnings, i.e., the amount remaining after the hard costs of producing the income. And yet there are some business owners who have committed to tithe on the gross revenues their business generates. The Holy Spirit must guide you in your particular situation. As you pursue the appropriate course for you, examine your motives. Don't look for ways to pay God less.

Since tithing involves heaven in your personal and business finances, it is in your best interest to tithe. To scheme and look for a loophole to offer the Lord less is foolish because it can diminish the blessings.

Enemies of Tithing on the Gross

Let's examine why many Christian business operators conclude that it is impossible to tithe on gross receipts. Modern businesses struggle under the staggering influence of the devourer, Satan. Enormous sums of business capital are funneled off to pay two things:

- taxes
- interest on debt

Because many modern businesses have rejected God's way and ignored his principles of increase, God has allowed the government, at enormous cost to taxpayers, to provide many of the services God ordained the church to supply.

After federal, state and local taxes are paid, the lenders are standing next in line. Then the labor, costs of goods and other services must be satisfied. What little, if any, that remains is called profit and it seems that God must get his portion there.

There is no simple solution to this dilemma. By following the advice in Chapters 13 and 14, the tax bite can be lessened but not fully eliminated. But you can do something about debt. Today most businesses, be they small home-based operations or giant conglomerates may not be able to tithe of gross revenues because they are highly leveraged, thus decimating present and future income. If you are following the advice contained in this book, you will take decisive measures to avoid or at least minimize borrowing to start the business or to operate it.

Furthermore, the ease in which the tithe can be applied to the gross income of a business depends upon the nature of the business itself.

In certain businesses, such as large supermarket chains the profit margin may be very small. Conversely, a service business may operate on a much larger margin. In this case, it would seem impossible for the grocery supermarket to tithe on the gross but possible for the service business to do so.

If the supermarket is operated the world's way, there is no way the Lord's tithe based upon the gross revenues could even be considered. But *what if* all assets were free of debt? *What if* inventory was free of debt? *What if* the windows of heaven were open upon that business? *What if* it was operated under biblical principles of increase? *What if* blessings abounded? *What if*...? Now can it be possible?

Consequently, if God has placed in your heart a desire to tithe on the gross revenues of your business, careful consideration must be exercised in the selection of the business and the way it is to be operated and financed.

If you choose to tithe on gross receipts you are not alone in this decision. There is usually one common denominator among businesses that tithe on the gross—they are debt free. Their growth may not be as meteoric or as spectacular as the highly leveraged ones, but by factoring in the "open windows of heaven," in the long run they can be miles ahead of their highly-leveraged competition.

The most important thing to recognize is that the tithe must be offered *in faith*, expecting God to respond exactly as he has promised. This attitude of faith is far more important than the amount of the tithe.

If a person truly believes the promises of Malachi 3 how could he or she be reluctant to tithe?

By offering God the firstfruits (the tithe must always be the first 10%) you will accomplish two things:

- You acknowledge He is the owner and lord of your business.

- You legally authorize heaven's involvement in the business.

The Kerr Letter

While I was conducting a seminar in California, an attendee handed me a lengthy handwritten letter that his deceased mother had received from Ruth Kerr, the widow of the founder of Kerr Jar Company. The following pages are some unedited excerpts from her inspiring letter written more than 40 years ago.

"It is with some trepidation that I am writing this letter for fear I might be misunderstood, but every time I pray for you and the successful outcome of your long pending lawsuit, a small still voice says 'Why don't you tell them about tithing' so I am going to give you my personal testimony, also Mr. Kerr's, which to me is next to my salvation the most wonderful experience I have ever had.

"Shortly after I met Al (Mr. Kerr) he told me how he became a tither. He read a book written by an evangelist friend of his who mentioned the story of Jacob in Genesis and made a vow 'If God will be with me, and will keep me in this way that I go, and will give me bread to eat and raiment to put on, so that I come again to my father's house in peace; then shall the Lord be my God; and this stone which I have set for a pillar, shall be God's house; and of all that Thou shalt give me, I will surely give the tenth unto Thee.' Genesis 28:20-22 inclusive.

"In Genesis 30:43 we read 'And the man increased exceedingly, and had much cattle and maidservants and menservants, and camels and asses.' God kept His Word just as He always does.

"Mr. Kerr had a double motive when he began to tithe, so he wrote on the flyleaf of his Bible, June 1, 1902, he too would tithe. In addition to believing God and wanting the results and blessings, he also felt tithing and the blessings which followed were wonderful, but this also was a sure way to prove to unbelievers that there was a God.

"When Mr. Kerr started tithing he was a salesman for a wholesale grocery house and just had a small salary per week and a small home with a mortgage on it.

"Within 3 months something wonderful happened. A German Jew from Germany came to Portland, Oregon with a patent for a fruit jar that sealed with a vacuum—something unheard of in this country. He tried to market it but women not understanding the vacuum principle were leery of it as they thought it would be very involved. In despair the inventor did not know what to do. Someone referred him to Mr. Kerr. After examining and testing it Mr. Kerr thought it had definite possibilities. The inventor said, 'I'll sell it to you,' to which Mr. Kerr replied, 'I don't have the money.' The inventor then offered to sell it for a very nominal fee, a small amount down and further small payments from time to time.

"Mr. Kerr borrowed $100, rented a tiny office, incorporated the Kerr Glass Mfg. Corp including in the articles [of incorporation], the clause that 10% of the net profits would go to the Lord's work, at the end of each year, which promise has been kept to this day—only Mr. Kerr increased it to 12% some years before his death and we keep it there.

"Since Mr. Kerr didn't know the first thing about making glass and certainly had no money to build a factory he boarded the train for San Francisco and asked the largest glass factory in the United States if they would make the jars for him and he would pay them as he sold them. They agreed and so the business continued on that basis for three years until April 6, 1906—and on that date came the startling news of a terrible earthquake, etc.

Mr. Kerr's friends in Portland said, 'Well Kerr, I guess you're done for,' to which he replied, 'I don't believe so. I made a vow 4 years ago to God and He has scrupulously kept His Word and I don't believe He is going back on me now.'

"The factory was the only building left standing in a three-mile square. The fire after the earthquake scorched the wooden fence on three sides and burned everything beyond for a mile and a half. Does God keep His Word? Indeed He does.

"In 1909 Mr. Kerr was able to buy a defunct glass plant in Altoona, Kansas and also acquired all the employees who had the 'know how' of glass making.

"Two years later the natural gas used for fuel played out. What to do? God had the answer.

"In the new state of Oklahoma there was another tither by the name of Charles Page who had built the town of Sand Springs, Oklahoma (6 miles from Tulsa), owned gas and oil wells galore, had brought in a big cotton mill, a steel plant, interurban railroad, water works, electric light plant and who also had on his land a glass company fully equipped but the latter had gone broke. Would Mr. Kerr run Mr. Page's defunct plant if Mr. Page would give him a 10-acre industrial site across the street on which to move his plant from Altoona? Mr. Kerr accepted with alacrity.

"By this time Mr. Kerr was selling his jars, caps and lids from the West to the Mississippi. He moved his offices from Portland, Oregon to Chicago, Illinois and began to sell all through the East and beyond into New England.

"When I met Mr. Kerr through a friend in 1912 he told me of this wonderful experience in tithing and gave God all the glory. I was so impressed I resolved to tithe right then and there. My first tithe only amounted to $1.25 a week, but I gave it regularly to my church and missions.

"We were married in 1913 and for nearly twelve years I was privileged to have my beloved companion by my side, then God took him home, and left me with six little youngsters ages 4-13. I wanted to die right then and there too but couldn't with six wee ones to care for. I did not plan to go into the business but in twelve months time the man who was running the business had a stroke and died, our sales manager died, followed shortly by our top salesman.

" 'I being in the way', God led me to take over, and in fear and trembling I did so. The factory was Mr. Kerr's separate property whereas the Kerr Glass Corp was the selling agency. The courts refused to recognize a portion of his will asking that 10% of everything except the Kerr Glass which paid 12% each year, was to be tithed and paid to 'the Lord's treasury' which was his name for his personal tithing account. The courts refused to recognize 'the Lord's treasury.'

"We incorporated the factory, put the 10% tithing clause in its articles of incorporation and I personally paid all his tithe on his estate on top of my own. It took me years to do it, but I wanted to carry out his wishes in every detail.

"All the children tithed from the time they were little tots out of their allowance and their earnings for little tasks they did each day.

"Clair, I have tithed for 49 years. I wouldn't give it up for anything in the world and with Solomon I can say, 'There hath not failed aught of any of His promises.' There used to be 80 glass companies. Today there are about 30 of our type. Either our competitors put them out of business or they went broke.

"On the contrary on Christmas Day Mr. Kerr came rushing down the steps saying over and over, 'I've got it, I've got it.' Competition had been extreme and our finances were at a very low ebb. I kept asking him what he meant and he said, 'The Lord sent us a Christmas present today, an idea for a jar sealing with a two-piece cap—you can throw the lid away after usage but you retain the screw band for years and use it over and over.' Much more economical than the first German invention where you had to throw the entire single cap away each time.

"We had samples made and experimented secretly night after night in our own kitchen until it was perfected and it was patented by the Patent Office the following August 15th.

"Our competitors ridiculed, laughed us to scorn, said the jars would leak air and contents all spoil—BUT none of these things happened and the new jars sold like hot cakes until we became the leader in the field. After 17 years when our patent expired, every competitor we had, came out with imitations. They have never yet been able to imitate our sealing composition.

"While home canning as a whole is on the decline, God again has stepped in and our jars can be equally used for freezing. Then too we manufacture in our three plants all kinds of commercial glassware and have the top reputation for 'quality ware.' This year we began the manufacture of plastic bottles and have already gone from one 8-hour shift to two.

"God has never let us down once, not even for a moment."

The letter from Mrs. Kerr contained several more hand-written pages. In them she describes how, after her husband's death, she continued the business. God gave her great favor and prospered her and the business. She ended the letter with these words:

"Personally I tithe my gross salary in addition to the two companies' tithe. It is such a joy and God's wonderful surprises are marvelous."

Just as God responded to Mr. Kerr's faithfulness in tithing, so he will respond as you tithe in faith. As your business grows and remains debt free, as you are faithful in the little things, God will deem you trustworthy of greater things. God discerns motives. If your heart commitment is to tithe from your gross revenues, God can and will provide the way.

Remember, he is your partner. It is his business. Let him guide you.

CHAPTER 10 | *START-UP CAPITAL*

How much will it cost to start your business? A realistic projection of start-up costs is vital to long-term success.

How much you will need to finance your undertaking is largely dependent on the type of business you are starting. For example, a home-based service company requires far less capital than a retail outlet that must purchase expensive inventory and fixtures before the first sale is made.

Your capital requirements will also depend upon the type of person you are. How frugal are you? Are you willing to sacrifice?

In the real estate field there is what is known as "sweat equity" where the buyer paints or otherwise provides the labor for fix-up to cover the down payment. If you don't have the required start-up capital, you may be able to substitute "sweat," take little or no salary initially and use creative ingenuity to minimize costs and avoid unnecessary expenses.

Sometimes people over-estimate the cost, but more frequently people underestimate how much it will cost to start the business.

Jesus said:

> Suppose one of you wants to build a tower. Will he not first sit down and estimate the cost to see if he has enough money to complete it? For if he lays the foundation and is not able to finish it, everyone who sees it will ridicule him, saying, "This fellow began to build and was not able to finish."
>
> Luke 14:28-30

Capital Requirements

How much do you need to build your "tower"? In the above passage Jesus used the words "first sit down." This statement suggests the first thing to do is to spend quality time determining the necessary capital requirements. You will need more than a hazy notion or general idea of the amount of cash required to start and keep your new business going.

If you have prepared a thoroughly thought-out business plan as suggested in Chapter 8, you will have calculated the capital requirements for getting the business started. Many experts suggest you allow at least a year's worth of overhead expenses. These expenses include real estate rent or mortgage payments, salaries and benefits, equipment, utilities, etc.

It is wise to anticipate the unexpected. If you will be operating a service business, anticipate increases in the costs of items such as paper, printing and advertising.

If you will be using raw materials, consider the possibility that higher costs of those raw materials may not be able to be passed along to new customers right away.

> A prudent man foresees the difficulties ahead and prepares for them; the simpleton goes blindly on and suffers the consequences.
>
> Proverbs 22:3

Be realistic. Often I observe that overhead and start-up costs are underestimated and the anticipated response of the marketplace is too optimistic. By wisely estimating the cost to "build your tower," you'll insure that you don't run out of money before the business can generate positive cash flow to cover expenses.

At the end of this chapter is a copy of the Small Business Administration's checklist for going into business. It provides a good basis for determining your initial capital outlay requirements.

Don't let your desire to go into business obfuscate or distort reality. Better to delay until you are adequately funded than to fail due to lack of sound judgment and planning.

To Borrow or Not to Borrow

Going deeply into debt to begin a new business is often a costly mistake. Some people have wrongly concluded that I am categorically opposed to debt in any form. Not so. I am categorically opposed to making debt a way of life. Your goal should be debt-free living personally and professionally.

While the Bible does not strictly prohibit debt, it clearly gives restrictive guidelines concerning its use and cautions against its abuse.

Conventional thinking sees debt as a means of using other people's money (OPM) to create leverage to control large assets. Such leverage can appear on paper to be a beneficial tool. But, if for some reason, the proforma (projection of revenues) is not attained, there's not enough money to service the debt. At that point, the lender will have a prior claim upon all income and you will become painfully aware of the truth found in Proverbs.

> The rich rule over the poor and the borrower is servant to the lender.
>
> Proverbs 22:7

Leverage is a two-edged sword. Under ideal circumstances leverage can increase overall yield; however, under adverse conditions, leverage will increase losses. If the statistics were available to show the number of businesses that have failed due to excessive debt, I believe it would astound you.

As your business grows and exceeds your projections, in time, there may be a place to judiciously and prayerfully employ debt. It may be appropriate to privately issue stock or even go public. In the meantime, if at all possible, your new business undertaking will best be capitalized from personal assets such as savings and the internal growth of the business.

Starting Smaller with Private Funds

Personal funding has many advantages. By using the word "personal," I am not necessarily referring to funds from your personal bank account. Capital may come from the sale of an asset such as a piece of real estate, a second car, an antique, mutual funds or other securities.

Do you have valuable assets you no longer need or use? What about that free-and-clear boat or motor home you have not used in months, or that lake property, or that valuable oil painting your rich uncle left you that you really don't like anyway?

There are people whose businesses don't require large inventory or expensive equipment who have funded their entire start-up capital requirements with the proceeds from a garage sale. You may be surprised how much you could net from a big garage sale and at the same time "de-junk" your life.

Consider the methods of raising capital employed by two different business persons in Jesus' parable. One man was a real estate developer, the other, a merchant of jewelry. Neither used OPM.

> The kingdom of heaven is like treasure hidden in a field. When a man found it, he hid it again, and then in his joy went and sold all he had and bought that field. Again, the kingdom of heaven is like a merchant looking for fine pearls. When he found one of great value, he went away and sold everything he had and bought it.
>
> Matthew 13:44-46

If you start your business with private funds, you won't have to worry about making loan payments or keeping investors happy during what might be lean start-up months or years. The more money you borrow, the more you will increase your fixed expenses. This makes it more difficult to survive any mistakes made during the initial learning process.

Think of it this way. By not borrowing, you can make mistakes more inexpensively and survive to tell others how to avoid them. Later, when you know how to plan for it better, you may, with the Lord's permission, judiciously borrow for growth, inventory or expansion.

Many great companies have become great through the use of internal funding from their own cash flow. Their growth may have been slow, but today they are solid and debt free for the glory of God.

There is a valuable lesson to be learned in Aesop's fable, *"The Tortise and the Hare."* It seems impossible that a slow moving "tortise" of a business could ever outpace the "hare" of a business. But if the "hare" is carrying a heavy debt load, the "tortise," free of debt, will ultimately be the winner.

Starting on a Shoestring

If you are starting on a shoestring, you are not alone. Many great companies prospering today had very humble beginnings. Although not a funding source per se, one of the most effective means of financing a new small business venture is to discover ways to begin for less.

An excellent book you may get from the public library is called *Starting On A Shoestring: Building A Business Without A Bankroll* by Arnold S. Goldstein. In this book Mr. Goldstein illustrates how to start a business with little or almost no capital.

Guard and Preserve Capital

To preserve your capital, if possible, minimize or try to avoid altogether, tying up large amounts of capital in fixed assets such as trade fixtures or real estate. The costs of these assets continue even if you fall short of projected sales.

In some situations it might be better to stay liquid by leasing rather than purchasing. You might even convince the landlord to pay the decorating and remodeling expenses to meet your requirements. Many times used fixtures and equipment can be bought at a substantial discount. There are stores that specialize in pre-owned office furniture and equipment.

Inventory Requirements

Initial inventory may require a large capital outlay. Could you minimize initial inventory requirements? Maybe the goods can be bought on consignment and not paid for until you sell them. Learn the art of negotiation. As a general rule, never accept the first price for anything.

Maybe you can persuade suppliers to allow short-term credit on your initial inventory although this will normally require some selling on your part. You will never know if you don't ask.

In the Gospel of Matthew, Jesus gave the formula to acquire not only answers to prayer, but any worthy pursuit. He advised:

> Ask and it will be given to you; seek and you will find; knock and the door will be opened to you. For everyone who asks receives; he who seeks finds; and to him who knocks, the door will be opened.
>
> Matthew 7:7,8

Explore every possibility before you seek outside capital. Maybe hiring an extra employee could be put off a few months.

Make sure you haven't overlooked hidden capital of your own. For example, if you own a whole life insurance policy, you can usually borrow the cash value of your policy. The policy remains in effect during the loan and the interest rate is usually substantially lower than bank rates.

It is generally wise to avoid the dangerous practice of raising start-up capital through a home equity loan. Be cautious, because a business failure could result in the loss of your home.

As a last resort, consider dipping into your IRA or other tax-deferred retirement account. Maybe you could take a lump sum distribution from your previous employment's retirement plan. Be aware though that if you're younger than 59½ you'll pay a 10% penalty plus the taxes due whenever retirement accounts are tapped.

Family Money

After you have exhausted the above suggestions, if you still need additional start-up capital, the next best place to turn is to your own family. Members of your family or your spouse's family will often invest in your business simply because they believe in you and your ability. The same applies to your friends. Many times they may not be as worried about a quick return as other investors might be. They may say, "Pay me back when you can…"

Beware! Close friendships and pleasant family relationships have been needlessly torn apart because the borrower was not able to meet his or her obligations in a way the lender thought they should have been. Remember, you have changed your relationship from a relative or a friend to that of a servant when you borrow.

Treat a loan from a family member as formally as you would any other business transaction. A loan document should be prepared stipulating the terms including the interest rate, frequency of the payment and/or the due date of the note.

Relying on a verbal agreement may cause tax problems. If the IRS views the loan as a gift the lender becomes subject to the federal gift tax rules and is required to pay taxes on the money if it is over $10,000.

If a relative desires not to charge you interest, make sure the loan is not over $100,000. If it is for more, the IRS will add what is commonly called imputed interest and your relative will be taxed as though he or she received interest, when in fact none was paid.

Imputed interest may also come into play for loans for more than $10,000 under certain situations. Check with your tax advisor.

By now my philosophy should be quite apparent. You should seek outside capital only as a last resort and only if it is absolutely necessary. Outside money, whether from relatives, friends, investors or institutional lenders, comes in two forms: "equity capital" and "debt capital."

Equity Capital

Equity capital is not a loan, it buys ownership in your busi ness. In a corporation, it is called common stock. In a partnership, it is called an ownership interest. If the business flourishes, the investor's yield is high; if the business languishes or fails, the investor will lose all or part of the capital invested.

If you must seek outside equity capital, before seeking institutional dollars, consider professional acquaintances as possible investors. There may be a local investment club or venture capital group to whom you could present your idea. Check with your CPA or investment advisor for referrals.

Debt Capital

By contrast, debt capital is a loan and it makes the investor a creditor with a legal claim to the business assets and, if you have personally guaranteed the loan, against your personal assets as well. They become the lender; you become the borrower. Remember the words of Solomon—they become the "ruler" and you the "servant." (Proverbs 22:7) A creditor has a prior claim and must be paid before the owner receives anything. Debt capital generally receives a fixed rate of return.

If you can't raise equity or debt capital from your friends or relatives, you have two other possible sources of money—the "private sector" and the "public sector."

Private Sector Financing

The private sector consists of institutions such as banks and savings and loans. They do not make equity investments as a general rule, but they may lend you some of the start-up capital if they can be convinced that your idea is viable and has good potential. They must be assured that you are solid and can repay the loan even if your business fails. The above applies to all institutional lenders—insurance companies, finance companies, pension funds, trusts, etc.

Only after you have been refused a loan from the bank can you apply with the public sector—the government. The United States Small Business Administration (SBA) has a variety of loan programs for new or expanding small businesses. In 1997, there were 52,700 SBA loans approved.

For new venture capital the 7(a) Program, known as the Loan Guarantee Plan, is most applicable. You borrow the money from the bank with a seven-to-ten-year pay back. The bank sets the interest rate. The SBA guarantees up to 80% of a loan up to $750,000 (the average is $230,000). There is no minimum; however, most lenders are reluctant to process commercial loans of less than $25,000.

Even with a SBA guaranteed loan, you will be expected to have some of your own capital invested in your business. The SBA makes loans for 50% to 70% of your start-up capital.

The interest rates of such loans are based on the prime rate as advertised in the *Wall Street Journal* according to the following schedule:

- Loans of less than seven years:
  prime rate plus 2¼%

- Loans of seven years or more:
  prime rate plus 2¾%

The maturity of an SBA guaranteed loan is based upon the following schedule:

- Working capital—five to seven years

- Fixed assets—seven to ten years

- Real estate—up to 25 years

There are some proposals that are ineligible for the SBA program such as religious organizations and their affiliates, magazines, newspapers, schools, TV or radio stations, real estate held for speculation, investment or rental.

To get the address of the SBA field office nearest you, call 800-368-5855 or write Small Business Administration, 1441 L Street N.W., Washington, D.C. 20416.

To get a loan through the SBA, you will have to demonstrate the ability to repay, have substantial collateral, have or hire management expertise, and be willing to contribute 25%-30% of the capital yourself or from your partners or stockholders.

Worksheet No. 2

Estimated Monthly Expenses Item	Your estimate of monthly expenses based on sales of $ _____ per year	Your estimate of how much cash you need to start your business (See column 3.)	What to put in column 2 (These figures are typical for one kind of business. You will have to decide how many months to allow for in your business.)
	Column 1	Column 2	Column 3
Salary of owner-manager	$	$	2 times column 1
All other salaries and wages			3 times column 1
Rent			3 times column 1
Advertising			3 times column 1
Delivery expense			3 times column 1
Supplies			3 times column 1
Telephone and telegraph			3 times column 1
Other utilities			3 times column 1
Insurance			Payment required by insurance company
Taxes, including Social Security			4 times column 1
Interest			3 times column 1
Maintenance			3 times column 1
Legal and other professional fees			3 times column 1
Miscellaneous			3 times column 1
Starting Costs You Have to Pay Only Once			Leave column 2 blank
Fixtures and equipment			Fill in worksheet 3 and put the total here
Decorating and remodeling			Talk it over with a contractor
Installation of fixtures and equipment			Talk to suppliers from who you buy these
Starting inventory			Suppliers will probably help you estimate this
Deposits with public utilities			Find out from utilities companies
Legal and other professional fees			Lawyer, accountant, and so on
Licenses and permits			Find out from city offices what you have to have
Advertising and promotion for opening			Estimate what you'll use
Accounts receivable			What you need to buy more stock until credit customers pay
Cash			For unexpected expenses or losses, special purchases, etc.
Other			Make a separate list and enter total
Total Estimated Cash You Need To Start		$	Add up all the numbers in column 2

NOTES

CHAPTER 11 | DEVELOPING A NETWORK

Years ago, the lyrics of a popular Gospel song were:

On the Jericho Road
There's room for just two.
No more and no less,
Just Jesus and you.

That may have been appropriate for the journey to Jericho but the journey to business success will involve others.

To be in business for yourself does not mean you must "go it alone." The central principle of management is to accomplish tasks through other people. Your chances of success will be greatly enhanced as you surround yourself with competent team members.

By law, a corporation must have a board of directors. In a sole proprietorship or a partnership you should have a board of advisors even though it's not required by law.

You need people who believe in you and who genuinely have your best interests at heart. You need people who can assist you in evaluating your ideas and who can help you determine if those ideas are truly viable. These mentors may or may not be those closest to you.

As you grow, your friends also must grow. If your friends are pulling you down or refuse to grow along with you, you may be forced to leave them behind and find new, positive friends to act as an influence in your life.

Paul felt strongly about this issue. He said:

> In the name of the Lord Jesus Christ, we command you, brothers, to keep away from every brother who is idle and does not live according to the teaching you received from us.
>
> II Thessalonians 2:6

Your relationships reveal who you are, and to a large extent, what you will become.

> He who walks with the wise grows wise, but a companion of fools suffers harm.
>
> Proverbs 13:20

No ongoing relationship will have a neutral impact on you. Either you will be drawing a person to your level or they will be drawing you to theirs. You are influencing or being influenced by every relationship.

Of course, God may bring people into your life for you to minister to and edify, but the subject matter here is how to draw people into your life who will inspire, affirm and edify you.

You need people who will seriously heed the instruction found in the Book of Hebrews.

> And let us consider how we may spur one
> another on toward love and good deeds.
>
> Hebrews 10:24

Your friends can act as a sounding board from which you can bounce ideas. Care must be taken to clearly explain to them that they must not simply say what they *think* you want to hear, but that they must try to be as objective as possible. As you grow and your business grows, it is of utmost importance for you to have a group who can mutually contribute or critique ideas in a non-judgmental, positive way.

> Plans fail for lack of counsel, but with
> many advisors they succeed.
>
> Proverbs 15:22

Let's consider other team members.

Finding the Right Accountant

Since the language of business is numbers and since many decisions must be made based upon numbers, you must select your accountant wisely. An accountant will help you set up your books and establish systems for handling cash receipts and disbursements.

Ask other business people in your same line of endeavor to recommend an accountant. A Certified Public Accountant (CPA) is suggested rather than one who is merely a general accountant or bookkeeper. A CPA must keep abreast of the constantly changing tax laws. Your CPA should act as a tax planner and not be merely a tax preparer. Look for someone well versed in the art of legal tax avoidance, not someone who will do things the easiest way possible.

If you have future aspirations of taking your business public, it is advisable to select a well-known firm because name recognition can lend credibility to your numbers.

Choosing an Attorney

Unless your business will be a sole proprietorship, you will probably need an attorney to form the corporation or draw the partnership agreement. Again, referrals from friends or business associates should be sought.

There are attorneys, and then there are competent attorneys. The irony is both charge about the same hourly fee.

Determine fees up front. Come to a clear understanding of the hourly fee. Sometimes senior attorneys can have junior associates handle your less complicated needs at a reduced rate.

Prepaid Legal Plans

Prepaid plans are usually for personal use such as will preparation, reviewing documents or for going to small claims court. Although such plans might work for a sole proprietorship, they probably won't work for a corporation or partnership.

Some smaller home-based business operators say they have had good experience with prepaid legal services for certain benefits that are offered. But before you sign up with any prepaid legal service, determine if they will let you use their services for business matters. Some won't.

If you are going to join a prepaid legal plan, choose a group that has been in business for at least three years and one that will give unlimited consultations or give at least 50 hours a year. Listed below are three firms with modest monthly fees that may meet the above guidelines.

> The Legal Service Plan of America
> 800-323-4620
>
> Caldwell Legal Services
> 800-222-3035
>
> Lawphone
> 800-255-3352

To avoid having to pay someone to reinvent the wheel, you should choose an attorney experienced in small business law in general and in your selected field specifically. If you plan to go public, choose one who has taken companies public before. You don't want to pay for his or her education, if you know what I mean.

Some people, operating on a tight budget, have purchased a book of legal forms or a computer program of legal forms from which they choose the appropriate ones and draw the minor documents themselves.

There are several legal software packages available that may be of interest to you. These programs provide templates of widely-used legal documents that allow you to fill in the blanks for things such as the names of the parties involved, dates, price, etc. Some popular ones are:

Do-It-Yourself Lawyer
Expert Software Incorporated
800-759-2562
Price $14.99

Quicken Complete Legal Collection
    Family Lawyer
    Business Law Partner
    Plain Language Law Dictionary
    American Bar Assoc. Family Legal Guide
Parsons Technology
800-779-6000
Price $49
Internet: //www.parsonstech.com

Legal LetterWorks
Round Lake Publishing Company
203-438-5255
Price: $79.95

Remember, legal computer software and forms books are not designed to replace your attorney. A lawyer has expertise; the packages don't.

Some advisors suggest that you take the prepared document to your attorney with this instruction, "Look at this and see if everything is legal and correct." Otherwise he or she may simply rewrite it, and you will have accomplished nothing by way of savings.

Choosing a Banker

Don't pick a bank; instead pick a banker. Choose a banker who is what I call a "people banker" as opposed to being a "numbers banker." Consider one who is eager to work with you.

Make it a point to visit frequently with your banker for a few minutes just about every time you go to the bank. Once you have established rapport and credibility, the loan for expansion will be much easier to obtain should you need it.

Choosing Other Team Members

Sooner or later, you may need a public relations firm, a management consultant, an advertising agency, or a board of directors. In the Lord's wise timing they will enter your life to help you achieve the success you deserve. The word "deserve" is used here because success and wealth don't go to those who need it most; success goes to those who, over time, have proven faithful in the small things. Pastor J. Don George of Irving, Texas encapsulates this message in three words beginning with the letter "d": "Details determine destiny."

Small Business Administration

The Small Business Administration publishes many low-cost books. Write them for a list of their publications. Their address is Small Business Administration, P.O. Box 46521 Denver, Colorado 80201-0030. Request *Resource Directory for Small Business Management*.

The Internal Revenue Service also has many free publications available just for the asking. They also offer excellent classes for the business owner. Check with the IRS for information concerning these classes and publications.

The Library

An afternoon visit to your local library may reveal a wealth of information. Get to know its resources. Your local library contains the combined wisdom of generations of high achievers. Search under "business," "management," "advertising," "self-improvement," and "taxes."

Leaders are readers. In addition to books, your library may offer workshops and lend vocational and motivational audiocassettes and videocassettes.

The Internet

Learn to go on-line with your computer to access the business information you need from the wealth of material found on the world-wide web. The internet is becoming a viable way of doing business and a way of life. The prices for access are minimal for the amount of information it provides. You can also use E-mail which, in many instances, eliminates long distance charges.

Magazines and Newsletters

The *Wall Street Journal* and *Forbes Magazine* are generally not as helpful to the small business person as, say, *Inc.* magazine or *Entrepreneur* magazine. Visit a newsstand and invest in a copy of these magazines to determine if you feel a subscription is worthwhile. Some people wisely make it a point to spend one afternoon a month in the public library reading the latest business magazines and financial publications.

People of God

> Blessed is the man who does not walk in the counsel of the wicked.
>
> Psalm 1:1

Ideally you should have a support group of men and women who know the Lord and his Word with whom you can pray and receive spiritual edification and direction. They should have a good grasp of biblical economics and believe in and apply biblical business practices.

> A godly man is a good counselor because he is just and fair and knows right from wrong.
>
> Psalm 37:30 (TLB)

Recommended Reading

Your handbook for business principles and practices is the Bible. God instructed Joshua:

> Do not let this Book of the Law depart from your mouth; meditate on it day and night, so that you may be careful to do everything written in it. Then you will be prosperous and successful.
>
> Joshua 1:8

Many authors of self-help, leadership and management books have unwittingly given principles from the Bible.

Unfortunately, many of them exclude God and his son, Jesus. They expect you to somehow implement these principles through your own willpower. This does not mean you should not read such books. But you should always recognize the divine factor that makes all truth work.

Paul identifies the source of the power. He says:

> For it is God himself whose power creates
> within you both the desire and the power
> to execute his gracious will.
>
> Philippians 2:13 (Weymouth Translation)

Pay special attention to the book of Proverbs. Proverbs has thirty-one chapters. If one chapter is read daily, the book would be read once per month. I know several successful business people who have adopted this discipline. Follow Solomon's advice and success will be a foregone conclusion.

> My son, do not forget my teaching, but
> keep my commands in your heart for they
> will...bring you prosperity.
>
> Proverbs 3:1,2

Even unbelievers will prosper if they follow Solomon's advice. But a believer will fail if he or she spurns the laws of success contained in Proverbs.

To help in the field of customer relations, I recommend the classic, *How To Win Friends And Influence People* written by Dale Carnegie back in the 1930s. And then there's that great inspirational best seller, *The Power of Positive Thinking* by Dr. Norman Vincent Peale.

Read *See You At The Top* by Zig Ziglar. Read Dr. Denis Waitley's and Brian Tracy's excellent books. Even though these books can be borrowed from your local library, don't. Buy them instead. They need to become a permanent part of your success library to be read and reread to enrich your life and make your business flourish.

Recommended Listening

By developing the audiocassette listening habit, you can

turn otherwise unproductive time while driving, waiting for appointments, shaving or applying makeup into a valuable listening experience.

See the order form at the end of this book for a list of resources my office has available.

The Nightingale-Conant Corporation is one of the world's leading producers of educational audiocassettes. Its catalog has a wealth of videocassettes and audiocassette albums covering business-related topics and powerful motivational materials. You can get a free catalog by calling toll-free 800-323-5552.

Re-member that its authors may not have the biblical background you may have. Depend upon the Holy Spirit to give you discernment between good and evil.

Some larger libraries have educational/motivational tapes available for checkout. Larger video rental outlets offer educational videos for a nominal rental fee. Start with Zig Ziglar's *GOALS*.

Brian Tracy's videos are high content and can provide profitable business ideas and concepts.

I emphasize again what I stated earlier—the Bible is the most important book. You can purchase the entire Bible on audiocassette. An economical producer of the Bible on audiocassettes is:

Bible on Tape (KJV or NIV)
2421 Aztec Road, N.E.
Albuquerque, NM 87107-4224
800-545-6552

Community Colleges

Most community colleges offer short inexpensive, non credit programs for the entrepreneur. They are usually taught by experienced owners and managers. Check them out.

Guard a Quiet-Time Appointment

Christians in business often get caught up in a whirlwind of activities and limit or forsake altogether the quintessential daily quiet time. The quiet time is a time to meditate on God's Word. It is a time to focus. It is a time for reflection upon your business calling and a turning to the Lord for ways and means to best fulfill it. Many find the early hours of the morning, before dawn, to be an ideal quiet time.

Especially when faced with a challenge, turn to the Lord.

> God is our refuge and strength, an ever-present help in trouble.
>
> Psalm 46:1

> In all your ways acknowledge him, and he will help you succeed.
>
> Proverbs 3:6

During the quiet time I recommend that you pray with a pen and paper in hand. Expect productive ideas and creative solutions to flow. Always bear in mind that God loves you and he wants you to succeed.

> The Lord be exalted who delights in the prosperity of his servant.
>
> Psalm 35:27

CHAPTER 12 | ADVERTISING AND PRICING

Once you are operating a business, how will your potential customers or clients hear about you? People may be looking for exactly what you have to offer, but the public can't take advantage of something if they don't know it exists, can they?

Your method of advertising will depend largely upon the type of business you have. A restaurant, for example, would usually have a grand opening special. It could advertise in the newspaper, use direct mail coupons and radio and television. But a bookkeeping service would probably use different media.

Consider using the Internet. The Internet and E-mail are revolutionizing the way the world does business. According to some forecasters, companies that are not doing business on the World Wide Web may not even be in business in the new millennium. If you don't know it by now, the Internet is no longer an option for small business; it is a necessity.

If you feel you cannot create your own web site there are professionals who can help you select the layout, design, background colors and include your company logo and pictures. Your web site can take your local company and give it a window to the world where your customers can find you 24-hours a days, 365-days a year.

If your product cannot be purchased directly through the Internet, include an option that lets potential buyers leave their name, phone number or other contact information with a request that someone call them with more information about a specific product.

After creating a company web site, the challenge will be to get people to visit it. You need to register the site with the Internet search engines that seek out information for users. *SitePromoter 2.0* can help you register your web pages on more than 150 search engines, directories and indexes. It also helps meet the requirements of each engine and directory and tells how to get the most publicity through them. Contact them at: http://www.sitepromoter.com.

The Nolo Press publishes a provocative book called *Marketing Without Advertising* by Michael Phillips and Salli Rasberry. It is worthwhile reading. The authors argue convincingly that most advertising is totally ineffective and is usually a waste of money. The book outlines a detailed plan to promote a business without cost-inefficient conventional advertising.

A Good Name

The best advertisement is actually very inexpensive. It is satisfied customers or clients.

Solomon said:

> A good name is more desirable than great riches, to be esteemed is better than silver or gold.
>
> Proverbs 21:1

Referrals may prove to be the best way to advance your business, especially if you are in a service business. Learn to ask for referrals. Give your customers or clients an incentive for introducing their sphere of influence to you and acquainting them with what your new business offers. A word from someone else holds more weight than self-promotion. Solomon instructed:

> Let another praise you, and not your own mouth: someone else and not your own lips.
>
> Proverbs 27:2

Many business owners have found that the most efficient way for their businesses to grow is by word of mouth. That is the way the gospel is to be spread and it's the way your business can grow. Paul told Timothy:

> The things you have heard me say in the presence of many witnesses entrust to reliable men who will also be qualified to teach others.
>
> II Timothy 2:2

"Give and it shall be given..."

Jesus gave the ultimate formula for having customers to respond liberally to you.

> Give and it will be given to you. A good measure, pressed down, shaken together and running over, will be poured into your lap. For with the measure you use, it will be measured to you.
>
> Luke 6:38

He was talking about a lifestyle of giving. The verse literally means to give and keep on giving. He said, "Give..." In the case of your business, give service, give quality, give exceptional value, give dependability.

For example, if you are an investment broker, make sure you give only well-researched, sound investment advice. If you are in the business of detailing cars, give attention to the extra details and go beyond the expectations of your customers.

If you will concentrate on giving quality, on being the best, on serving, then growth and bigness will ultimately take care of themselves.

Solomon asked:

> Do you see a man skilled in his work? He will serve before kings, he will not serve before obscure men.
>
> Proverbs 22:29

Target Your Audience

If you feel you must advertise, think and analyze before you spend money. Make sure your target audience's eyes will see what your advertising dollar is buying.

Don't be unduly influenced to invest in Yellow Page advertising if it will not be productive for you. If your business is something like a 24-hour plumbing operation, the Yellow Pages is a vital link to your prospective customer. However, if you offer a bookkeeping service such advertising may not produce a single new customer.

Remember if you discover the Yellow Pages is not working, you can't go to the telephone company and cancel it. You must continue paying monthly until that book expires— even if you move and change telephone numbers.

Every molecule of you and your business should exude success. People don't want to do business with a loser. Make your company look successful. After all, the Law of Genesis states that everything reproduces after its own kind.

One of your greatest public relations agents is a successful image. Keep your office, your showroom, your restrooms and your cars clean; stay well groomed personally.

It is generally worthwhile to create a professional image with appropriate matching letterheads, invoices, company brochures and business cards.

Remember what God told Samuel:

> Man looks at the outward appearance, but the Lord looks at the heart.
>
> I Samuel 16:7

In regard to outward appearances, men are not like God because only God always sees beyond outward appearances. Your customers are initially impressed and moved to action by what they see—i.e., your outward image.

With a computer and a laser printer you may be able to design your own letterhead, cards, labels and brochures.

Check out paper companies such as Paper Direct and Quill who have colorful pre-designed stock.

Maybe you can create a business logo from public domain clip art. There are thousands of images of art in public domain that are free for use by anyone. They are available on CD-ROM from computer supply houses and over the Internet.

By thinking creatively you may be able to put two or more of these images together and perhaps add a few words in a distinctive typeface of your choice and create your own logo. To do this, you will need a graphics image program but many of these can be obtained as freeware or shareware as well.

If you feel you cannot create your own professional looking image, get help from a professional in designing a distinct and unique logo that will give your business instant recognition. A good graphic designer can help tie all your materials together—company receipts, invoices, business cards, stationery, envelopes, etc.

For a classic touch, order "thank you" cards personalized with your logo and matching envelopes. Follow up sales and presentations with a "thank you" note. This action reaps high dividends.

Economize anywhere except in the areas that will meet your customers' eyes and in the area of getting quality employees. Of even more importance than your printed material, are your employees and sales people who represent you and your business.

Now let's focus on pricing. How do you arrive at a fair price for your product or service? In order for customers to part with their money, the price they pay for an item must be regarded as "fair" and congruent with their perception of its worth. There is a fine line here. If the price is considered low, the merchant runs the risk of having the customer doubt the quality of the product but if it is perceived to be too high, the customer will simply not buy.

After the cost of goods and overhead, your challenge will be to establish an acceptable price range that will give an adequate profit and still be considered a good value by the customer or client.

In some cases, the price may be set by your major competitors. If you do not maintain parity or price below your competitor, naturally customers will not buy from you.

Usually small business operators arrive at the retail price based upon the cost of the merchandise. But to remain in business that retail price must cover not only the cost of the merchandise but operating expenses such as rent, labor, utilities, advertising, insurance, telephone, printing, etc. *and* an appropriate amount as a profit.

When some small business operators discover how little the major chains pay for the exact item they offer, they get a rude awakening to what is known as "economy of scale." You may be purchasing the unit by a gross or two, but the major chain may purchase a half million or more. Naturally their per-unit cost will be less. This is no reason to despair though.

Beating the Competition

Where you can rise and shine brighter than your national competitors is in the area of overhead. Many major companies are buckling under an oppressive debt load. A large percentage of every sale goes to service debt. This is especially true of the companies that have fallen victim to hostile take-overs. Leveraged buyouts increase the debt load. These companies may be plagued with huge payrolls of "unprofitable servants." They must fund medical plans, profit-sharing plans for employee retirement, pay huge retainers to attorneys to defend themselves against frivolous lawsuits and pay outlandish insurance premiums to cover the myriad of liabilities they face.

Furthermore, these publicly traded companies have stockholders who are expecting and demanding dividends.

Value-Added Technique

Some small business people can handily compete by using the value-added technique. As an example, even though the small business's wholesale cost of a bicycle may be equal to a national chain's retail price, the small business may be able to get more for the same bike by adding a special seat or a light-and-horn package or special treatment. Or a sporting goods store may offer lessons as a freebie for buying the tennis racquet from them, etc. Allow God to instruct you in this area.

> I am the Lord your God who teacheth thee to profit, which leadeth thee by the way thou shouldest go.
>
> Isaiah 48:17,18 (KJV)

Lastly, the national chain does not have you. *You* make your customers or clients feel important. *You* give service. *You* exude the love of the Lord. The national chain may not have the Lord's favor as *you* do. *You* can have the Lord giving promotion.

> Promotion cometh neither from the east, nor from the west nor from the south.
>
> Psalm 75:6

The inference of the above verse is that promotion comes from the direction north, indicating God's throne.

Claim the promise of Psalm 1. Resolve to be the person who is:

> ...like a tree planted by the streams of water, which yields its fruit in season and whose leaf does not wither. Whatever he does prospers.
>
> Psalm 1:1-3

Can you compete? Yes, you can! The question should be, can they compete against you? If you have adopted the philosophy presented in this book, you will not be struggling under huge debt payments, you will have learned how to get value out of every dollar spent and you will be walking in God's favor.

Markup Formula

The majority of small retailers use a keystone markup in pricing; they simply double the cost. If an item costs $20, the amount the consumer would be charged is $40. However, this technique may or may not enable you to make a profit. Remember, the key to staying in business is to turn a profit. Someone wisely said, "Nobody ever went broke making a profit." Tragically, many small business operators don't know if they are making a profit.

If, for example, you are selling ice cream cones, analyze the facts. How many ice cream cones must you sell to break even? Obviously, if the sales do not reach that level, you will be operating at a loss, or in common vernacular, operating in the red.

After you have estimated your costs of overhead, as explained earlier in this book, estimate your annual gross sales. In the case of an ice cream shop, how many cones can you reasonably expect to sell each day? Multiply that amount by the number of days you are open each year.

Now divide the annual cost of overhead by the number of cones to be sold each year. This will reveal how many cents of each cone sale goes for rent, telephone, payroll, including yours, etc. (These expenses are known as overhead.)

Now deduct the actual costs of the ice cream, cone, napkins and all other product costs.

What remains is your profit? Don't forget you deserve a profit. Remember you have made an investment. You have paid for things like trade fixtures and signs, maybe franchise fees, etc. Your price must reflect an amount that will render an acceptable yield on your investment as a profit.

At a later date, if you want to sell your business, its value will be determined by how much profit it generates. Let's say you want a 10% profit. By doing your homework and reading the various trade journals and publications for your type of business, you determine that the normal overhead costs expressed as a percentage is 35% of the gross sales. Since the profit of 10% plus the overhead of 35% totals 45%, the cost of goods must be 55% (100% less 45%) because it must total 100% of the selling price.

If you know the product cost is 60¢ per cone, you divide that amount by 55% or .55 and you will get $1.09. If you can sell each cone for $1.09, you will cover all costs and make a 10% profit. Now you must determine if the public will pay $1.09 for each cone. If that amount is higher than the market will support, you must look for ways to cut your costs of product or overhead. If you can't, you must face the fact that an ice cream shop is not a viable idea.

Other Resource Material

Order a free listing of SBA's publications entitled *SBA's Resource Directory for Small Business Management* from the Small Business Administration (SBA). For the local SBA field office nearest you, dial 800-8-ASK-SBA or download from SBA on-line: http://www.sba.gov.

Also the publication *Learn the Going Wage Rate* evaluating the cost of adding new personnel can be obtained from the Bureau of Labor Statistics, 202-606-6220 or on-line: http://stats.bis.gov/ocshome.htm.

Do-It-Yourself Advertising & Promotion details how to find the appropriate medium for your message and your budget can be obtained from John Wiley & Sons, Inc., 605 Third Ave., New York 10158.

Basic Profit Mechanics—How to Make Money in Your Business analyzes costs and sets prices for maximum profits can be obtained from Global Management Exchange, Box 1249, Friday Harbor, Washington 98250. 800-360-6166.

With a lot of God-inspired common-sense, you will be able to operate in a perfect price range and succeed profitably in a competitive environment.

CHAPTER 13 | *TAXES*

Like it or not you have a partner in your business—Uncle Sam. He's a demanding partner and he insists you operate the business according to his rules.

Tax laws are never static; they are ever changing. I have used my best efforts to compile the tax information contained in this chapter and to verify its accuracy *as of the date of this writing*.

This chapter is not written as a definitive guide to U.S. tax law. My intent is to offer you a broad overview of tax laws as they pertain to and affect small business.

The assistance of a competent professional such as a Certified Public Accountant (CPA) or an attorney skilled in tax law is recommended before the implementation of any tax or legal material contained in this book.

Due to the complexities of the IRS tax laws, this material may seem tedious. You may be tempted to skip this chapter altogether or at least put off reading it until later, but it will be in your best interest to wade through it now.

When you start your own business in this country, even a part-time business operated out of your home, you automatically qualify for many powerful tax deductions you otherwise cannot take as an individual.

Being a part of the kingdom of God does not exempt you from paying taxes. Both Jesus and Paul addressed the issue of a Christian's obligation to pay taxes.

Jesus said:

> Give to Caesar what is Caesar's, and to God what is God's.
>
> Matthew 22:21

Paul instructed:

> If you owe taxes, pay taxes.
>
> Romans 13:7

Personal Income Taxes

Your goal should be to give Caesar no more than Caesar is due. Even the law of the land states:

> Anyone may so arrange their affairs so that their taxes are as low as possible. No one owes any public duty to pay more than the law demands.
> — Judge Learned Hand

Ignorance of tax law causes many Christians to overpay taxes annually. Paying no more taxes than the law demands requires you to become familiar with tax law. Begin by requesting Publication 17, *Your Federal Income Tax*, from the IRS. This free publication covers your personal income tax. All tax forms and publications cited in this chapter may be obtained by calling 800-829-3676 or your local IRS office.

Business
Income Taxes

For an in-depth study of small business tax benefits, request the Internal Revenue Service to send you its free Publication 334, entitled *Tax Guide for the Small Business.*

As a practical measure, this publication should be ordered annually so you keep abreast of all changes in the tax laws. Since the tax laws change, the latest edition of Publication 334 can serve as a resource to update this book.

Are you aware that more Americans *overpay* taxes than *underpay* them? Furthermore, are you aware that most tax fraud is in the area of understating income rather than overstating deductions? Your tax liability is probably one of your greatest expenditures—usually greater than housing, transportation or health costs. In this chapter you'll learn the beneficial impact starting and operating a business can have on your federal income taxes.

Even though a business can be a powerful tax shelter, I don't suggest starting one for the sake of the tax benefits alone. Your purpose in starting a business should be to make a profit. The tax advantages are a great fringe benefit of being in business.

The Ultimate
Tax Shelter

You have probably heard the old saying that the only two

things in life that are certain are death and taxes. In a jocular vein, someone once said, "One good thing can be said about death—it does not get worse every time Congress meets." Let me remind you again, since Congress continues to meet, the tax information contained in this chapter will continue to change.

Most of the great tax shelters previously used to put high-income earners in the zero tax bracket have been severely weakened or eliminated altogether. Fortunately the small business still affords powerful tax incentives even after the devastation of the Tax Reform Act of 1986.

From a tax standpoint, to be in business and to be eligible for the additional tax benefits, you must have a "product or a service you regularly offer to the public with the *intent* to produce a profit." That's it. That is the IRS's definition of being in business. Notice its definition does not require a corporation, a specified amount of money or even an office for that matter.

If a small business is operated at a loss as a sole proprietorship, your taxable income derived from your regular job or investments will be reduced by the amount of loss your small business shows. This loss is subject to the limitations discussed later in this chapter. This loss is entered on Line 12 of your Individual Tax Return (Form 1040) thereby reducing your Adjusted Gross Income.

If your first year's business income is $4,000, it will be recorded on a Schedule C. Then on that same form you will off-set the income by the expenses. If the expenses are $6,000, the difference, a negative $2,000, is transferred to Line 12 of Form 1040, thus reducing your taxable income. Isn't that great?

Foreigners frequently marvel at the absolute freedom in
this great country—freedom to pursue wealth to the extent
of one's potential. It is reported that individuals from some
so-called "Third World" nations have made application to
open a business in their country over a decade ago and
they are still waiting for approval. What a pity! By contrast,
in our land there are thousands of businesses that require
no licenses and very little if any money to begin. Opportunities are waiting everywhere.

Generally *all business* expenses are tax deductible. The preceding sentence says it all. The beauty is that a surprising
number of activities you do or did as an individual, once
you are in business, can become tax deductible. Once you
are in business, many assets you buy and use anyway, such
as your automobile, video camera, VCR, or computer may
be partially or even totally tax deductible to the extent they
are used in your business. This is true even if you buy
them on credit.

In 1987 the deduction for sales tax on personal property
was disallowed as a deduction for an individual taxpayer.
However, as a small business operator, the sales tax on supplies you purchase to be used in your business is still
deductible as a business expense.

Sales tax paid when you buy a capital asset such as a car to
be used in your business is added to the basis and recovered through depreciation.

Personal interest is not deductible but business and investment interest is. When you borrow money to purchase a computer, a video camera, a car or any other asset you will use in your business, even in your part-time business, the business interest portion is deductible.

For a business expense to be deductible it must meet these three IRS rules:

1. It must truly be a business expense as contrasted with a personal expense. For example, a real estate brokerage license fee is a deductible expense whereas a fishing license fee (that is, if you are not a commercial fisherman) is a personal expense and therefore not deductible as a business expense.

2. To quote the IRS, the expense must be "ordinary and necessary," meaning that the expense must be one commonly accepted in your business and an expense "appropriate and helpful in developing and maintaining your trade or business."

3. The amounts must be reasonable.

PARTIAL LIST OF POSSIBLE DEDUCTIBLE EXPENSES			
Account books	Coffee service	Gifts to customers	Professional
Accounting fees	Collection expense	Interest on	journals
Advertising	Commissions	business debt	Property taxes
Auditing fees	Consultant fees	Inventory	Publications
Automobile	Contractor's fees	Janitorial service	Reference books
expenses	Conventions	Ledgers	Rent
Bad debts	Cost of goods sold	Legal expenses	Repairs
Bank service	Country club dues	Liability insurance	Research and
charges	Credit bureau fees	Licenses	experimentation
Bonding fees	Credit card fees for	Loss on sale of	Safe deposit box
Bookkeeping	merchants	business assets	Salaries
services	Depreciation	Machinery	Salaries-spouse
Books (useful life	Dues	Magazines	and/or children
1 year or less)	Education	Merchant's	Sales tax
Burglar alarm	expenses	associations	Service charges
service	Electricity	Minor repairs	Small tools
Burglary (see	Employer's taxes	Moving expenses	Stationery
Casualty losses)	Employment	Night watch	Subscriptions
Business	agency fees	service	Supplies
associations	Entertainment	Office furnishings	Telephone
Business cards	Equipment	Office in home	Tools (useful life
Business gifts	Extended coverage	Office supplies	1 yr or less)
Business	insurance	Passport fees for	Trademarks
interruption	Fees for services	business trip	Travel away from
insurance	Fees to	Patents	home
Business license	organizations	Payroll and	Uniforms
Casualty losses	Fire insurance	withheld payroll	Union dues
Charitable	Fire losses	Periodicals	Utilities
contributions	Freight	Permit fees	Vehicles
Cleaning	Garbage	Postage	
Clothing, special	Gas	Professional fees	

Read the above list of possible deductions carefully. See how many items on the list are expenses you incur whether you have a small business or not. To the extent you use them in your business, they now become deductible.

It is easy to see that most legitimate business expenses are deductible. Did you notice there is an exception in the list of deductible expenses—start-up expenses are missing?

Start-Up Expenses

The costs you incur before you actually open for business, things such as organizational expenses, rent, telephone and advertising expense, attorney's fees to draft your lease, corporate charter or other documents, if incurred as a start-up expense, are NOT deductible. Your strategy should be to make your first sale as early as possible in order to make some of the above mentioned expenses tax deductible.

Even the non-deductible start-up expenses are not lost. You can elect to do one of two things with them:

1. Depreciate the start-up expenses over a five-year period, or

2. Capitalize them and have no deduction until such time as you sell your business or simply quit. To capitalize them means you add them to your cost or basis. Your accountant can help you determine the best way to handle these start-up expenses.

Hobby Losses

Another notable exception to deductible business expenses is called "hobby losses." Remember, to be in business there must be an *intent* to make a profit. The test to determine if an activity is for profit is to ascertain if that activity is operated like a business and shows a profit in any three out of five consecutive years. This means you can show a tax loss for two consecutive years. But by the third year, if you show no taxable income, the IRS can deem your activity a hobby and not a business. At the end of two years of loss, you can file Form 5213 that can give you a total of five years to show a taxable profit. If you file this form, your chances of an audit go up appreciably, therefore consider twice before filing it.

Incidentally, the three-out-of-five-year policy mentioned above is not a tax law, only an IRS rule. The burden of proof is on the IRS, not you.

Remember I wrote earlier that ignorance of the tax laws causes many people to overpay federal income taxes year after year. Well, I recently talked to a man who had what he called a hobby in woodworking. He showed me some of his work. It was beautiful. With great pride, he told me how much money some of his pieces were bringing at a local flea market. When I asked him if his business generated much tax shelter for his other income, he looked bewildered and said, "This is a hobby, not a business."

If he treats the activity as a hobby, it can never be a tax shelter. True, there may be some marginal tax benefits, but he will never be able to shelter other income. Here's why. All income generated from a hobby is taxable and can only be offset by the expenses of carrying on that hobby.

As a hobby, if he sold $2,500 worth of woodworking in a year, then deductions can be taken *up to* $2,500. These deductions are treated as miscellaneous itemized deductions on Schedule A of his Form 1040 and can only be claimed if all his itemized miscellaneous deductions exceed 2% of his adjusted gross income.

If, on the other hand, his woodworking is treated as a business (remember, it can be a part-time business), he is entitled to the 27 expense categories listed on Schedule C.

There is no 2% limitation on those deductions.

As you will learn later in this chapter, he can take a deduction of up to $18,500 for 1998 for the purchase of capital items such as a saw or a sander. He can depreciate his shop. He can write off the transportation costs for materials and finished products. If these total expenses are greater than the gains, the losses can then offset his other income.

The determining factor as to whether a hobby is a business or not is intent. The predominant intent and motive in performing the activity must be profit.

Another factor the IRS may look at to determine the status of the activity is the businesslike way in which the activity is conducted. To pass this test, I suggest a separate business checking account be opened, business cards be printed, an assumed name be obtained, etc.

Tips for Greater Deductions

1. Find legitimate business uses for assets such as your motor home, boat or plane.

2. If you operate as a corporation, talk to your CPA or tax attorney about the benefits of an "S" corporation election.

3. Combine vacations with business trips.

4. Use as many personal items as possible in your business—typewriter, VCR, home computer, cassette recorder, etc.

5. Use your automobile or truck in your business.

6. Hire your children in your business and thereby make some or all of the amount of their allowances deductible.

7. If possible, convert personal debt to business debt so you can write-off the interest.

8. Make part of your home expenses deductible by setting up an office in it.

Reason
for Taxes

Congress seems to favor the development of business. The reason for tax laws in this country is not only to raise revenue for the Federal Treasury, but it is also to create incentives to induce people to do what is best for our country and economy—start businesses. Congress knows a small company operated out of a garage has the potential to someday become a major employer and taxpayer such as Apple Computer or Texas Instruments.

You, as an individual taxpayer, have limited means to shelter your earned income:

1. You can fill out the Schedule A of Form 1040 and deduct your interest on two homes, take charitable contribution deductions, etc.

2. You can use Form 2106 to deduct some expenses you may incur as an employee.

3. You can use Form 3903 if you've moved and met the criteria to deduct moving expenses.

On the other hand, observe how generous the tax laws are to those in business. Look at the many deductions which are available to you on these forms:

Sole proprietorship	— Schedule C
Partnership	— Schedule K
Corporation	— Form 1120

Therefore when you choose a business, choose one with the potential of being profitable; choose one you enjoy; choose one you are naturally gifted to do; and also, if possible, choose one that uses your major personal assets such as your car, computer, VCR, car phone and your recreational vehicle for business purposes. After all, Uncle Sam is your partner. Let him pay his way!

What Is a Deduction?

What is a deduction anyway? It is an expense that directly reduces your taxable income. Personal deductions such as mortgage interest and church contributions are allowed *only* if deductions are itemized on Schedule A. But business deductions are deducted from gross income even if itemized deductions are not claimed. If you can generate enough deductions to offset your taxable income entirely, you will pay no income taxes.

Entertainment

Fully 50% of the cost of feeding and entertaining your prospects, customers, clients, suppliers and professional advisers, including the cost of your own meal can be a tax deduction for you if the entertainment meets what the IRS calls the "directly related test." This requirement may be met in one of the following three ways:

1. The Directly Related Test

You must be able to demonstrate a business motive for the entertainment. For example, you arrange to meet your friend for lunch. Your purpose in having lunch together is to introduce him or her to your business opportunity. Naturally you pick up the tab and leave an appropriate tip. Fifty percent of this cost, including tips and taxes can be deducted from your gross income.

Here's how you do it. When you prepare your tax return, use the Schedule C. Record your total entertainment expense on Line 24b. Subtract 50% on Line 24c and enter the 50% figure on Line 24d. Thus your taxable income is reduced by this entertainment expense.

What if you entertained your prospect on a hunting trip or on a yacht or at a restaurant? If the directly related test can be passed, it is possible to deduct it. However, the IRS presumes entertainment during hunting or fishing trips or on a yacht is not conducive to business discussion or activity. It is incumbent on you to prove otherwise, if you wish to claim the deduction.

2. Clear Business Setting Test

You must be able to demonstrate you had no significant motive for incurring the expenses other than to further your business. For example, after an opportunity meeting for a multi-level company, you take your new recruit to a restaurant to discuss strategies for getting him or her off to a successful start. Normally you would have gone straight home, but in order to help further your business you incur this entertainment expense; therefore, the cost is 50% deductible.

3. Services Performed Test

The expense meets the directly related test if it was directly or indirectly made for the benefit of an individual as compensation for services or as a taxable prize or award. For example, you provide a vacation trip to Jamaica as a prize to the sales representative who reaches a sales quota. The value of the vacation will be taxable to the winner but the cost is deductible to you because it is a directly related entertainment expense.

Keep Essential Records

The key to deducting these entertainment expenses is to keep records to support the deduction. You are required to keep a record book (your daily pocket calendar is adequate) in which you record the time the expense was incurred, with whom, the place, how much you spent and the business purpose.

I suggest you have a receipt for the expense even though the IRS rules say you don't have to have a receipt if the expense is under $25. If the expense is over $25, you must have a receipt for the expense. Without these records, your deductions may be disallowed if you are audited.

The amount deductible for meals and entertainment expense is 50% of the total bill, provided that business was specifically discussed at the meal. Be aware that the IRS is more likely to audit excessive entertainment expense, so cover yourself well. For more information, ask the IRS to send you Publication 463, *Travel, Entertainment and Gift Expenses.*

Education
Expenses

How about education expenses such as tuition, course fees, books, etc.? They are deductible if the education is to maintain or sharpen your skills in your *present* line of work. You can enjoy great tax deductions and at the same time improve your professional skills by taking seminars, workshops or college courses, even if they lead to a degree.

Education expenses are *not* deductible if the education is to qualify you for a *new* field or to meet the *minimum* educational requirements of your present job. It sounds irrational, but that's the way it is.

Any magazines, books (including this one), newsletters, audiocassettes or videocassettes that relate to your business are tax deductible.

The next time you visit the mall, go to the business section of a bookstore. Uncle Sam, your business partner, can help you purchase books that relate to business, management, business ideas, marketing, advertising, record keeping and success in general.

Business Gifts

You can deduct the cost of a business gift to an individual of up to $25 per person for any tax year. Incidental costs such as gift wrapping, postage, insurance or even engraving are not included in calculating the cost limitation of the gift.

A gift to the spouse of a person you are doing business with is considered an indirect gift to the person with whom you're doing business and is not deductible. But if both spouses have business connections with you, you can give a gift of up to $25 to each of them and claim a deduction.

A gift may cost more than $25, but only $25 will be eligible for the deduction. You and your spouse are treated as one taxpayer if you both give business gifts to the same person. Even if you have separate businesses, are separately employed or file separate returns, only one of the gifts can be deducted.

There is a special exception to this $25 business gift deductibility limitation. Items costing $4 or less on which your name is permanently imprinted and are part of identical items distributed, are fully deductible and are not counted in determining the limitation. These can be items like pens, mugs or appointment books bearing your name and telephone number.

One year I gave my clients a cleverly designed business card file they could set on their desk. Since it bore my name and met the $4 test, it did not count against the $25 limitation if I wanted to further ingratiate myself to them with additional gifts.

Suppose you want to treat a favorite customer to tickets to the symphony or to a play. This would be considered a legitimate business deduction if it meets the cost test mentioned above.

However, if you accompany your customer or client to the event, there are different rules that apply. If you go along, you can deduct the cost of the tickets as a business expense only if it passes the business discussion test. You must talk business immediately preceding the show or immediately after. Furthermore, if you go, you can only deduct 50% of the cost; however, there is no $25 limitation.

It is important to keep records of your deductible gift giving. Your records should reflect the cost of the gift, the date given and the name of the person receiving it.

Insurance

An individual is able to deduct 45% in years 1998 and 1999, 50% in year 2000 and 2001, 60% in 2002, 80% in 2003 thru 2005, 90% in 2006 and 100% in 2007 and thereafter of the cost of health insurance premiums paid.

The remainder of personally paid health insurance (in this case, 55% in 1998) is deductible on Schedule A of your Form 1040 only if your medical expenses are more than 7.5% of your adjusted gross income (AGI) floor.

On the other hand, the insurance coverage paid for your employees is 100% deductible. So is yours, if you are employed by your corporation but the insurance must be provided to other employees of the corporation as well. All other premiums paid on other types of business insurance are also deductible.

WHAT KINDS OF INSURANCE DO I NEED?

In this day of litigation, take special care to be adequately insured. The kinds of insurance to be considered are:

Fire —	• covers loss in case of fire
Extended Coverage —	• covers loss from storms, explosions, smoke damage and damage from a vehicle
Liability —	• covers bodily injury or damage to other's property
Disability —	• covers loss of personal income due to a disabling illness or injury
Errors & omissions —	• coverage for a business' mistakes, either by omission or malfeasance
Life insurance —	• on owner, partners or key employees
Property Damage —	• covers damage done to property of others. Example: smoke damage to adjoining property
Vandalism & Malicious Mischief —	• as the name implies
Theft Coverage —	• covers protection from burglary and robbery
Product Liability —	• covers the business in the event the user of a product sues
Business Interruption —	• pays you what you would have earned while your business is closed due to fire, etc.
Worker's Compensation —	• provides disability and death benefits to employees injured or killed on the job. This is mandatory in most states.
Automobile Insurance —	• covers the business vehicle. Unfortunately the premiums are higher than personal use vehicles.
Business Owner's Package —	• is a package combining most or all the above in one policy

I generally recommend independent agents since they are not tied to one company. Shop around until you find someone sensitive to your needs and budget.

IMPORTANT: Make sure independent contractors who do work for you have worker's compensation on themselves and on those to whom they may subcontract work. If not, I would reconsider using them because you may be liable if there is injury to the contractors or their people.

Travel Expense

One of the great tax deductions available to you as a small business operator is that travel related to your small business becomes a legitimate tax write-off. Your strategy should be to psychologically make the business trip satisfy your yearning to get away. There is no reason you cannot enjoy a business trip, is there?

Granted, for a trip to be deductible, the primary purpose must be business related. But there is no law that says a vacation cannot be planned around a legitimate business purpose and consequently make all or at least a substantial part of the trip tax deductible. As long as a spouse or other family members traveling with you are co-owners or employees of your small, even part-time business, and you can demonstrate that they have a valid business reason for accompanying you, their expenses are deductible as well.

Even if family members accompanying you have no business purpose for being there, you may still deduct the full auto mileage, auto rental and hotel expenses (if your room rate is not increased by the additional persons accompanying you). You may deduct any other expenses you would have incurred had you been traveling alone. You cannot deduct their food or airline tickets in such cases. If possible, make it your strategy to find some legitimate business purpose for your family to accompany you and thus make all related expenses deductible.

Consider some of these ways to deduct travel expenses:

- **Meeting with current or potential clients**

    If your business is in the field of direct sales, the primary purpose of a trip could be to offer your product or service to a prospect.

- **Visiting with owners of a similar business in order to learn from them**

  Such a visit can provide a wealth of information as you observe their success systems. Be prepared to demonstrate to the IRS that what you learned or experienced was directly connected to your business.

- **A trip to buy products for resell**

  If audited, you may have to justify that you had to see the products, something you could not do by looking at a catalog.

- **Trade shows, business conventions, conferences or association meetings**

  Travel to a business seminar is deductible. Keep a complete itinerary of the convention or the seminar as part of your records. In order to qualify for the deduction the lecturers must be live and not viewed by video only. It is reasoned that you could have rented the videos and viewed them at home. Unfortunately, travel to investment seminars is no longer deductible.

- **Setting up distributors for your product or service**

  You may want to travel across the country to interest a potential independent distributor to become a part of your sales team. Such a trip can be totally deductible.

For all such trips you may deduct all business expenses incurred including air fares, rental cars, meals and entertainment (subject to the 50% rule), laundry or any other expense you can justify as a business-related expense.

If you extend your business trip a few days for leisure activities and if you can justify that you had to be at that geographical location to conduct the business activity, the whole transportation cost is deductible. This does not include lodging and food costs during the leisure time.

The test to decide whether or not the primary purpose of the trip is business is to determine the amount of time you spent on business or the need to be in that spot to conduct the business or attend the convention.

Travel Abroad

The tax deductible business trip can even be abroad; however, special rules apply. Trips outside of the United States must be one week or less in length, not counting the day you leave but counting the day you return. If the trip lasts over one week, you must spend three days on business for every one day of pure vacation time. If you spend more than 25% of the time abroad as personal vacation days, you can only deduct the business percentage of the trip. However, if you conduct business on Friday and Monday but not on the weekend, you can count the weekend as two business days.

Cruise Ships

If your business association promotes a convention aboard

a cruise ship, special rules apply. First, you must be able to show that the convention is directly related to your business. You may deduct up to $2,000 per year for attending cruise ship conventions if all the ports-of-call are in the United States or its possessions (including Puerto Rico, U.S. Virgin Islands and Guam), Mexico, Canada, Barbados or Jamaica and if the ship is U.S. registered. Consider Hawaii or Alaska.

You can deduct the cost of travel to a business destination even if the mode of transportation is a cruise ship. A special rule applies. Be sure you contact the IRS for the limitations and regulations.

Automobile

An automobile is one example of an asset most of us have whether we're in business or not. The car can be a costly expense amounting to thousands of dollars annually. Fortunately, once in business, the business portion of the automobile can be partially or totally "written off" as a business expense.

All costs of operating the vehicle for business use are deductible with one notable exception—commuting between your home and your usual place of business. This is true even if you drive to a different job location everyday.

There is an exception, however. If you drive to several job locations each day then only the mileage to the first stop and from the last stop to your home is not deductible. Strategize to make your stops more advantageous from a tax angle.

Not only can the costs of operating the vehicle be deducted, but the cost of the automobile itself can be depreciated over a period of time. See the in-depth study of depreciation later in this chapter.

There are two ways to deduct the operating expenses of your automobile:

- the actual expense method
- the standard mileage allowance

The Actual Expense Method

The *actual expense method* requires more record keeping. Keep itemized records of all auto expenses such as:

gasoline and oil	insurance	tires
parking and tolls	repairs	cleaning
license fees, etc.	maintenance	taxes

These expenses must be prorated or divided between the non-deductible personal use, such as going to the grocery store or church and business use, such as going to see a prospect or to a business seminar.

As an example, say you drive a total of 20,000 miles during a year—15,000 miles are in connection with your business. In this case, 75% (15,000 divided by 20,000) of the operating expenses are deductible as a business expense and 25% are not deductible. Example:

$1,000 gasoline expense for year
x 75% business use
$750 can be deducted

The easiest way to ascertain business use is to keep a small notebook in your car and log all business usage. Use the Daily Mileage Log provided at the end of this chapter.

The Standard
Mileage Allowance

The *standard mileage allowance* is the easy way of writing off automobile expenses and because of recent increases in the allowable amount per mile, it may be the most liberal. For 1998, simply deduct 32½ cents per mile for every business mile driven.

> CAUTION: *This method is in lieu of depreciation and the other expenses used with the actual expense method except you can deduct parking and tolls.*

For the fifth straight year, the IRS has increased its flat mileage allowance. In 1998, all miles you drive for business earn the full 32½ cents per mile.

If your car is a gas hog or if you drive so little that the depreciation deduction is spread over fewer miles, you may still be able to beat the standard mileage allowance. In every case, check it both ways and, of course, choose the bigger deduction. This choice affects later tax years.

If, in the first year, you elect to use the actual expense method and deduct actual costs and depreciation, you may not elect to use the standard allowance for that car in a later year and vice versa.

You cannot change methods after you've started.

The standard mileage allowance method requires you to keep a log as well. There is no getting around a log. If you want the deduction, there must be a mileage log.

In this log book, you will record the odometer readings for

the beginning and the ending of the tax year. Throughout the year keep a log of all business mileage driven in this auto. You need this data to prove business use.

Subtract the beginning of the year mileage from the ending of the year mileage. This gives you the overall mileage, both personal and business for the year. Add up all the business miles driven during the year. Divide this year-end total of business miles by the year-end overall total miles driven to determine the percent of business usage of your vehicle(s). A good format for keeping a record of your mileage is shown below.

Daily Mileage Log

Codes For Each Automobile
    A Car 1 _____
    B Car 2 _____
    etc.

Codes For Type Mileage:
    10__   Business
    20__   Personal
    30__   Medical
    40__   Educational
    etc.

Example: "10A" would be business mileage for Car 1. So when you total all your "10A's" you would know how far you drove for business in Car 1.

Date	Description	Mileage Code	Beginning Mileage	Ending Mileage	Net Mileage

The standard mileage allowance may not be used if you lease your vehicle or if you operate more than one vehicle at a time for business use in any one business. Use Form 2106 as the worksheet but take the deduction on Schedule C and the depreciation on Form 4562.

Some non-business mileage is also deductible. In 1998 for mileage driven for charitable purposes, the deduction is 14 cents per mile. For medical purposes, the deduction is 10 cents per mile. For more information request IRS Publication 917, *Business Use Of A Car.*

Depreciation

When you use property having a useful life of more than one year in your small business, the government permits you to get back what you paid for the property by depreciating it. You do this by deducting a portion of its cost on your tax return each year.

Such assets are treated differently than a business expense. An expense is written off in the year it is incurred, but a business asset must be depreciated over a period of time. Depreciating an asset means its cost is recovered by writing it off over a specified number of years (the recovery period) regardless of whether the asset is new or used at the time it is put into service in your business. Get IRS's Publication 534, *Depreciation,* for complete instructions about how to claim this deduction.

Examples of property that can be depreciated are buildings, vehicles, machinery, furniture and equipment. In order for property to be depreciated:

- It must be used in a business for the production of income.

- It must have a determinable life.

- It must have a life longer than one year.

- It must be something that wears out or loses value.

An Expense Item vs. a Capital Item

A copier is an example of an asset that can be depreciated.

But copier supplies, such as paper and toner, are expensed. Do you see the difference? Any small tool is expensed whereas a major piece of machinery must be depreciated and not expensed.

If you buy a small cassette recorder for $50, it is not a capital asset but it is expensed as a business deduction in the year of its acquisition. On the other hand, if a high-speed tape duplicator is purchased for $2,000, it is a capital asset and will be depreciated over a period of years.

You are allowed to depreciate the total cost of the asset including sales tax, installation costs and freight charges. It's immaterial that the acquisition may have been financed. If you did finance the purchase, don't forget to expense the interest because business interest is deductible even though personal interest is not.

Assets Converted From Personal Use

If you purchase an asset as a personal item and later convert it to business use, you can depreciate the original cost or the market value at the time of conversion, whichever is less. Items serving both a business use and a non-business or personal use are depreciated to the extent they are used for business. This means that only the part used in your business can be depreciated.

> *Example:* If you use a video camera 40% of the time (by actual written log of time used) for personal use such as video taping your children's birthdays, and 60% of the time for business use such as recording business presentations, then you can depreciate 60% of the cost or basis.

Office in Home

If your business is located within a building you own, the building may be depreciated.

If your place of business is in your home, then a home-office deduction is available if a room or even a portion of a room meets the following guidelines.

It must be <u>exclusively</u> used on a regular basis as either of the following:

(1) The principal place of the business, or

(2) As a meeting place for clients, customers or patients in the normal course of business, or

(3) In the taxpayer's trade or business if the portion used is a separate structure not attached to the dwelling unit.

If the taxpayer is an employee, a deduction is allowed only if the home office is maintained for the convenience of the employer.

In 1993, the U.S. Supreme Court handed down a decision that effectively eliminated the ability of many individuals to claim tax deductions for home-office expenses such as depreciation, utilities and repairs. The basic effect of the decision was to deny a home-office deduction to the many individuals who use their home offices exclusively and regularly for some functions related to their trade or business (for example, administrative work) but whose "principal place of business" is deemed to be elsewhere. In this situation a home-office deduction may not be claimed unless the home office satisfies numbers two and three above.

In view of the fact that a growing number of individuals are managing their business activities from their homes, Congress has modified the law, effective for taxable years beginning after December 31, 1998, to provide that a home office qualifies as a "principal place of business" if:

(1) The home office is used by the taxpayer to conduct administrative or management activities of a trade or business *and*

(2) There is no other *fixed* location of the trade or business where the taxpayer conducts *substantial* administrative or management activities of the trade or business.

Thus, even if an individual also carries out administrative or management activities while traveling (for example, from a hotel room or a car), the home-office deduction will still be available. Similarly, if an individual does occasional paperwork or other administrative tasks at a fixed location of the business outside the home, it will still be possible to claim a home-office deduction if the other requirements are met.

Note that the expansion of the "principal-place-of-business" rule does not preclude a deduction with respect to a home office that meets the previous tests for being considered a principal place of business. Thus, taxpayers who have no other place of business other than their home office or who can show that the home office is their principal place of business will still be eligible for deductions provided all other requirements are met.

If you are a sole proprietor who uses your home for scheduling your appointments, doing research, keeping books or ordering supplies, you can deduct home-office expense if there is no other fixed location for such activities.

Figuring Home-Office Depreciation

You generally determine the depreciation of your home office by dividing the square footage of the office area by the total square footage of your home. This gives the percentage of your home being used for business purposes. Multiply this percentage by the cost basis in your home to determine the amount you can recover through depreciation. Your cost basis should be your acquisition costs plus any capital improvements you've made. Land is considered a permanent asset and cannot be depreciated.

Example of Figuring Home-Office Depreciation

James is in the mail order business and has an office in his home that meets IRS requirements for deducting expenses for the business use of the home. His office is 400 square feet. His home is 2,000 square feet.

400 square feet divided by 2,000 square feet = 20%

Since his house costs $120,000 and the lot is worth $20,000 ($120,000 - $20,000 = $100,000), 20% of $100,000 is $20,000 which will be depreciated over a period of 27½ years as explained later in this chapter.

Also be aware that 20% of the utilities, maid service, property taxes, mortgage interest, insurance, repairs, security service fees, decorating and all other expenses related to the care and upkeep of the property can be expensed in the year of their payment. Refer to IRS Publication 334 for directions on computation.

If James rents the house, of course, he cannot depreciate it but he can deduct 20% of the rent as a direct expense write-off in the year he pays it.

Home-Office Deduction Limitation

The home-office tax deduction is limited by the net income the business produces. This means you can only claim this deduction for a given year in which your business actually makes money. See "Deduction Limit" in IRS Publication 587, *Business Use of Your Home.*

If the business you conduct out of your home shows a tax loss, then part of your home-office expenses are not deductible that year. The depreciation or rent, utilities and insurance may be deducted only to the extent there is no loss; however, any unused loss may be carried (with some adjustments) to a future profitable year and deducted then. Interest and property taxes on the home office may be deducted regardless of a tax loss.

The total deductions you can take (with depreciation taken last) cannot be more than your gross income from your home-based business minus the sum of:

(1) The business percentage of the otherwise deductible mortgage interest, real estate taxes and casualty and theft losses

(2) The business expenses that are not attributable to the business use of your home such as salaries and supplies

Let's go back to the mail order business that James operates out of his home. Remember his home office is 20% of his home.

Here is how he would figure the allowable loss:

Gross sales	$13,000
Less cost for goods sold	7,000
Gross income	6,000
Less 20% of the mortgage interest and real estate taxes	3,000
Balance	3,000
Less business expenses allowed in full (postage, salaries, etc.)	2,000
Gross income limit	1,000
Less other expenses allocable to business use of the home: maintenance, insurance and utilities (20%)	800
Limit on further deduction	$200
Depreciation $1,600	
Carryover to future years ($1,600 - 200=)	$1,400

Since the depreciation, in this case $1,600, must be taken last, James can only deduct $200 of the depreciation this tax year because of the gross income limit. However, $1,400 can be carried over to next year, subject to the income limits of that year.

Here are the steps taken to arrive at the deductible operating expenses and depreciation for the office in the home:

Step 1   Reduce the gross sales from the business activity in your home by the business portion of deductible home mortgage interest, real estate taxes and casualty losses.

Step 2   From the balance of income arrived at from

Step 1, deduct business expenses, such as salaries, subscriptions, dues, telephone and supply costs that could be claimed even if you did not have an office in the home.

Step 3   From the balance of income under Step 2, if any, you deduct office operating expenses such as maintenance, utilities, insurance and cleaning services.

Step 4   If a balance still remains under Step 3, you deduct allocable depreciation up to the amount of remaining business income.

The amount of ad valorem real estate taxes, home mortgage interest or casualty losses not allocable to the home office under Step 1 may be claimed as itemized deductions on Schedule A on your Form 1040.

Sale of Home

If you sell your home, there is a catch in the depreciation expense. Ordinarily, when you sell your house you may postpone paying capital gain on the sale of the old house if you buy another one. This applies to the total value of the property, except for the portion you have depreciated for business use. Check with your CPA.

Asset Expensing
(Section 179)

Before we discuss how to compute depreciation, let us first examine what is known as "asset expensing" or the "first-year expensing" deduction. As a small business person you may be able to avoid the depreciation calculation on personal property assets, that is, assets other than real estate, altogether by electing to use asset expensing (Section 179 of the IRS code). This will allow you to write off up to $18,500 in 1998 on assets you would normally have to depreciate as a capital item.

Any amount taken through asset expensing is taken in lieu of regular depreciation. You simply expense the item or items up to the limit in the year you put it or them into service (not necessarily when purchased) just like you would any other business expense.

Use Form 4562, *Depreciation and Amortization*, to make your election and to report your Section 179 deduction. The $18,500 in 1998 maximum applies to each taxpayer and not to each business you operate.

To be eligible for asset expensing, the asset must be used at least 51% of the time for business use.

This write-off cannot exceed the total taxable income from all businesses and W-2 income for the year not counting the Section 179 deduction, but the unused portion can be carried forward to the next year as long as it does not exceed the taxable income for the new year.

Unfortunately, if you didn't utilize this benefit in a previous year due to ignorance of its availability, you cannot amend your previous tax return to claim it.

There is a restriction that might affect some small business persons reading this. If you purchase more that $200,000 in depreciable assets in any one year, the $18,500 maximum is reduced dollar for dollar by the amount in excess of $200,000. This means if you purchase $218,500 or more in 1998 you are allowed no asset expensing.

Seek competent tax counsel from your CPA or tax attorney

to determine if you should use asset expensing. Many businesses lose money the first year or two and consequently owe no tax, so why waste the write-off? It might be advantageous to depreciate the assets and have the write-off when you really have income you need to shelter. Remember, to be in business there must be the intent to make a profit.

Recovery
Period

The "Recovery Period" or the period of time you have to write-off the asset is as follows:

RECOVERY PERIODS FOR DEPRECIATION					
3 year	5 year	7 year	27.5 years	31.5 years	39 years
Tractor trailer trucks Race horses over 2 yrs old Any horse over 12 yrs old	Cars Light trucks Research equipment Computers Alternative energy equipment Heavy trucks Trailers Buses Cattle Sheep Goats Copiers Typewriters	Most machinery Equipment Furniture Fixtures Display cases Signs Office equipment Cellular phones Fax machines Refrigerators Video VCR	Residential rental real estate	All real estate placed in service before May 13, 1993	All real estate placed in service after May 13, 1993.

Two Types of
Depreciation

Now that you know the write-off periods, here are two of the depreciation methods used for business assets:

MACRS

1. Modified Accelerated Cost Recovery System (Modified ACRS or MACRS)—This method allows for faster write-off in the first few years and smaller write-offs in later years.

Straight Line

> 2. Straight Line—With this method you distribute the write-off equally over the recovery period except for the first and last years as explained below. Non-residential buildings must use this straight-line method.

	DEPRECIATION RATE FOR RECOVERY PERIOD					
	3-YEAR ASSETS		5-YEAR ASSETS		7-YEAR ASSETS	
Year	Method 1 MACRS	Method 2 Straight Line	Method 1 MACRS	Method 2 Straight Line	Method 1 MACRS	Method 2 Straight Line
1	33.33%	16.67%	20%	10%	14.29%	7.14%
2	44.45%	33.33%	32%	20%	24.49%	14.29%
3	14.81%	33.33%	19.2%	20%	17.49%	14.29%
4	7.41%	16.67%	11.52%	20%	12.49%	14.28%
5			11.52%	20%	8.93%	14.29%
6			5.76%	10%	8.92%	14.28%
7					8.93%	14.29%
8					4.46%	7.14%

RESIDENTIAL RENTAL PROPERTY *Straight line over 27.5 years* *Mid-month convention*												
Month Property Placed in Service												
Year	1	2	3	4	5	6	7	8	9	10	11	12
1	3.485%	3.182%	2.879%	2.576%	2.273%	1.967%	1.667%	1.364%	1.061%	.758%	.455%	.152%
2-9	3.636%	3.636%	3.636%	3.636%	3.636%	3.636%	3.636%	3.636%	3.636%	3.636%	3.636%	3.636%
10	3.637%	3.637%	3.637%	3.637%	3.637%	3.637%	3.636%	3.636%	3.636%	3.636%	3.636%	3.636%
11	3.636%	3.636%	3.636%	3.636%	3.636%	3.636%	3.637%	3.637%	3.637%	3.637%	3.637%	3.637%
12	3.637%	3.637%	3.637%	3.637%	3.637%	3.637%	3.636%	3.636%	3.636%	3.636%	3.636%	3.636%
13	3.636%	3.636%	3.636%	3.636%	3.636%	3.636%	3.637%	3.637%	3.637%	3.637%	3.637%	3.637%
14	3.637%	3.637%	3.637%	3.637%	3.637%	3.637%	3.636%	3.636%	3.636%	3.636%	3.636%	3.636%
15	3.636%	3.636%	3.636%	3.636%	3.636%	3.636%	3.637%	3.637%	3.637%	3.637%	3.637%	3.637%
16	3.637%	3.637%	3.637%	3.637%	3.637%	3.637%	3.636%	3.636%	3.636%	3.636%	3.636%	3.636%
17	3.636%	3.636%	3.636%	3.636%	3.636%	3.636%	3.637%	3.637%	3.637%	3.637%	3.637%	3.637%
18	3.637%	3.637%	3.637%	3.637%	3.637%	3.637%	3.636%	3.636%	3.636%	3.636%	3.636%	3.636%
19	3.636%	3.636%	3.636%	3.636%	3.636%	3.636%	3.637%	3.637%	3.637%	3.637%	3.637%	3.637%
20	3.637%	3.637%	3.637%	3.637%	3.637%	3.637%	3.636%	3.636%	3.636%	3.636%	3.636%	3.636%
21	3.636%	3.636%	3.636%	3.636%	3.636%	3.636%	3.637%	3.637%	3.637%	3.637%	3.637%	3.637%
22	3.637%	3.637%	3.637%	3.637%	3.637%	3.637%	3.636%	3.636%	3.636%	3.636%	3.636%	3.636%
23	3.636%	3.636%	3.636%	3.636%	3.636%	3.636%	3.637%	3.637%	3.637%	3.637%	3.637%	3.637%
24	3.637%	3.637%	3.637%	3.637%	3.637%	3.637%	3.636%	3.636%	3.636%	3.636%	3.636%	3.636%
25	3.636%	3.636%	3.636%	3.636%	3.636%	3.636%	3.637%	3.637%	3.637%	3.637%	3.637%	3.637%
26	3.637%	3.637%	3.637%	3.637%	3.637%	3.637%	3.636%	3.636%	3.636%	3.636%	3.636%	3.636%
27	3.636%	3.636%	3.636%	3.636%	3.636%	3.636%	3.637%	3.637%	3.637%	3.637%	3.637%	3.637%
28	1.97%	2.273%	2.576%	2.879%	3.182%	3.485%	3.636%	3.636%	3.636%	3.636%	3.636%	3.636%
29							0.152%	.0455%	.0758%	1.061%	1.364%	1.667%

NONRESIDENTIAL RENTAL PROPERTY *Straight line over 39 years* *(Placed in service on or after May 13, 1993)*												
Month Property Placed in Service												
Year	1	2	3	4	5	6	7	8	9	10	11	12
1	2.461	2.247	2.033	1.819	1.605	1.391	1.177	0.963	0.749	0.535	0.321	0.107
2-39	2.564	2.564	2.564	2.564	2.564	2.564	2.564	2.564	2.564	2.564	2.564	2.564
40	0.107	0.321	0.535	0.749	0.963	1.177	1.391	1.605	1.819	2.033	2.247	2.461

Which method is best for your given circumstance? A competent tax adviser can assist you in making a determination. If you need higher deductions now to off-set large business income, elect the Modified ACRS.

However, if you have reduced your taxes to zero, you do not need the deduction. In that case elect the straight-line method which may afford the deduction later when your taxable income is greater.

Half-Year Convention

Except for real property, (e.g., buildings), both methods above do not allow you to deduct a full year's depreciation the first year, You are allowed only a half year's depreciation the first year. This is called the "half year convention." At the end of the period allowed, you add the remaining half year's depreciation. This, in essence, adds an additional year to the depreciation period; thus a seven-year property is actually written off over eight years.

Last Quarter Purchases

Be aware that if more than 40% of your depreciable assets other than real estate are purchased in the last quarter of the year, you must group the assets according to the quarter in which they were purchased. This is a rather complicated computation that requires four separate depreciation computations. You must calculate quarter by quarter. It is so complicated that it is advisable to simply avoid it by not buying more than 40% of your depreciable assets in the last three months of the year or seek the help of a competent tax preparer in making the computation.

Figuring Straight Line

To figure straight line depreciation for real estate, you divide the cost (without land) by 27½ years for residential property or 39 years for all other real estate. This gives you the annual depreciation for each year except for the first and last year as explained earlier in this chapter.

For real estate, the building is depreciated by what is called the "mid-month convention." No matter what month of the year or which day of the month you acquire the property, you are allowed one-half month's depreciation for that month and the full depreciation for the remaining months of the year thereafter.

There is a special limitation on the deduction for a passenger car used in business. You cannot just use the Depreciation Table. The total deduction that may be claimed may not exceed $3,160 for the first year of the recovery period. The maximum depreciation is $5,000 for the second year; $3.050 for the third year; $1,775 for years four and five; and $1,775 until fully depreciated.

The above maximum annual ceiling figures are based on 100% business usage of the auto. If business use is less, the maximum annual limits must be reduced to reflect the actual business-use percentage.

In 1998, the luxury excise tax added to the price of luxury cars has been dropped to 8%. The tax applies to the amount of the sales price of an automobile that exceeds $36,000.

"Listed property" is a term applied to certain equipment

that may be used for both personal and business purposes. Listed property includes but is not limited to passenger cars, cellular phones, computers, boats, airplanes, and any photographic, sound, or video recording equipment that could be used for entertainment or recreational purposes.

Remember, you can only depreciate that percentage of the asset that is used for business purposes. What happens when a business asset is used less than 50% of the time for business purposes?

If the percentage is 50% or less, for certain "listed" property, you must figure the depreciation on the percentage of business use using the straight-line method not the alternate MACRS recovery period. You cannot use the accelerated method (MACRS) or first-year expensing deduction (Section 179). Refer to IRS Publication 534 for complete instructions.

Your strategy is to make sure any major assets such as the video recorder, the camera, the computer, or the cellular phone are used at least 51% of the time for business purposes. Then you can use both MACRS and first-year expensing.

If business use in a later year drops to 50% or less, MACRS and any first-year depreciation are subject to "recapture." Remember, keep a log of actual use.

Selling an Asset

Laws that apply when you sell an asset that has been depreciated are somewhat complex. They depend on how many years you've depreciated the asset, how much write-off you've taken, and what method of depreciation you've used.

Your "adjusted cost basis" is what remains after you subtract the total amount of depreciation written off in the past from the cost of the asset.

If you should sell an asset for more than the remaining cost basis (adjusted cost basis), a taxable event occurs. The profit is taxable as gain and should be recorded as income. Because this income will be treated differently from your earned income on your tax return, you must keep all your calculations and papers to give copies to your accountant who does your tax return.

On the other hand, if the selling price is lower than the adjusted cost basis, a tax-deductible loss occurs that will also be shown on your tax return. It is a good idea to keep a file folder labeled "Tax Return Info for (year)" handy for accumulating facts for your tax return.

Be sure to record the sale of the asset on your Equipment Worksheet form at the end of this chapter.

Discarding an Asset

When you discard or junk a fully depreciated asset, there is no profit or loss as far as bookkeeping is concerned. Simply record the discarding of the item(s) on your Equipment Worksheet. If, however, the item is only partially depreciated and becomes worthless, you can write off the un-depreciated portion of the cost in the year that the asset becomes worthless.

Be sure to record the junking of the asset on your Equipment Worksheet.

Here is an example of the Equipment Worksheet and Depreciation Schedule. A copy for your use is at the end of this chapter.

Equipment Worksheet & Depreciation Schedule

	Description	Date of Acqui-sition	Life	Method	Basis	Removals	ITC or Other Reductions	Accumulated Depreciation Previous	19___ Depreciation	
1										1
2										2
3										3
4										4
5										5
6										6
7										7
8										8
9										9
10										10
11										11
12										12
13										13
14										14

Estimated Tax

Income taxes are due on a pay-as-you-go basis. They are payable through withholding or quarterly payments. Most small business operators' incomes are not subject to withholding, therefore they are required to make estimated quarterly tax installment payments.

To avoid a penalty, for individuals these installments must be at least 90% of the current year's taxes or 100% of the prior year's taxes. These payments are due on:

April 15	September 15
June 15	January 15 of the following year

If you file your individual tax return and pay the balance of the tax due by January 31, you don't have to pay the final estimate separately. Individuals use Form 1040-ES and a corporation uses Form 1120-W. These forms and remittances must be deposited in a bank authorized to accept estimated tax deposits.

Request Publication 505, *Tax Withholding and Estimated Taxes* from the IRS.

Corporate Estimated Tax

If your business is a corporation and has taxable income, it must also make estimated tax payments as early as the fourth month of its first tax year. To avoid penalties, corporations must pay 100% of the taxes shown on the return or 100% of the prior year's taxes.

Your corporation will be issued a coupon book preprinted with your tax identification number. The coupons are to be used for deposits of all types of federal taxes, corporate income taxes, payroll tax deposits and federal unemployment taxes.

Form 1099

You must report to IRS any payments of $600 or more made to any one person during the year. The form to use is 1099-MISC. This form must be issued for rent, commissions, royalties, annuities and compensation for services. For interest paid, use Form 1099-INT.

Always remember to get the Social Security number or tax ID number of anyone to whom you make payment *before you give them their check*. You can be penalized by IRS if you do not use the payee's Social Security number when you file the Form 1099. Form 1099s and summary Form 1096 are due to IRS by February 28 each year. A copy of Form 1099 must be sent to the payee by January 31.

Fortunately Form 1099s are not required to be sent to corporations or government agencies; nor issued with payments for merchandise, telephone, freight or storage; or sent with rent made to a real estate agent.

Form SS-4

As a sole proprietorship, use your Social Security number on all tax forms and licenses unless you hire employees, in which case you must obtain an Employer Identification Number (EIN, sometimes called a federal ID number). This number is easily obtained by filing Form SS-4. There is no fee charged.

Once you obtain the EIN you will automatically receive quarterly and year-end payroll tax forms that you must fill out even if you don't have employees for that particular period. So, in order to avoid unnecessary paperwork, don't apply for a number until you have employees.

On the other hand, partnerships and corporations must have an EIN number even if they do not have employees. See the sample Form SS-4 at the end of this chapter.

If you need the Employer Identification Number fast, you may follow these simple steps to have it issued over the phone:

1. Complete a Form SS-4.

2. Call the IRS service center for your state. While you are on the phone get their fax number.

3. An IRS representative will issue an EIN over the phone.

4. Write that EIN number in the upper right corner of the Form SS-4 above the phrase "Official Use Only".

5. Fax your SS-4 to the IRS at the number you obtained earlier. Your original SS-4 <u>should</u> <u>not</u> <u>be</u> <u>mailed</u> to the IRS. Fax service can only be used to send SS-4s with EINs issued by the IRS over the phone or sign, date and mail the Form SS-4 in an envelope within 5 days to the IRS service center for your state.

Hiring Employees

Once you begin paying salaries you become, in essence, an agent of the U.S. government to collect taxes from your employee(s). Request a business tax kit from your local IRS office. Make sure the kit contains Circular E, *Employer's Tax Guide*. It contains up-to-date withholding tables for income tax and Social Security taxes to be withheld.

Payroll taxes, as discussed in the next paragraph, can be automatically calculated by using most integrated software accounting packages. We recommend America's #1 best-selling accounting software, *QuickBooks* by Intuit.

In addition to a Social Security tax of 7.65% of gross wages which is deducted from an employee's earnings up to $68,400 for 1998, the employer must pay from the employer's funds another 7.65%, making a total Social Security tax of 15.30% on the first $68,400 of income for 1998. There is an additional 1.45% Medicare hospital insurance tax on all monies above the $68,400. There is no wage limit on Medicare taxes; everything is taxable.

The employer also must pay for federal and state unemployment insurance for an employee. Be aware of these hidden costs when hiring an employee.

As a <u>self-employed</u> person, you must pay the total FICA tax yourself. In 1998, it is 15.30% on the first $68,400 and there is a 2.90% Medicare hospital insurance tax on all monies above the $68,400. You can deduct one-half of your self-employment tax on Line 25 of Form 1040.

Spouse

The law now requires the payment of Social Security taxes when you hire your spouse. This of course, allows your spouse to qualify for Social Security income when he or she retires.

Form W-4

When a new employee is hired, you must furnish him or her with a Form W-4 or a W-4A which will give you the number of withholding allowances the employee is claiming. The form must be completed by all employees and returned to you by October 1.

If an employee doesn't complete the form, you are required to withhold taxes on the basis of one allowance, if single, and two allowances, if married. You are required to report to IRS the names of all employees who claim 10 or more allowances or who claim exemptions from withholding if his or her wages would normally exceed $200 per week.

As a practical matter, encourage your employees to claim only enough allowances to cover their tax liability. If he or she over withholds and gets a refund, it is like giving the government an interest-free loan.

Form I-9

Employers must have an employee fill out an I-9 at the beginning of employment. This information is used by employers as a record to determine eligibility of an employee to work in the U.S.

The form will be kept by the employer and made available for inspection by officials of the U.S. Immigration and Naturalization Service, the Department of Labor and the Office of Special Counsel for Immigration Related Unfair Employment Practices.

An individual may not begin employment unless this form is completed since employers are subject to civil and criminal penalties if they do not comply with the Immigration Reform and Control Act of 1986.

Employers must retain completed I-9s for three years after the date of hire or one year after the date employment ends, whichever is later. They are not to be mailed to IRS.

Form W-2

By January 31 of each calendar year, you must furnish each employee with a Form W-2 showing the taxable wages paid during the preceding year and the taxes withheld. The form along with a W-3 summary form is to be filed by you with IRS by February 28.

Hiring Your Children

Instead of giving an allowance to your children, consider

hiring them or even your grandchildren and make some or all of what you give them tax deductible. They can clean the office, wash the business car, run business errands, address mail, etc. The salary you pay them will be deductible to you as a bona fide business expense.

They will not be required to file a tax return if they earn less than $4,250 for 1998. Of course they must do the work for which they are paid. Salaries paid to children under 18 are not subject to Social Security tax.

Independent Contractors

If it is possible for anyone providing services for your business to be considered an "independent contractor," rather than an employee, it is certainly to your advantage. If they are not classified as employees, you do not have to pay social security, unemployment tax, state unemployment tax, withhold federal or state income tax or purchase worker's compensation.

But you cannot just call someone an independent contractor to avoid withholding on him or her. The IRS Code is very strict on what constitutes an employee vs. an independent contractor.

Recently the IRS has focused extra attention on what it deems widespread abuse of contract labor. It claims the abuse is costing the government $1.6 billion per year.

IRS provides Form SS-8 to help you determine if a person qualifies as an independent contractor, or whether he or she must be treated as an employee. The following chart should help you define the functions:

SOME FACTORS USED TO DETERMINE IF ONE IS AN INDEPENDENT CONTRACTOR

1. The compensation should be on a project by project basis; not necessarily an hourly or weekly income.

2. There should be no exclusivity of arrangement. That is to say, an independent contractor may do work for someone else if he or she so desires.

3. The insurance should be paid by the independent contractor and he or she should not participate in company retirement plans or drive a company car.

4. The independent contractor should not be bound to your office or shop but have the liberty to perform his or her service or complete the project at his or her own home or office without your direct supervision.

An independent contractor is a person who works for a fixed period to accomplish a specific job for a person who can't specifically tell him or her how, when or where to do that job.

The independent contractor pays self-employment taxes and deducts his or her expenses on a Schedule C. He or she is considered self-employed and receives from you a 1099-MISC rather than a W-2, provided you pay him or her $600 or more per year.

Sales and
Use Tax

In most states, sales taxes are collected by the business entity that sells, leases or rents taxable items or services and are paid to the proper taxing authority. However, some purchasers may claim an exemption from paying sales tax on items they are purchasing for resale, exemption or direct payment exemption certificate, when appropriate. Check with your accountant as to when this is used.

While the business entity is supposed to collect the tax at the time of a taxable transaction, the entity remains liable for the tax until it is paid to the state.

The business entity must remit tax to the state on all taxable transactions, whether or not tax was collected. If sales tax is not collected for taxable services, the business can be held responsible for unpaid taxes.

Use tax is applicable when purchases are made, no sales tax is paid and the products are used (rather than resold) in the business of the purchaser. Use tax (charged at the same rate as sales tax) is then due on these purchases. This situation frequently arises when fixed assets are purchased from out-of-state vendors.

Contact your State Comptroller's office about your liability for sales and use taxes.

How Long Should Business Records Be Kept

The following chart is simply a guide and is not intended to be a list of legal time requirements for keeping records. You should consult your legal counsel for statutory requirements.

HOW LONG SHOULD BUSINESS RECORDS BE KEPT?

4 Years	6 Years	7 Years	10 Years	Permanent
Budgets General Correspondence Insurance policies (after expiration) Petty cash records Travel records of employees	Employee time reports Equipment repair records Employee expense reports Freight bills and claims	Accident reports after they are settled Accounts payable invoices & ledgers Accounts receivable ledger Employee applications after the employee is terminated Contracts Credit and collections correspondence Depreciation records after disposition of property or investment Fixed asset records after disposition of property or investment Forms after disposition of property or investment Inventory reports Invoices (issued and received) Leases after termination of the lease Mortgages after disposition of property or investment Notes (cancelled) Payroll checks, earnings records, withholding and exemption certificates, Forms 941 etc., personnel files after employment is terminated Securities (brokerage slips)	Check registers Cash journals General journals Payroll journals Property tax records Sales and use tax returns Bank statements Cancelled checks after disposition of property or investment	Capital stock info such as certificates, transfers, etc. Charter, by-laws, and articles of incorporation Annual financial reports Deeds and easements Annual tax returns Journal entries (year end) Minutes of corporation Patents, copyrights and trademark info Retirement and pension records General ledger

Equipment Worksheet & Depreciation Schedule

	Description	Date of Acquisition	Life	Method	Basis	Removals	ITC or Other Reductions	Accumulated Depreciation Previous	19___ Depreciation	
1										1
2										2
3										3
4										4
5										5
6										6
7										7
8										8
9										9
10										10
11										11
12										12
13										13
14										14
15										15
16										16
17										17
18										18
19										19
20										20
21										21
22										22
23										23
24										24
25										25
26										26
27										27
28										28
29										29
30										30
31										31
32										32
33										33

Equipment Worksheet & Depreciation Schedule

	Remaining Balance	19___ Depreciation	Remaining Balance	19___ Depreciation	Remaining Balance	19___ Depreciation	Remaining Balance	
1								1
2								2
3								3
4								4
5								5
6								6
7								7
8								8
9								9
10								10
11								11
12								12
13								13
14								14
15								15
16								16
17								17
18								18
19								19
20								20
21								21
22								22
23								23
24								24
25								25
26								26
27								27
28								28
29								29
30								30
31								31
32								32
33								33

Daily Mileage Log

Codes For Each Automobile
   A Car 1 _____
   B Car 2 _____
etc.

Codes For Type Mileage:
   10__   Business
   20__   Personal
   30__   Medical
   40__   Educational
   etc.

Example: "10A" would be business mileage for Car 1. So when you total all your
   "10A's" you would know how far you drove for business in Car 1.

Date	Description	Mileage Code	Beginning Mileage	Ending Mileage	Net Mileage

Form **SS-4**

(Rev. December 1995)

Department of the Treasury
Internal Revenue Service

Application for Employer Identification Number

(For use by employers, corporations, partnerships, trusts, estates, churches,
government agencies, certain individuals, and others. See instructions.)

▶ Keep a copy for your records.

EIN _____

OMB No. 1545-0003

Please type or print clearly.

1 Name of applicant (Legal name) (See instructions.)

2 Trade name of business (if different from name on line 1)	**3** Executor, trustee, "care of" name
4a Mailing address (street address) (room, apt., or suite no.)	**5a** Business address (if different from address on lines 4a and 4b)
4b City, state, and ZIP code	**5b** City, state, and ZIP code

6 County and state where principal business is located

7 Name of principal officer, general partner, grantor, owner, or trustor—SSN required (See instructions.) ▶ _____

8a Type of entity (Check only one box.) (See instructions.)

☐ Sole proprietor (SSN) _____

☐ Partnership   ☐ Personal service corp.

☐ REMIC   ☐ Limited liability co.

☐ State/local government ☐ National Guard

☐ Other nonprofit organization (specify) ▶ _____

☐ Other (specify) ▶

☐ Estate (SSN of decedent) _____

☐ Plan administrator-SSN _____

☐ Other corporation (specify) ▶ _____

☐ Trust   ☐ Farmers' cooperative

☐ Federal Government/military ☐ Church or church-controlled organization

(enter GEN if applicable) _____

8b If a corporation, name the state or foreign country (if applicable) where incorporated	State	Foreign country

9 Reason for applying (Check only one box.)

☐ Started new business (specify) ▶ _____

☐ Hired employees
☐ Created a pension plan (specify type) ▶

☐ Banking purpose (specify) ▶ _____

☐ Changed type of organization (specify) ▶ _____

☐ Purchased going business

☐ Created a trust (specify) ▶ _____

☐ Other (specify) ▶

10 Date business started or acquired (Mo., day, year) (See instructions.)	**11** Closing month of accounting year (See instructions.)

12 First date wages or annuities were paid or will be paid (Mo., day, year). **Note:** *If applicant is a withholding agent, enter date income will first be paid to nonresident alien. (Mo., day, year)* . . . . ▶

13 Highest number of employees expected in the next 12 months. **Note:** *If the applicant does not expect to have any employees during the period, enter -0-. (See instructions.)* . . . ▶	Nonagricultural	Agricultural	Household

14 Principal activity (See instructions.) ▶

15 Is the principal business activity manufacturing? . . . . ☐ Yes ☐ No
If "Yes," principal product and raw material used ▶

16 To whom are most of the products or services sold? Please check the appropriate box.   ☐ Business (wholesale)
☐ Public (retail)   ☐ Other (specify) ▶   ☐ N/A

17a Has the applicant ever applied for an identification number for this or any other business? . . . . ☐ Yes ☐ No
Note: *If "Yes," please complete lines 17b and 17c.*

17b If you checked "Yes" on line 17a, give applicant's legal name and trade name shown on prior application, if different from line 1 or 2 above.
Legal name ▶   Trade name ▶

17c Approximate date when and city and state where the application was filed. Enter previous employer identification number if known.

Approximate date when filed (Mo., day, year)	City and state where filed	Previous EIN

Under penalties of perjury, I declare that I have examined this application, and to the best of my knowledge and belief it is true, correct, and complete.

	Business telephone number (include area code)
	Fax telephone number (include area code)

Name and title (Please type or print clearly.) ▶

Signature ▶   Date ▶

Note: *Do not write below this line. For official use only.*

Please leave blank ▶	Geo.	Ind.	Class	Size	Reason for applying

For Paperwork Reduction Act Notice, see page 4.   Cat. No. 16055N   Form **SS-4** (Rev. 12-95)

_____   _____
                    _____

U. S. Department of Justice   **I-9**   OMB No. 1115-0136
Immigration and Naturalization Service   **Employment Eligibility Verification**

═══

Please read instructions carefully before completing this form. The instructions must be available during completion of this form. ANTI-DISCRIMINATION NOTICE. It is illegal to discriminate against work eligible individuals. Employers CANNOT specify which document(s) they will accept from an employee. The refusal to hire an individual because of a future expiration date may also constitute illegal discrimination.

Section 1. Employee Information and Verification. To be completed and signed by employee at the time employment begins

Print Name: Last	First	Middle Initial	Maiden Name

Address (Street Name and Number)	Apt. #	Date of Birth (month/day/year)

City	State	Zip Code	Social Security #

I am aware that federal law provides for imprisonment and/or fines for false statements or use of false documents in connection with the completion of this form.

I attest, under penalty of perjury, that I am (check one of the following):

☐ A citizen or national of the United States
☐ A Lawful Permanent Resident (Alien # A _____)
☐ An alien authorized to work until _____
(Alien # or Admission #)

Employee's Signature	Date (month/day/year)

Preparer and/or Translator Certification. (To be completed and signed if Section 1 is prepared by a person other than the employee.) I attest, under penalty of perjury, that I have assisted in the completion of this form and that to the best of my knowledge the information is true and correct.

Preparer's/Translator's Signature	Print Name

Address (Street Name and Number, City, State, Zip Code)	Date (month/day/year)

Section 2. Employer Review and Verification. To be completed and signed by employer. **Examine one document from List A OR examine one document from List B _and_ one from List C** as listed on the reverse of this form and record the title, number and expiration date, if any, of the document(s)

	List A	OR	List B	AND	List C
Document title:	_____		_____		_____
Issuing authority:	_____		_____		_____
Document #:	_____		_____		_____
Expiration Date (if any):	_____		_____		_____
Document #:	_____				
Expiration Date (if any):					

CERTIFICATION – I attest, under penalty of perjury, that I have examined the document(s) presented by the above-named employee, that the above-listed document(s) appear to be genuine and to relate to the employee named, that the employee began employment on (month/day/year) _____ **and that to the best of my knowledge the employee is eligible to work in the United States. (State employment agencies may omit the date the employee began employment).**

Signature of Employer or Authorized Representative	Print Name	Title

Business or Organization Name Address (Street Name and Number, City, State, Zip Code)	Date (month/day/year)

Section 3. Updating and Reverification. To be completed and signed by employer

A. New Name (if applicable)	B. Date of rehire (month/day/year) (if applicable)

C. If employee's previous grant of work authorization has expired, provide the information below for the document that establishes current employment eligibility.

Document Title:	Document #:	Expiration Date (if any):

I attest, under penalty of perjury, that to the best of my knowledge, this employee is eligible to work in the United States, and if the employee presented document(s), the document(s) I have examined appear to be genuine and to relate to the individual.

Signature of Employer or Authorized Representative	Date (month/day/year)

Form W-4 (1998)

Purpose. Complete Form W-4 so your employer can withhold the correct Federal income tax from your pay. Because your tax situation may change, you may want to refigure your withholding each year.

Exemption from withholding. *If you are exempt, complete only lines 1, 2, 3, 4, and 7, and sign the form to validate it. Your exemption for 1998 expires February 16, 1999.*

Note: *You cannot claim exemption from withholding if (1) your income exceeds $700 and includes unearned income (e.g., interest and dividends) and (2) another person can claim you as a dependent on their tax return.*

Basic instructions. If you are not exempt, complete the Personal Allowances Worksheet. The worksheets on page 2 adjust your

withholding allowances based on itemized deductions, adjustments to income, or two-earner/two-job situations. Complete all worksheets that apply. They will help you figure the number of withholding allowances you are entitled to claim. However, you may claim fewer allowances.

New—Child tax and higher education credits. For details on adjusting withholding for these and other credits, see **Pub. 919,** Is My Withholding Correct for 1998?

Head of household. Generally, you may claim head of household filing status on your tax return only if you are unmarried and pay more than 50% of the costs of keeping up a home for yourself and your dependent(s) or other qualifying individuals.

Nonwage income. If you have a large amount of nonwage income, such as interest or dividends, you should consider making estimated tax payments using Form 1040-ES. Otherwise, you may owe additional tax.

Two earners/two jobs. If you have a working spouse or more than one job, figure the total number of allowances you are entitled to claim on all jobs using worksheets from only one W-4. Your withholding will usually be most accurate when all allowances are claimed on the W-4 filed for the highest paying job and zero allowances are claimed for the others.

Check your withholding. After your W-4 takes effect, use Pub. 919 to see how the dollar amount you are having withheld compares to your estimated total annual tax. Get Pub. 919 especially if you used the Two-Earner/Two-Job Worksheet and your earnings exceed $150,000 (Single) or $200,000 (Married). To order Pub. 919, call 1-800-829-3676. Check your telephone directory for the IRS assistance number for further help.

Sign this form. Form W-4 is not valid unless you sign it.

Personal Allowances Worksheet

A Enter "1" for **yourself** if no one else can claim you as a dependent . . . . **A** _____

B Enter "1" if:
- You are single and have only one job; or
- You are married, have only one job, and your spouse does not work; or
- Your wages from a second job or your spouse's wages (or the total of both) are $1,000 or less.

. . **B** _____

C Enter "1" for your **spouse**. But, you may choose to enter -0- if you are married and have either a working spouse or more than one job. (This may help you avoid having too little tax withheld.). . . . . **C** _____

D Enter number of **dependents** (other than your spouse or yourself) you will claim on your tax return . . . . **D** _____

E Enter "1" if you will file as **head of household** on your tax return (see conditions under **Head of household** above) . **E** _____

F Enter "1" if you have at least $1,500 of **child or dependent care expenses** for which you plan to claim a credit . . **F** _____

G **New—Child Tax Credit:** • If your total income will be between $16,500 and $47,000 ($21,000 and $60,000 if married), enter "1" for each eligible child. • If your total income will be between $47,000 and $80,000 ($60,000 and $115,000 if married), enter "1" if you have two or three eligible children, or enter "2" if you have four or more . . . . **G** _____

H Add lines A through G and enter total here. **Note:** This amount may be different from the number of exemptions you claim on your return. ▶ **H** _____

For accuracy, complete all worksheets that apply.
- If you plan to **itemize or claim adjustments to income** and want to reduce your withholding, see the Deductions and Adjustments Worksheet on page 2.
- If you are **single,** have **more than one job,** and your combined earnings from all jobs exceed $32,000 OR if you are **married** and have a **working spouse or more than one job,** and the combined earnings from all jobs exceed $55,000, see the Two-Earner/Two-Job Worksheet on page 2 to avoid having too little tax withheld.
- If **neither** of the above situations applies, **stop here** and enter the number from line H on line 5 of Form W-4 below.

- - - - - - - - - - - - - - **Cut here and give the certificate to your employer. Keep the top part for your records.** - - - - - - - - - - - -

Form **W-4** Department of the Treasury Internal Revenue Service	**Employee's Withholding Allowance Certificate** ▶ For Privacy Act and Paperwork Reduction Act Notice, see page 2.	OMB No. 1545-0010 **1998**

1 Type or print your first name and middle initial	Last name	**2** Your social security number

Home address (number and street or rural route)	**3** ☐ Single ☐ Married ☐ Married, but withhold at higher Single rate. Note: *If married, but legally separated, or spouse is a nonresident alien, check the Single box.*
City or town, state, and ZIP code	**4** If your last name differs from that on your social security card, check here and call 1-800-772-1213 for a new card . . . . . . ▶ ☐

5 Total number of allowances you are claiming (from line H above or from the worksheets on page 2 if they apply) . **5** _____

6 Additional amount, if any, you want withheld from each paycheck . . . . **6** $ _____

7 I claim exemption from withholding for 1998, and I certify that I meet **BOTH** of the following conditions for exemption:
- Last year I had a right to a refund of **ALL** Federal income tax withheld because I had **NO** tax liability **AND**
- This year I expect a refund of **ALL** Federal income tax withheld because I expect to have **NO** tax liability.
If you meet both conditions, enter "EXEMPT" here . . . . ▶ **7** _____

Under penalties of perjury, I certify that I am entitled to the number of withholding allowances claimed on this certificate or entitled to claim exempt status.

Employee's signature ▶ _____ **Date** ▶ _____ , 19 ___

8 Employer's name and address (Employer: Complete 8 and 10 only if sending to the IRS)	**9** Office code (optional)	**10** Employer identification number

Cat. No. 10220Q

Deductions and Adjustments Worksheet

Note: *Use this worksheet only if you plan to itemize deductions or claim adjustments to income on your 1998 tax return.*

1   Enter an estimate of your 1998 itemized deductions. These include qualifying home mortgage interest, charitable contributions, state and local taxes (but not sales taxes), medical expenses in excess of 7.5% of your income, and miscellaneous deductions. (For 1998, you may have to reduce your itemized deductions if your income is over $124,500 ($62,250 if married filing separately). Get Pub. 919 for details.)   **1** $_____

2   Enter:
  $7,100 if married filing jointly or qualifying widow(er)
  $6,250 if head of household
  $4,250 if single
  $3,550 if married filing separately   **2** $_____

3   **Subtract** line 2 from line 1. If line 2 is greater than line 1, enter -0-   **3** $_____
4   Enter an estimate of your 1998 adjustments to income, including alimony, deductible IRA contributions, and education loan interest.   **4** $_____
5   **Add** lines 3 and 4 and enter the total   **5** $_____
6   Enter an estimate of your 1998 nonwage income (such as dividends or interest)   **6** $_____
7   **Subtract** line 6 from line 5. Enter the result, but not less than -0-   **7** $_____
8   **Divide** the amount on line 7 by $2,500 and enter the result here. Drop any fraction   **8** _____
9   Enter the number from Personal Allowances Worksheet, line H, on page 1   **9** _____
10   **Add** lines 8 and 9 and enter the total here. If you plan to use the Two-Earner/Two-Job Worksheet, also enter this total on line 1 below. Otherwise, **stop here** and enter this total on Form W-4, line 5, on page 1   **10** _____

Two-Earner/Two-Job Worksheet

Note: *Use this worksheet only if the instructions for line H on page 1 direct you here.*

1   Enter the number from line H on page 1 (or from line 10 above if you used the Deductions and Adjustments Worksheet)   **1** _____
2   Find the number in **Table 1** below that applies to the **LOWEST** paying job and enter it here   **2** _____
3   If line 1 is **GREATER THAN OR EQUAL TO** line 2, subtract line 2 from line 1. Enter the result here (if zero, enter -0-) and on Form W-4, line 5, on page 1. **DO NOT** use the rest of this worksheet   **3** _____

Note: *If line 1 is **LESS THAN** line 2, enter -0- on Form W-4, line 5, on page 1. Complete lines 4–9 to calculate the additional withholding amount necessary to avoid a year end tax bill.*

4   Enter the number from line 2 of this worksheet   **4** _____
5   Enter the number from line 1 of this worksheet   **5** _____
6   **Subtract** line 5 from line 4   **6** _____
7   Find the amount in **Table 2** below that applies to the **HIGHEST** paying job and enter it here   **7** $_____
8   **Multiply** line 7 by line 6 and enter the result here. This is the additional annual withholding amount needed   **8** $_____
9   **Divide** line 8 by the number of pay periods remaining in 1998. (For example, divide by 26 if you are paid every other week and you complete this form in December 1997.) Enter the result here and on Form W-4, line 6, page 1. This is the additional amount to be withheld from each paycheck   **9** $_____

Table 1: Two-Earner/Two-Job Worksheet

Married Filing Jointly				All Others			
If wages from LOWEST paying job are—	Enter on line 2 above	If wages from LOWEST paying job are—	Enter on line 2 above	If wages from LOWEST paying job are—	Enter on line 2 above	If wages from LOWEST paying job are—	Enter on line 2 above
0 - $4,000	0	38,001 - 43,000	8	0 - $5,000	0	70,001 - 85,000	8
4,001 - 7,000	1	43,001 - 54,000	9	5,001 - 11,000	1	85,001 - 100,000	9
7,001 - 12,000	2	54,001 - 62,000	10	11,001 - 16,000	2	100,001 and over	10
12,001 - 18,000	3	62,001 - 70,000	11	16,001 - 21,000	3		
18,001 - 24,000	4	70,001 - 85,000	12	21,001 - 25,000	4		
24,001 - 28,000	5	85,001 - 100,000	13	25,001 - 42,000	5		
28,001 - 33,000	6	100,001 - 110,000	14	42,001 - 55,000	6		
33,001 - 38,000	7	110,001 and over	15	55,001 - 70,000	7		

Table 2: Two-Earner/Two-Job Worksheet

Married Filing Jointly		All Others	
If wages from HIGHEST paying job are—	Enter on line 7 above	If wages from HIGHEST paying job are—	Enter on line 7 above
0 - $50,000	$400	0 - $30,000	$400
50,001 - 100,000	760	30,001 - 60,000	760
100,001 - 130,000	840	60,001 - 120,000	840
130,001 - 240,000	970	120,001 - 250,000	970
240,001 and over	1,070	250,001 and over	1,070

Privacy Act and Paperwork Reduction Act Notice. We ask for the information on this form to carry out the Internal Revenue laws of the United States. The Internal Revenue Code requires this information under sections 3402(f)(2)(A) and 6109 and their regulations. Failure to provide a completed form will result in your being treated as a single person who claims no withholding allowances. Routine uses of this information include giving it to the Department of Justice for civil and criminal litigation and to cities, states, and the District of Columbia for use in administering their tax laws.

You are not required to provide the information requested on a form that is subject to the Paperwork Reduction Act unless the form displays a valid OMB control number. Books or records relating to a form or its instructions must be retained as long as their contents may become material in the administration of any Internal Revenue law. Generally, tax returns and return information are confidential, as required by Code section 6103.

The time needed to complete this form will vary depending on individual circumstances. The estimated average time is: **Recordkeeping** 46 min., **Learning about the law or the form** 10 min., **Preparing the form** 1 hr., 10 min. If you have comments concerning the accuracy of these time estimates or suggestions for making this form simpler, we would be happy to hear from you. You can write to the Tax Forms Committee, Western Area Distribution Center, Rancho Cordova, CA 95743-0001. **DO NOT** send the tax form to this address. Instead, give it to your employer.

 Printed on recycled paper   *U.S. Government Printing Office. 1997 · 419-119*

CHAPTER 14 | THE SCHEDULE C

To demonstrate how a small business can be a powerful tax shelter, let's illustrate with a hypothetical part-time home-based business operated by Tom.

Tom's W-2 shows income of $31,000 from his regular job. Tom's new part-time business is with a network marketing organization that markets nutritional products. His first year's receipts total $10,200. Not bad, considering the limited time he has invested in his new business. He anticipates spending more time building a customer base and recruiting a sales organization of independent marketing representatives next year.

This is Tom's first year to report business income, so let's look over his shoulder as he fills out the IRS Form 8829 and the Schedule C portion of his Form 1040. (See a filled in Schedule C example on page 14-11.)

> **NOTE**: There is a difference in the way business expenses and office-in-home expenses are reported on a tax return. For example, insurance on the computer is a business expense and would be reported directly on Schedule C. On the other hand, the business portion of your homeowner's insurance is an office-in-home expense and would be reported on Form 8829. All *expenses related to the office in home* such as taxes, utilities, home

insurance and other expenses related to the upkeep of the business portion of the house are reportable on IRS Form 8829 and the total is brought forward to line 30 on Schedule C. The computations on Form 8829 determine what can be deducted in the current year if your business is operating at a loss and what expenses (if any) must be carried forward to the next year.

At the end of this chapter is a Form 8829 and a Schedule C.

Use Form 8829 to record such items as the business portion of home insurance, taxes, utilities and other expenses related to the upkeep of the house. The adjusted total on Form 8829 is then transferred to line 30 on the Schedule C. If there are office-in-home expenses not used, they can be carried forward to a later year.

Let's examine a Schedule C example:

Line 1   *Gross receipts* or *sales.* Remember his gross receipts were $10,200. He enters that amount on Line 1.

Line 2   *Returns and allowances.* On Line 2 he enters a refund he gave a customer, $34.

Line 3   After subtracting Line 2 from Line 1, he enters the result, $10,166.

Line 4   By following the steps on page two, Lines 33-40 of Schedule C, Tom arrives at the *cost of the goods* he sold. He enters that amount, $3,400.

Line 5   By subtracting Line 4 from Line 3 he arrives

at his *gross profit* and enters that amount, $6,766.

Line 6   Since his vitamin sales were the only source of income, he enters nothing on this line.

Line 7   By adding Lines 5 and 6 (in his case, zero) he now has his *gross income*, $6,766, which he enters.

Tom has now finished Part I and is ready to offset this income with expenses by filling in Part II, Lines 8-27 on Schedule C.

Line 8   *Advertising.* On this line Tom puts $1,300, the cost of a classified ad, the printing of a promotional brochure and mailing costs.

Line 9   *Bad debts.* Tom realized that he would not be able to collect $39 from a bad check from a customer who moved without leaving a forwarding address. Since Tom is using the accrual method of accounting he can deduct that amount here.

Line 10   *Car and truck expenses.* Since this is the *first year* Tom has used his second car in his business and for some personal use, he can make a one-time choice to use either the actual operating costs of his car during business trips OR deduct a flat IRS allowance of 32½ cents per mile for all business mileage traveled in 1998 whichever one gives him the greater write off. But he has to figure it both ways. If he does not choose the IRS mileage allowance the first year, he cannot choose it in a later year. Tom logged accurate records of the actual costs of operating that vehicle and applied his percentage of business usage to it. He answers the questions in Part IV. He spent $1,470 for gas, oil, tolls, repairs, etc. last year.

Since he used the second vehicle 55% of the time in business, he enters $809.

Line 11   *Commissions and fees.* Because the two sales representatives Tom recruited are independent contractors, they will be filling out their own Schedule C. Tom didn't pay them a commission; the MLM company did and they will supply these representatives with a Form 1099 if their earnings exceed $600. Tom leaves this line blank.

Line 12   *Depletion.* Tom leaves this line blank since it does not apply to his business.

Line 13   *Depreciation and Section 179 deduction.* When Tom adds up the depreciation allowable on the business portion of his car and the business portion of the computer he purchased, he had $2,938.

Line 14   *Employee benefit program.* He leaves this blank since it doesn't apply to his business.

Line 15   *Insurance.* The premium to cover the new computer and other office equipment he bought, totals $115.

We need to remind Tom that in the future when he shows a profit, medical insurance premiums for himself, his spouse and his dependents are deductible on Form 1040, Line 26, provided his net earned income from the business is at least equal to the deduction. In this example, it is not and therefore he may not deduct medical insurance this year. The percentages he may be able to deduct are 45% in year 1998 and

1999, 50% in years 2000 and 2001, 60% in year 2002, 80% in years 2003-2005, 90% in year 2006 and 100% in years 2007 and thereafter.

Line 16   *Interest.* On Line 16b he puts $3,875. This is the business portion of the interest paid on the automobile as well as the interest paid on a bank loan for start-up capital and money to purchase the business computer. Deduction, $3,875.

Line 17   *Legal and professional services.* He consulted with his attorney about a business matter. He enters his bill of $150.

Line 18   *Office expense.* Tom goes through all his receipts, credit card invoices and canceled checks for postage, paper, copies and other consumable office supplies. Deduction, $237.

Line 19   *Pension and profit-sharing plans.* He leaves this blank. He's thinking, "Maybe next year…"

Line 20   *Rent on business property.* He rented a mini-storage unit for $75 per month to warehouse inventory. His deduction, $900 ($75 for 12 months) goes on Line 20b.

Line 21   *Repairs.* Tom paid $55 to have the business typewriter repaired and cleaned. He enters $55.

Line 22   *Supplies.* Tom puts nothing on this line. He has already shown his supplies in another category.

Line 23   *Taxes and licenses.* His business does not require a license or franchise tax, so he leaves this line blank but he does have social security taxes on his wife in the amount of $165.

Line 24a   *Travel.* Tom's trip to attend a business seminar, including his airfare and lodging, is $400. While out of town he had his clothes cleaned for $15. Total deduction, $415.

Line 24b *Total meals and entertainment.* One hundred percent (100%) of his food and entertainment while on the trip to a business seminar as well as entertainment throughout the year to discuss his business opportunity with friends and prospects is entered on Line 24b. The amount is $500.

Line 24c Enter $250 which is 50% of Line 24b.

Line 24d Subtract Line 24c from Line24b for a deduction of $250.

Line 25 *Utilities and telephone.* This line assumes you have an office outside of your home where you pay the utilities. For utilities for the business portion of the house, use Form 8829. A separate business telephone and long-distance cost is deductible. Deduction, $240.

Line 26 *Wages.* Tom hires his spouse to assist in the business. He pays her $1077. He pays his children $600 as wages for business errands. This line is for wages only; the payroll taxes are reported on *Line 23 Taxes and Licenses.* Total deduction, $1,677.

Line 27 *Other expenses.* These other expenses listed below are itemized in Part V of Schedule C. The total on Line 48 is brought forward to Line 27.

To improve his skill as a small business

operator, he invested in 2 home-study pro-grams including this one. Deduction, $175.

He opened a business account at his bank and incurred service charges including check printing charges of $62.

A business newsletter and a subscription to a trade publication equal $210.

Line 28   *Total expenses.* Tom totals the expenses listed on Lines 8-27. To earn the gross income on Line 7, he spent, $13,612.

Line 29   *Net profit or (loss).* The difference in Tom's gross income (Line 7) and his total expenses (Line 28) is ($6,846). In Tom's case he is operating at a tax loss so this is a negative figure.

Since he operated at a taxable loss, he must check the appropriate box on the bottom of Schedule C. To claim the loss as an offset against other income such as the salary from his full-time job, he must be able to check the box on Line 32a and then he may enter the loss on Line 12 of Form 1040 and Line 2 of Schedule SE.

If Tom is entitled to claim an office-in-home deduction, he can deduct the business portion of the taxes and mortgage interest on Schedule A regardless of the above loss. The other expenses are carried forward to the next year. Again, Form 8829 is where all expenses and computations as to which expenses are deductible are made for the office in home and the total is carried to line 30 of Schedule C.

There are two additional points—recapture and self employment tax.

What About Recapture?

Firstly, there is no recapture. This means that he does not have to give back his losses in the future when his business begins operating at a taxable profit. There is no recapture even if he should stop his business.

Self-Employment Tax

Secondly, had Tom's business shown a profit he would have owed self-employment tax but since Tom operated at a taxable loss he owes none.

I believe Tom's case clearly illustrates how the small business affords one of the better tax shelters in America today. Use it while you can.

Net Operating Loss (NOL)

If the tax loss your small business generates exceeds your other income, the excess, known as a net operating loss (NOL) may be carried back three years and then forward 15 years. The loss carried back to a prior year offsets the income for that year and entitles you to a refund.

The Net Operating Loss is not simply the business loss shown on your tax return. It is a complicated combination of business and non-business income and deductions. It is complex but it can save you a substantial amount of money.

How to Figure
an NOL

Be sure to get professional help when working with Net
Operating Losses. For more information, get IRS publication 536, *Net Operating Loss*.

Form **8829**

Department of the Treasury (O)
Internal Revenue Service

Expenses for Business Use of Your Home

▶ File only with Schedule C (Form 1040). Use a separate Form 8829 for each home you used for business during the year.

▶ See separate instructions.

OMB No. 1545-1266

19

Attachment
Sequence No. **66**

Name(s) of proprietor(s)

Your social security number

Part I	Part of Your Home Used for Business			
1	Area used regularly and exclusively for business, regularly for day care, or for storage of inventory or product samples. See instructions	1		
2	Total area of home	2		
3	Divide line 1 by line 2. Enter the result as a percentage	3		%

● For day-care facilities not used exclusively for business, also complete lines 4–6.

● All others, skip lines 4–6 and enter the amount from line 3 on line 7.

4	Multiply days used for day care during year by hours used per day	4		hr.
5	Total hours available for use during the year (365 days × 24 hours). See instructions	5	8,760	hr.
6	Divide line 4 by line 5. Enter the result as a decimal amount	6	.	
7	Business percentage. For day-care facilities not used exclusively for business, multiply line 6 by line 3 (enter the result as a percentage). All others, enter the amount from line 3 ▶	7		%

Part II	Figure Your Allowable Deduction				
8	Enter the amount from Schedule C, line 29, **plus** any net gain or (loss) derived from the business use of your home and shown on Schedule D or Form 4797. If more than one place of business, see instructions			8	

See instructions for columns (a) and (b) before completing lines 9–20.

		(a) Direct expenses	(b) Indirect expenses		
9	Casualty losses. See instructions	9			
10	Deductible mortgage interest. See instructions	10			
11	Real estate taxes. See instructions	11			
12	Add lines 9, 10, and 11	12			
13	Multiply line 12, column (b) by line 7	13			
14	Add line 12, column (a) and line 13			14	
15	Subtract line 14 from line 8. If zero or less, enter -0-			15	
16	Excess mortgage interest. See instructions	16			
17	Insurance	17			
18	Repairs and maintenance	18			
19	Utilities	19			
20	Other expenses. See instructions	20			
21	Add lines 16 through 20	21			
22	Multiply line 21, column (b) by line 7	22			
23	Carryover of operating expenses from 1996 Form 8829, line 41	23			
24	Add line 21 in column (a), line 22, and line 23			24	
25	Allowable operating expenses. Enter the **smaller** of line 15 or line 24			25	
26	Limit on excess casualty losses and depreciation. Subtract line 25 from line 15			26	
27	Excess casualty losses. See instructions	27			
28	Depreciation of your home from Part III below	28			
29	Carryover of excess casualty losses and depreciation from 1996 Form 8829, line 42	29			
30	Add lines 27 through 29			30	
31	Allowable excess casualty losses and depreciation. Enter the **smaller** of line 26 or line 30			31	
32	Add lines 14, 25, and 31			32	
33	Casualty loss portion, if any, from lines 14 and 31. Carry amount to **Form 4684**, Section B			33	
34	Allowable expenses for business use of your home. Subtract line 33 from line 32. Enter here and on Schedule C, line 30. If your home was used for more than one business, see instructions ▶			34	

Part III	Depreciation of Your Home			
35	Enter the **smaller** of your home's adjusted basis or its fair market value. See instructions	35		
36	Value of land included on line 35	36		
37	Basis of building. Subtract line 36 from line 35	37		
38	Business basis of building. Multiply line 37 by line 7	38		
39	Depreciation percentage. See instructions	39		%
40	Depreciation allowable. Multiply line 38 by line 39. Enter here and on line 28 above. See instructions	40		

Part IV	Carryover of Unallowed Expenses to 1998		
41	Operating expenses. Subtract line 25 from line 24. If less than zero, enter -0-	41	
42	Excess casualty losses and depreciation. Subtract line 31 from line 30. If less than zero, enter -0-	42	

For Paperwork Reduction Act Notice, see page 3 of separate instructions.   ✲ *Printed on recycled paper*   Cat. No. 13232M   Form **8829**

SCHEDULE C
(Form 1040)

Department of the Treasury (U)
Internal Revenue Service

Profit or Loss From Business
(Sole Proprietorship)

▶ Partnerships, joint ventures, etc., must file Form 1065.

▶ Attach to Form 1040 or Form 1041.   ▶ See Instructions for Schedule C (Form 1040).

OMB No. 1545-0074

19

Attachment
Sequence No. **09**

Name of proprietor

Social security number (SSN)

A Principal business or profession, including product or service (see page C-1)

B Enter principal business code (see page C-6) ▶

C Business name. If no separate business name, leave blank.

D Employer ID number (EIN), if any

E Business address (including suite or room no.) ▶ ....
City, town or post office, state, and ZIP code

F Accounting method: (1) ☐ Cash   (2) ☐ Accrual   (3) ☐ Other (specify) ▶ ....

G Did you "materially participate" in the operation of this business during 1997? If "No," see page C-2 for limit on losses. ☐ Yes ☐ No

H If you started or acquired this business during 1997, check here . . . . ▶ ☐

Part I   Income

1	Gross receipts or sales. **Caution:** If this income was reported to you on Form W-2 and the "Statutory employee" box on that form was checked, see page C-2 and check here ▶ ☐	1	10200
2	Returns and allowances	2	34
3	Subtract line 2 from line 1	3	10166
4	Cost of goods sold (from line 42 on page 2)	4	3400
5	**Gross profit.** Subtract line 4 from line 3	5	6766
6	Other income, including Federal and state gasoline or fuel tax credit or refund (see page C-2)	6	
7	**Gross income.** Add lines 5 and 6 ▶	7	6766

Part II   Expenses. Enter expenses for business use of your home only on line 30.

8	Advertising	8	1300	19 Pension and profit-sharing plans	19	
9	Bad debts from sales or services (see page C-3)	9	39	20 Rent or lease (see page C-4): a Vehicles, machinery, and equipment	20a	
10	Car and truck expenses (see page C-3)	10	809	b Other business property	20b	900
11	Commissions and fees	11		21 Repairs and maintenance	21	55
12	Depletion	12		22 Supplies (not included in Part III)	22	
13	Depreciation and section 179 expense deduction (not included in Part III) (see page C-3)	13	2938	23 Taxes and licenses	23	165
				24 Travel, meals, and entertainment: a Travel	24a	415
14	Employee benefit programs (other than on line 19)	14		b Meals and entertainment . 500		
15	Insurance (other than health)	15	115	c Enter 50% of line 24b subject to limitations (see page C-4) . 250		
16	Interest: a Mortgage (paid to banks, etc.)	16a	3875	d Subtract line 24c from line 24b	24d	250
	b Other	16b		25 Utilities	25	240
17	Legal and professional services	17	150	26 Wages (less employment credits)	26	1677
18	Office expense	18	237	27 Other expenses (from line 48 on page 2)	27	447
28	**Total expenses** before expenses for business use of home. Add lines 8 through 27 in columns ▶				28	13612

29 Tentative profit (loss). Subtract line 28 from line 7 . . . . | 29 | <6846>

30 Expenses for business use of your home. Attach **Form 8829** . . . . . . | 30 |

31 **Net profit or (loss).** Subtract line 30 from line 29.
 • If a profit, enter on **Form 1040, line 12,** and ALSO on **Schedule SE, line 2** (statutory employees, see page C-5). Estates and trusts, enter on Form 1041, line 3.
 • If a loss, you MUST go on to line 32. | 31 | <6846>

32 If you have a loss, check the box that describes your investment in this activity (see page C-5).
 • If you checked 32a, enter the loss on **Form 1040, line 12,** and ALSO on **Schedule SE, line 2** (statutory employees, see page C-5). Estates and trusts, enter on Form 1041, line 3.
 • If you checked 32b, you MUST attach **Form 6198.**

32a ☒ All investment is at risk.
32b ☐ Some investment is not at risk.

For Paperwork Reduction Act Notice, see Form 1040 instructions.   Cat. No. 15786J   Schedule C (Form 1040)

Schedule C (Form 1040) 1997   Page **2**

Part III	**Cost of Goods Sold** (see page C-5)		

33   Method(s) used to
value closing inventory: **a**   Cost   **b**   Lower of cost or market   **c**   Other (attach explanation)

34   Was there any change in determining quantities, costs, or valuations between opening and closing inventory? If "Yes,"
attach explanation . . . .   ☐ Yes   ☐ No

35	Inventory at beginning of year. If different from last year's closing inventory, attach explanation	**35**	
36	Purchases less cost of items withdrawn for personal use.	**36**	
37	Cost of labor. Do not include salary paid to yourself	**37**	
38	Materials and supplies	**38**	
39	Other costs	**39**	
40	Add lines 35 through 39	**40**	
41	Inventory at end of year	**41**	
42	**Cost of goods sold.** Subtract line 41 from line 40. Enter the result here and on page 1, line 4	**42**	*3400*

Part IV	**Information on Your Vehicle. Complete this part ONLY if you are claiming car or truck expenses on line 10 and are not required to file Form 4562 for this business. See the instructions for line 13 on page C-3 to find out if you must file.**

43   When did you place your vehicle in service for business purposes? (month, day, year) ▶ _____ .

44   Of the total number of miles you drove your vehicle during 1997, enter the number of miles you used your vehicle for:

a Business _____   **b** Commuting _____   **c** Other _____

45   Do you (or your spouse) have another vehicle available for personal use? . . . .   ☐ Yes   ☐ No

46   Was your vehicle available for use during off-duty hours? . . . .   ☐ Yes   ☐ No

47a   Do you have evidence to support your deduction? . . . .   ☐ Yes   ☐ No

  b   If "Yes," is the evidence written? . . . .   ☐ Yes   ☐ No

Part V	**Other Expenses.** List below business expenses not included on lines 8 - 26 or line 30.	
	EDUCATION	*175*
	BANK CHARGES	*62*
	DUES & SUBSCRIPTIONS	*210*
48	**Total other expenses.** Enter here and on page 1, line 27	**48**	*447*

STF FED2615F 2

SCHEDULE SE
(Form 1040)

Department of the Treasury
Internal Revenue Service (U)

Self-Employment Tax

▶ See Instructions for Schedule SE (Form 1040).

▶ Attach to Form 1040.

OMB No. 1545-0074

19

Attachment
Sequence No. **17**

Name of person with **self-employment** income (as shown on Form 1040)

Social security number of person
with **self-employment** income ▶

Who Must File Schedule SE

You must file Schedule SE if:

- You had net earnings from self-employment from **other than** church employee income (line 4 of Short Schedule SE or line 4c of Long Schedule SE) of $400 or more, **OR**
- You had church employee income of $108.28 or more. Income from services you performed as a minister or a member of a religious order **is not** church employee income. See page SE-1.

Note: *Even if you had a loss or a small amount of income from self-employment, it may be to your benefit to file Schedule SE and use either "optional method" in Part II of Long Schedule SE. See page SE-3.*

Exception. If your only self-employment income was from earnings as a minister, member of a religious order, or Christian Science practitioner **and** you filed Form 4361 and received IRS approval not to be taxed on those earnings, **do not** file Schedule SE. Instead, write "Exempt–Form 4361" on Form 1040, line 47.

May I Use Short Schedule SE or MUST I Use Long Schedule SE?

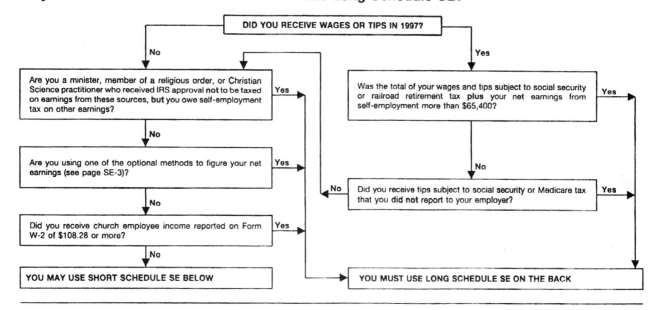

Section A—Short Schedule SE. Caution: *Read above to see if you can use Short Schedule SE.*

1	Net farm profit or (loss) from Schedule F, line 36, and farm partnerships, Schedule K-1 (Form 1065), line 15a	**1**		
2	Net profit or (loss) from Schedule C, line 31; Schedule C-EZ, line 3; and Schedule K-1 (Form 1065), line 15a (other than farming). Ministers and members of religious orders, see page SE-1 for amounts to report on this line. See page SE-2 for other income to report	**2**		
3	Combine lines 1 and 2	**3**		
4	**Net earnings from self-employment.** Multiply line 3 by 92.35% (.9235). If less than $400, **do not** file this schedule; you do not owe self-employment tax . . . . ▶	**4**		
5	**Self-employment tax.** If the amount on line 4 is: • $65,400 or less, multiply line 4 by 15.3% (.153). Enter the result here and on **Form 1040, line 47.** • More than $65,400, multiply line 4 by 2.9% (.029). Then, add $8,109.60 to the result. Enter the total here and on **Form 1040, line 47.**	**5**		
6	**Deduction for one-half of self-employment tax.** Multiply line 5 by 50% (.5). Enter the result here and on **Form 1040, line 26**	**6**		

For Paperwork Reduction Act Notice, see Form 1040 instructions.   Cat. No. 24557Q   **Schedule SE (Form 1040)**

Schedule SE (Form 1040)   Attachment Sequence No. **17**   Page **2**

Name of person with **self-employment** income (as shown on Form 1040)	Social security number of person with **self-employment** income ▶	┊ ┊

Section B—Long Schedule SE

Part I — Self-Employment Tax

Note: *If your only income subject to self-employment tax is* **church employee income,** *skip lines 1 through 4b. Enter -0- on line 4c and go to line 5a. Income from services you performed as a minister or a member of a religious order* **is not** *church employee income. See page SE-1.*

A   If you are a minister, member of a religious order, or Christian Science practitioner **and** you filed Form 4361, but you had $400 or more of **other** net earnings from self-employment, check here and continue with Part I . . . . . ▶ ☐

1	Net farm profit or (loss) from Schedule F, line 36, and farm partnerships, Schedule K-1 (Form 1065), line 15a. **Note:** *Skip this line if you use the farm optional method. See page SE-3* . .	**1**		
2	Net profit or (loss) from Schedule C, line 31; Schedule C-EZ, line 3; and Schedule K-1 (Form 1065), line 15a (other than farming). Ministers and members of religious orders, see page SE-1 for amounts to report on this line. See page SE-2 for other income to report. **Note:** *Skip this line if you use the nonfarm optional method. See page SE-3.*	**2**		
3	Combine lines 1 and 2	**3**		
4a	If line 3 is more than zero, multiply line 3 by 92.35% (.9235). Otherwise, enter amount from line 3	**4a**		
b	If you elected one or both of the optional methods, enter the total of lines 15 and 17 here . .	**4b**		
c	Combine lines 4a and 4b. If less than $400, **do not** file this schedule; you do not owe self-employment tax. **Exception.** If less than $400 and you had **church employee income,** enter -0- and continue ▶	**4c**		
5a	Enter your **church employee income** from Form W-2. **Caution:** *See page SE-1 for definition of church employee income* **5a**			
b	Multiply line 5a by 92.35% (.9235). If less than $100, enter -0-	**5b**		
6	**Net earnings from self-employment.** Add lines 4c and 5b	**6**		
7	Maximum amount of combined wages and self-employment earnings subject to social security tax or the 6.2% portion of the 7.65% railroad retirement (tier 1) tax for 1997	**7**	65,400	00
8a	Total social security wages and tips (total of boxes 3 and 7 on Form(s) W-2) and railroad retirement (tier 1) compensation **8a**			
b	Unreported tips subject to social security tax (from Form 4137, line 9) **8b**			
c	Add lines 8a and 8b	**8c**		
9	Subtract line 8c from line 7. If zero or less, enter -0- here and on line 10 and go to line 11 . ▶	**9**		
10	Multiply the **smaller** of line 6 or line 9 by 12.4% (.124)	**10**		
11	Multiply line 6 by 2.9% (.029).	**11**		
12	**Self-employment tax.** Add lines 10 and 11. Enter here and on **Form 1040, line 47**	**12**		
13	**Deduction for one-half of self-employment tax.** Multiply line 12 by 50% (.5). Enter the result here and on **Form 1040, line 26** . . . **13**			

Part II — Optional Methods To Figure Net Earnings (See page SE-3.)

Farm Optional Method. You may use this method **only** if:
- Your gross farm income[1] was not more than $2,400, **or**
- Your gross farm income[1] was more than $2,400 and your net farm profits[2] were less than $1,733.

14	Maximum income for optional methods	**14**	1,600	00
15	Enter the **smaller** of: two-thirds (⅔) of gross farm income[1] (not less than zero) **or** $1,600. Also, include this amount on line 4b above	**15**		

Nonfarm Optional Method. You may use this method **only** if:
- Your net nonfarm profits[3] were less than $1,733 and also less than 72.189% of your gross nonfarm income,[4] **and**
- You had net earnings from self-employment of at least $400 in 2 of the prior 3 years.

Caution: *You may use this method no more than five times.*

16	Subtract line 15 from line 14	**16**		
17	Enter the **smaller** of: two-thirds (⅔) of gross nonfarm income[4] (not less than zero) **or** the amount on line 16. Also, include this amount on line 4b above	**17**		

[1]From Schedule F, line 11, and Schedule K-1 (Form 1065), line 15b.   [3]From Schedule C, line 31; Schedule C-EZ, line 3; and Schedule K-1 (Form 1065), line 15a.
[2]From Schedule F, line 36, and Schedule K-1 (Form 1065), line 15a.   [4]From Schedule C, line 7; Schedule C-EZ, line 1; and Schedule K-1 (Form 1065), line 15c.

CHAPTER 15 | *BOOKKEEPING*

When people think of bookkeeping they often visualize themselves agonizing over columns that won't balance and wearing their fingers to a stub pounding an adding machine with a stream of tape hanging from it. Bookkeeping needn't be that way especially now with the advent of the personal computer.

A business person must keep books because the IRS requires it. But even if the government did not require you to keep records, it is to your benefit to do so anyway. To run your business efficiently and profitably, you must have the information only a set of books can provide. Good records show the true financial picture. They reveal your true profit or loss. Only with a good set of books can you make decisions based on the facts not on supposition.

> Any enterprise...profits wonderfully by keeping abreast of the facts.
>
> Proverbs 24:3,4 (TLB)

This chapter covers bookkeeping for the sole proprietorship form of ownership, not for a corporation or partnership, although there are similarities between the three.

Don't Mingle Personal and Business Expenses

If you are operating your business as a sole proprietorship, it is easy to fall into the trap of commingling your personal and business expenses. Bookkeeping safeguards against this and helps you maintain the separateness so vital to the success of a small business, especially one operated out of your home.

A lack of accurate financial records is a prevalent contributor to failures in small businesses. After all expenses such as rent, insurance, taxes, payroll, utilities, advertising and other overhead, your books will reveal where you must price your product or service in order to make a profit.

Computerized Bookkeeping

If you haven't already, you should soon be entering the computer age and investing in a personal computer (PC) or a Macintosh for your small business. You will find a vast array of bookkeeping software programs available to you.

QuickBooks

A top-selling business financial software program is *QuickBooks* published by Intuit. It has a suggested retail price of around $100. It is as easy to use as filling in a blank check. Once you fill in the check on the screen, *QuickBooks* takes it from there. It prints the checks, creates and updates the check register, categorizes spending, reconciles the bank accounts, slashes data entry time (type a few characters and it instantly fills in the rest), provides a multitude of reports and graphs, produces profit and loss statements, balance sheets, budgets, audits, forecasts cash flow, tracks payroll, jobs, clients, properties and more.

Quickbooks will enable you, without the assistance of an accountant, to keep a double entry set of books with a general ledger, journals, profit and loss statement, balance sheet, accounts payable, accounts receivable, invoicing, inventory, billing, budgeting, etc.

QuickBooks can also be purchased on CD-rom. This version gives you various accounting ratios that can help you operate your business to the maximum by calculating the return on capital invested, return on equity, break-even point, etc.

But if you don't have a computer yet and you wish to learn more about these valuable calculations of ratios, your library should be able to help you. Also you may call the general information number for the Small Business Administration, 800-827-5722.

Before paying retail for any computer program, check the ads in the computer magazines and mail order catalogs. Often you will find substantial savings. Many catalog companies offer overnight delivery for a small charge.

Computer
User Groups

Most major cities have computer user groups that meet regularly. They can be a great source for hardware and software information, networking and getting your questions answered. Some clubs have special interest groups (SIGs) in QuickBooks, desktop publishing, investments, etc.

Opening a Bank Account

When you start your business, one of the first things you must do is to open a business checking account. The absolute necessity of keeping your personal finances and your business finances separately cannot be over-emphasized. You must look upon your small business as an entity separate from yourself.

Since the start-up expenses for your new business are not deductible from a tax viewpoint, it will be advantageous to open this account as early as possible. The business checking account is one of the signals the IRS looks for to determine the starting point of the small business.

For your businesses account, select a bank that is not only conveniently located but one with a banker with whom you can relate.

You will find a wide disparity between the service charges of banks. Such costs can add up to a significant expense, so let the costs be one of the determining factors in choosing a bank. You may find that some large banks, especially those that are part of a giant holding company, may not cater to small business accounts. Their service fees can nibble you to death. You may find that a smaller bank may be more eager for your business.

Your bank account can serve as a bookkeeping tool. In order to have a record of your earnings, deposit all income from the business, whether check or cash, into the business bank account. When you record the deposit into the checkbook be sure to write a brief description of *what* the deposit consists of and *where* it comes from.

Once the bank account is opened, if possible pay all business bills by check. The small items that do require cash can be paid from a petty cash fund. Keep only a small amount in this fund and try to use the fund as infrequently as possible and then only when there is no practical way to write a check. An inexpensive metal box or a vinyl zipper money bag available at office supply stores will serve well as a petty cash container.

In the following example, $50 will be used as the amount in petty cash. Some businesses may require more, some less. To start a petty cash fund:

1. Write a check for $50 (or whatever amount you determine) payable to "petty cash."

2. Cash the check.

3. Put the money in the petty cash container along with a piece of accounting worksheet paper and a pencil.

4. Each time you take money out of petty cash, record on the worksheet the date, the payee, the amount and what it was for. Keep your cash receipts in the container.

5. When the amount starts to get low, total the worksheet entries.

6. Add the cash remaining in the box to the total on the worksheet. The items on your worksheet plus the cash still remaining in the box should equal $50. If it does, you have balanced and are ready to make out another check to "petty cash" for an

amount sufficient to bring the cash back up to $50. *The amount of the check will be the total of the worksheet entries.*

7. Staple all the old cash receipts to the worksheet and file them.

8. Put the new cash in the petty cash container along with a new worksheet.

From time to time you may be tempted to compromise "penny-any" things such as putting the change from a purchase into your pocket instead of putting it back in the petty cash box or buying a book of stamps from petty cash and using some for personal use. Don't.

Jesus said:

> Whoever can be trusted with very little can also be trusted with much.
>
> Luke 16:10

Personal Draws

When you want to take some of your profit from your sole proprietorship business, do it with a personal draw. You make a withdrawal by writing a check to yourself from your business account and depositing that check into your personal account. Once it is deposited in your personal account you can pay for personal items such as groceries, your house payment, and any other non business expenses.

If you use some of your product for personal use, you will treat it like a personal draw also.

In a sole proprietorship form of ownership, you are self

employed for tax purposes. There is no salary or withholding for the owner, simply a draw.

So instead of having withholding taken from his or her paycheck, the owner pays estimated tax quarterly from the monies in his or her personal checking account. It is very important to pay estimated taxes when due to avoid penalties and interest that may accrue for non payment. In other words, don't wait until the end of the year to pay estimated taxes. The IRS has forms to help you compute your estimated tax due.

Employees of a Sole Proprietorship

However, when you have an employee or employees, you, as the owner of a sole proprietorship, must treat them the same way corporations do. You must do the following:

- Obtain an employer's identification number from the IRS by filling out and filing a Form SS-4.

- Obtain Circular E from the IRS to use to determine the payroll withholding deposits.

- Obtain a state unemployment number from your state.

- Fill out and file Form 941 and the state unemployment forms quarterly.

- File Form 940 annually.

Income Tax Withholding Records

Regardless of the number of employees, you must maintain all records pertaining to payroll taxes. The following is a list of the types of records you need:

- Name, address and Social Security number of each employee. Have employee fill out a W-4.

- Have employee fill out an IRS Form I-9. This is a statement relating to employee's nonresident alien status.

- Amount and date of each payment of wages.

- Amount of wages subject to withholding in each payment.

- Amount of withholding tax collected from each payment.

- Reason the taxable amount is less than the total amount, if it is.

- Market value and date of non cash compensation.

- Information about payments made under sick-pay plans.

- Withholding exemption certificates.

- Agreements regarding the voluntary withholding of extra cash.

- Dates and payments to employees for non business services.

- Requests for different computation of withholding taxes.

Social Security (FICA) Tax Records

- Amount of each payment subject to FICA tax.

- Amount and date of social security (FICA) tax

collected from each payment. Explanation of the difference, if any.

- Gross wages paid during quarter.

- Gross wages paid from previous quarters during calendar year.

- Total amount paid during the calendar year.

- Amount subject to unemployment tax.

- Amount of contributions paid into the state unemployment fund.

Until you invest in a computer and *QuickBooks* with its excellent, easy-to-use payroll program, consider a good pegboard or "write-it-once" system. These can be purchased at most office supply stores.

There are basically two ways to keep books:

single entry
double entry

The single entry system is designed to keep the paperwork to a minimum and at the same time provide the basic information needed to satisfy the IRS and to manage your business.

The double entry system provides cross checks and balances, thereby minimizing errors. Each transaction requires two entries, a debit and a credit. It is by far the best system.

As pointed out earlier, *QuickBooks* uses the double entry system and will handle the debits and credits for you. But until you buy a computer which should be as soon as possible, there is a system called "an entry and a half" that combines both single- and double-entry systems as shown in this chapter.

Regardless of whether your books are single, double or an entry and a half, you must choose between two accounting methods —"cash" or "accrual."

Cash Method of Accounting

With the *cash method*, income is reported as received and expenses are recorded <u>only</u> <u>when</u> <u>paid</u>, not when they are incurred. In other words, if you charge a business expense in December on your credit card but don't pay your credit card statement until January, the expense is deducted in January not December.

With the cash method, unpaid credit sales and expenses you owe but haven't paid yet do not show up on your books. This may give a distorted picture of your income and expense.

Accrual Method of Accounting

On the other hand, the *accrual method* records the income whether it is received or not and records expenses whether paid or not. Transactions, cash or credit, are recorded <u>when</u>

incurred, <u>not</u> <u>when</u> <u>paid</u>. Accrual accounting requires more effort than cash accounting, but it gives a truer picture of what is happening. When you buy supplies or merchandise, because you record it when you order it, you know how much money you are going to need at the end of the month. Money that people are obligated to pay you this year, whether paid in this year or next year, is this year's income. Any deductible item you become obligated to pay this year is a deduction for this year. The good news is you can get deductions for bills you haven't paid yet; the bad news is you pay taxes on income you haven't received yet.

If you are in manufacturing or in a business that stocks and sells parts, federal law says you must use the accrual method for such inventory. If you have no inventory you can use either method.

> *NOTE: Once a method is selected, whether cash or accrual, written permission from the IRS must be received in order to change methods.*

Accounting Year

Determine the dates of your fiscal year before you begin entering transactions in your books. Every company has a fiscal year sometimes referred to as the accounting year. For most companies, this fiscal year is the same as the calendar year, that is January through December. In this book we use the calendar year as the fiscal year.

Types of Businesses

There are basically three types of businesses. They each use a basic accounting system but with their own unique chart of accounts.

A chart of accounts is a listing of the various account names and their respective numbers. An example of a typical Chart of Accounts is shown on page 15-17

Service-Type Business

1. *A service business*—This type of business must keep track of the services it sells. If there are customers who charge their purchases, there must be a method of invoicing, a way to monitor the length of time between sending the invoice and receiving payment and a system of follow-up letters.

   If there are employees, obtain an employer's identification number from the IRS by filling out a Form SS-4. Also obtain a Circular E from the IRS that contains the payroll tables necessary to figure withholding taxes. (See a sample Form SS-4 in Chapter 13.)

   You will need a time sheet form to show the hours worked.

   Payroll was discussed in greater detail a few pages earlier in this chapter under the heading, "Employees of a Sole Proprietorship".

Retail or Wholesale Type Business

2. *A Retail or Wholesale Business*—A retail or wholesale business uses the same basic accounting system as a service business with the addition of a system for keeping track of goods on order and, once they are received, a way to verify the price on those invoices.

   Included in this type business are your "accounts payable," e.g., suppliers who allow you to purchase on credit rather than pay cash. There must also be a method of controlling inventory and recording the items sold. This allows you to monitor how quickly your goods are moving and when you will need to reorder.

Most small businesses use a physical inventory method and take an inventory at least once a year. The accounting records used as an example in this book follow this method. The financial statements prepared during the year will be reasonably accurate if the inventory does not fluctuate substantially.

QuickBooks provides a good inventory control system but if you don't have a computer yet the following forms will suffice until you do.

Inventory

"Perpetual inventory" records can be kept on index cards or on ledger sheets with a separate page for each type item. You can tell at a glance what is on hand or on order, how long it takes to receive an order and what your balance on hand is. Below is an example of an Inventory Control card.

Inventory Control Card					
Item *Auto Oil Additive*					
Cost *$2.25* Supplier *Acme Oil*					
Ordered		**Received**			
Quantity	Date	Quantity	Date	Sold	Balance
25	*1/18*				
		25	*2/1*		*25*
				|||| |||	*17*
				|||| ||||	*8*
50	*2/15*				
		50	*3/1*		*58*

Manufacturing Type Business

3. *A Manufacturing Business*—In addition to using the same accounting systems as described for a retail or wholesale business, a manufacturing business requires a production and manufacturing cost system that allows you to monitor how much and how many products you are producing and how long it is taking to manufacture your products.

Your small business can operate quite successfully with simplified versions of the systems mentioned above.

There is another version of *QuickBooks* called *QuickBooks Pro* for companies requiring an accounting package that does job costing, time costs management, estimating, etc.

A checkbook can be turned into a highly effective purchase and payment system by the use of proper coding of the checks. This will be covered later in this chapter.

Bookkeeping, Sequence of Events

The sequence of events for keeping a simple set of books looks like this.

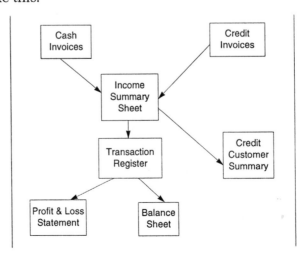

There are blank copies of all the forms used in this book at the end of the chapters where they are introduced.

Create a
Chart of Accounts

Step 1

Create your own customized Chart of Accounts with a list of account names like those shown later in this chapter.

These account names are grouped together under the categories listed below:

>   Assets
>   Liabilities
>   Capital
>   Income
>   Expenses

Review the account names shown on the Chart of Accounts on page 15-17 and from each category, choose a few that apply to your particular business.

Instead of having only one Sales Income account, you may want to use several sales account names such as Retail Sales, Wholesale Sales, Mail Order Sales, etc., because you may want to maintain additional detail to determine the source of the income.

If you operate a service-type business you will probably have income account headings such as Income, Commissions Income, Miscellaneous Income, etc.

The same applies to expenses. You may have Advertising,

Insurance, Telephone, etc. You can customize your accounts based upon your particular requirements. Usually 15 to 20 accounts are sufficient for a small business, but you can use as many names from each category as you need.

If the Chart of Accounts shown on page 15-17 does not fit your type of business, be creative and design your own. Account names within the various categories are numbered as shown below, e.g., asset accounts can use any of the numbers from 1000 to 1999, etc.

Classification of Categories

1000 - 1999	Assets
2000 - 2999	Liabilities
3000 - 3999	Proprietorship (Capital)
4000 - 4999	Income
5000 - 7999	Expenses

The sample Chart of Accounts shown on the next page is for a sole proprietorship and will give you some idea of the various account names you may wish to use.

CHART OF ACCOUNTS

ASSETS

1000 Cash In Bank
1040 Accounts Receivable
1050 Less: Allowance For Bad Debts
1070 Inventory

1200 Prepaid Expenses
1220 Utility Deposits
1240 Land
1250 Buildings

1260 Less: Accum. Depreciation-Bldg.
1280 Office Furniture and Equipment
1290 Less: Accum. Deprec. Furniture
1300 Auto
1310 Less: Accumulated Deprec.Auto

LIABILITIES

2000 Accounts Payable
2020 Notes Payable
2080 Sales Tax Payable

2100 Payroll Taxes Payable
(includes FICA and Withholding)

2120 Mortgages Payable
2140 Loans

CAPITAL

3000 (Name of proprietor), Capital
3020 (Name of proprietor), Withdrawals

3030 Accumulated Profit & Loss

INCOME

4000 Retail Sales
4080 Wholesale Sales

4120 Sales- Services
4160 Miscellaneous Income

4200 Commissions/Bonuses

EXPENSES

5000 Advertising
5040 Auto
5080   Insurance
5120   Fees & Licenses
5160   Gas or Diesel
5200   Repairs
5240   Tires
5280   Parking Fees & Tolls
5320 Bank Loan Interest
5360 Contract Labor
5400 Depreciation
5440 Dues & Subscriptions

5480 Entertainment
5520 Family Labor
5560 Freight Paid
5600 Insurance
5640 Interest
5680 Legal & Accounting
5720 Maintenance Expense
5760 Miscellaneous Expense
5800 Office Rental
5840 Office Supplies
5880 Payroll
5920   Payroll Taxes

5960 Taxes
6020 Postage
6060 Rent
6080 Sample Products
6100 Telephone
6140 Travel
6180 Utilities
   COST OF SALE ACCOUNTS
6820 Products Purchased For Resale
6860 Material And Supplies
6900 Freight In

NON-DEDUCTIBLE ITEMS:

7000 Credit Card Payments
7020 Petty Cash Checks
7030 Miscellaneous

CODE FOR BUSINESSES:
Example:
Business A — Profit Enterprises

Business A — _____
Business B — _____
Business C — _____
Business D — _____

CODE FOR CREDIT CARDS:
Example:
C1 — VISA

C1 — _____
C2 — _____
C3 — _____
C4 — _____
C5 — _____

Definitions of the
Chart of Accounts

ASSET ACCOUNTS:

1000   *Cash in Bank* — Regular checking account
        including deposits, transfers, checks
        written, etc.

1020   *Savings Acct* — A savings account including
        deposits, withdrawals, interest earned, etc.

1040   *Accounts Receivable* — Monies owed to the
        company

1050   *Less: Allowance For Bad Debts* — This
        allowance can only be used by those who
        are on the *accrual* basis

1070   *Inventory* — Items on hand to be sold to
        others

1200   *Prepaid Expenses* — Expenses paid in
        advance such as annual insurance
        premiums paid when the policy is renewed

1220   *Deposits* — Monies paid as deposits for
        utilities, telephone, etc. They remain in the
        deposit account until they are refunded.

1240   *Land* — All purchases of land. Land cannot
        be depreciated like buildings, furniture and
        equipment can.

1250   *Buildings* — Includes all purchases of
        buildings whose expected useful life for tax
        purposes is more than one year. These
        assets are to be depreciated.

1260   *Less: Accumulated Depreciation-Bldg* —

When depreciation is figured for tax purposes on *Buildings* the figure goes here. This account holds the accumulation of all depreciation from the date the *Building* is placed in service until the date of the sale or disposition of the asset.

1280   *Office Furniture and Equipment* — All purchases of furniture and equipment whose cost exceeds the minimum set by the company and the expected life exceeds one year. For example, a tape duplicator costing $2000 would be placed in this account whereas a tape recorder at $100 would be placed in an expense account called *Office Supplies*.

1290   *Less: Accumulated Depreciation - Furniture* — This account holds the depreciation for account *1280 Office Furniture and Equipment*. The offset account is the expense account called Depreciation.

1300   *Auto*

1310   *Less: Accumulated Depreciation - Auto*

LIABILITY ACCOUNTS:

2000   *Accounts Payable* — This account is used only when a company is on the *accrual* basis. At the time a bill is made, the expense is debited and this account is credited.

If you are using this account, print it each month just as you do your check register to retain the detail. The details of your checks will show up here not in your check register if you are using the *accrual* method.

2020   *Notes Payable* — This account holds the principal due on notes for funds borrowed for a period of twelve months or less.

2080   *Sales Tax Payable* — Holds tax collected on sales. At the time of recording a sale, the amount of the sale less sales tax is placed in an income account and the sales tax is placed in this account. Periodically the accumulation is deposited with your State Comptroller, either through your bank or directly to the State. These deposits are used to fill out your State Sales Tax form.

2100   *Payroll Taxes Payable* (includes FICA and Withholding) — All payroll taxes withheld from an employee's pay is accumulated here. Periodically the accumulation is deposited with the IRS either through your bank or directly to the IRS. These deposits are used quarterly to fill out your IRS Form 941 and state employment reports.

2120   *Mortgages Payable* — Initially when you are setting up your set of books the balance of the mortgage will go here. Then each month as you pay your mortgage the principal part of your payment will be placed here. If you don't know the principal amount each month, you can make a journal entry later to reflect the principal.

2140   *Loans*

CAPITAL ACCOUNTS:

3000   *(Your name), Capital*

3020   *(Your name), Withdrawals* — In a sole

proprietorship, this account is the place to take out monies for personal use. It is not an income or an expense when you take monies out for personal use.

3030   *Accumulated Profit & Loss* — This is a running total of the difference between your income and your expenses.

INCOME ACCOUNTS:

4000   *Retail Sales*

4080   *Wholesale Sales*

4120   *Sales- Services*

4160   *Miscellaneous Income*

4200   *Commissions/Bonuses*

EXPENSE ACCOUNTS:

5000   *Advertising*

5040   *Auto*

5080   *Auto Insurance*

5120   *Auto Fees & Licenses*

5160   *Auto Gas or Diesel*

5200   *Auto Repairs*

5240   *Auto Tires*

5280   *Parking Fees & Tolls*

5320   *Bank Loan Interest*

5360   *Contract Labor*

5400   *Depreciation* — This account offsets all the

asset accounts such as *Less: Accumulated Depreciation-Bldg, Less: Accumulated Depreciation- Furniture*, etc.

5440   *Dues & Subscriptions*

5480   *Entertainment*

5520   *Family Labor*

5560   *Freight Paid*

5600   *Insurance*

5640   *Interest*

5680   *Legal & Accounting*

5720   *Maintenance Expense*

5760   *Miscellaneous Expense* — Don't put a lot into this account. Try to be more descriptive and find other accounts that will better describe what the check is used for.

5800   *Office Rental*

5840   *Office Supplies*

5880   *Payroll*

5920   *Payroll Taxes*

5960   *Taxes*

6020   *Postage*

6060   *Rent*

6080   *Sample Products*

6100   *Telephone*

6140   *Travel*

6180   Utilities

COST OF SALE ACCOUNTS:

6820   Products Purchased For Resale

6860   Material And Supplies

6900   Freight In

Creating the
Cash Receipt

Step 2

Record the sale on an individual receipt or cash register tape at the time you make the sale. Which of these two forms you use will depend upon the volume of your business. The cash register is necessary only if your business does scores of transactions daily such as a grocery store. For most businesses, a cash receipt will suffice. These can be purchased at an office supply store in inexpensive, pre-printed, pre-numbered books.

Use a separate receipt for each sale. The receipt should be filled out in duplicate (one for you, one for the customer) and should include:

1. Company name, address and telephone number

2. Receipt number

3. If it is a credit sale, write CREDIT SALE and write the name of the credit card used—MasterCard or Visa, etc.

4. Date of sale

5. Customer's name and address

6. Brief description of what was sold

7. Amount of purchase without sales tax or handling charges (called the "net amount" in this book)

8. Sales tax and/or handling charges shown separately

9. Total amount received including sales tax and/or handling charges (called the "gross amount" in this book)

Below is a example of a *cash receipt.* This receipt is used for all sales in which you do not extend credit. Credit sales will be addressed later.

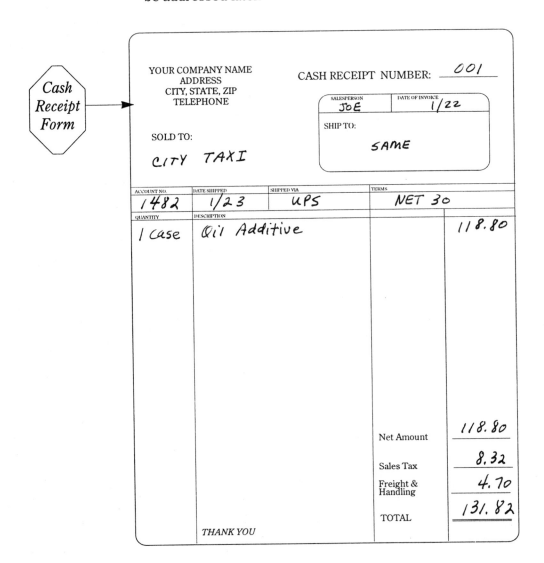

Step 3

From the *cash receipts* slips for the day

- Add up all the "net amounts" without including sales tax.

- Post your total to the Taxable Sales column on the Income Summary Sheet.

- Total up all the sales tax from the cash receipts for the day.

- Record the total sales tax on the same line on your Income Summary Sheet.

- If there are any non-taxable sales, add them up and post them on the Income Summary.

- Total the figures across the line and post the sum in the Total Sales column. This total should equal the total of all cash receipts for the day including sales tax and non-taxable items.

- Place a check mark in the Cash column to show that this group of receipts was from cash sales.

- Staple all the invoices together and mark today's date on the top one.

- Record this same date on the Income Summary under the Period Invoices Cover column.

- File the receipts according to date. The sum of the Total Sales column is the amount you will put in the bank. Each day's deposit should have its own bank deposit ticket.

Income Summary - Month of _____

For Cash Sales

Period Invoices Cover	Cash	Credit	Bank Deposit	Taxable Sales	Sales Tax	NON-TAXABLE SALES		TOTAL SALES
						FREIGHT	WHOLESALE	
1/22 — 1/24	✓			475 20	33 28	18 80		527 28

At the time you make the bank deposit, you will record in your Transaction Register the total amount of the deposit broken down into the proper account as shown on the Income Summary Sheet such as sales, sales tax, non-taxable entries. See the following examples.

Transaction Register - Month of

For Cash Sales

Date	Check #	Credit Card Code	Cash	Deposited	Reconciled	Accounting Code	Description	Amount	Check Balance Forward 1,560	
1/24				✓		4000A	Invoices 1/22 - 1/24	475 20		1
						2080A	SALES TAX	33 28		2
						6900A	FREIGHT IN	18 80		3
								527 28	2087 28	4
										5
										6
										7
										8
										9
										10
										11

A *credit invoice* form is to be used if the purchase is charged. Below is an example:

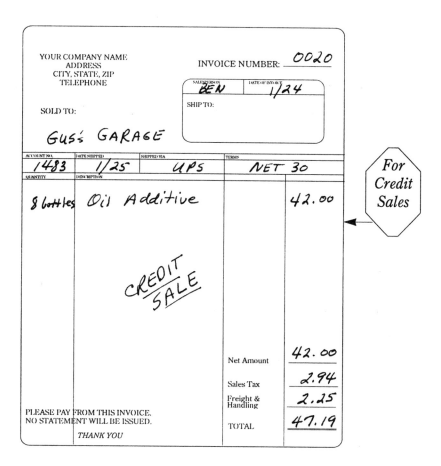

Record the *credit invoices* the same way as you did cash invoices. Place a checkmark in the column headed Credit. Just as you did for the cash receipts, staple all your invoices together and mark on the front the dates covered and record them on the Income Summary.

Income Summary - Month of _JANUARY_

For Credit Sales

Period Invoices Cover	Cash	Credit	Bank Deposit	Taxable Sales	Sales Tax	NON-TAXABLE SALES		TOTAL SALES
						FREIGHT	WHOLESALE	
1/22 - 1/24		✓		4200	294	225		4719

Transaction Register - Month of _JANUARY_

For Credit Sales

Date	Check #	Credit Card Code	Cash	Deposited	Reconciled	Accounting Code	Description	Amount	Check Balance Forward 2087.28
1/24						4000A	Invoices 1/22 - 1/24	4200	1
						2080A	SALES TAX	294	2
						6900A	FREIGHT IN	225	3
								4719	4
									5

With the credit invoices you have one more step. You must post the invoices to a Credit Customer Summary. This is simply a way to keep up with each customer to whom you have extended credit. As the customer pays, you mark him or her off the Credit Customer Summary sheet. File these credit invoices according to the date.

Credit Customer Summary

For Credit Sales

Date	Customer	Invoice No.	Total Sales Amount	Date Paid	Memo
11/23	AJAX DELIVERY	003	3240		NOTICE SENT 12/28
12/19	ELITE LIMOUSINE	006	1479	1/15	
1/24	GUS'S GARAGE	0020	4719		

If you have only a few sales each day, you may choose to post once every few days. It is not necessary to stick to one time frame for posting. If you have heavy volume one week, you may post more often. But don't allow the paper-work to accumulate. It can become a nightmare when invoices are out of order or missing.

Return of Merchandise

When you have a return of merchandise, either cash or credit, handle it as if it were a negative sale.

1. Prepare a separate invoice and mark it in big red letters, "RETURN" or "REFUND."

2. Copy all the information from the original sales slip including the sales tax amount.

3. Include the return slip with the *current* batch of receipts or invoices.

4. When you total the amounts on the receipts or invoices as previously instructed, subtract the amounts on the REFUND receipts or invoices as part of the batch.

Transaction Register

The Transaction Register is a way of recording expenses that allows a form of "accrual" accounting. The following example demonstrates how it works. Here are a few ground rules:

- This one Transaction Register can record up to 24 businesses if they all use the same checking account. Business #1 will be "A," Business #2 will be "B," Business #3 will be "C," etc. For example, if you record an expense check to the Daily News for advertising, and you are keeping track of more than one business, you will write in the Code column "5000A." This code will signify Advertising (Account 5000) for "A" which is Business #1.

- An indefinite number of your credit cards can be recorded. You need to assign each of your credit cards a number such as C1 for Visa, C2 for American Express, C3 for Mastercard, etc.

- This Register also accommodates cash transactions as well as deposits.

- If you have a check or deposit that needs to be divided into several different accounts, simply list the amounts one under another, draw a line and total the check on the next blank line below.

- The Check Balance Forward column is a running total of your bank account. You will notice that not all entries from the Amount column are a part of the Check Balance column. Items for which you do not write checks or make deposits will not be included in the Balance Forward column, only in the Amount column.

- Your Transaction Register is also used to record a cash or credit transaction even though you don't write a check for it. You expense the item when you make it, not when you pay it. For example, if you charge $50 at an office supply store on your Visa card, you expense it to Account 5840. When you do pay your Visa, all the items should have already been expensed because you recorded the expense as you made it. In this case your check to pay Visa will be coded as a non-deductible expense such as 7000 Credit Card Payment account. When you receive your Visa statement, check to see that all the expenses listed on their statement are shown on your Transaction Register including interest. You cannot deduct an expense twice.

• The "Reconciled" column is for you to place check marks as you reconcile your bank account at the end of the month. Usually a form showing how to reconcile your checks is on the back of the statement from your bank.

Below is a copy of the Transaction Register with several entries filled in. You can see how easily this system works. Let's say you make out a check to One Stop Supply for merchandise and included in the amount you pay is $240 to One Stop and $7.50 for freight for a total of $247.50. It would be recorded as follows:

Transaction Register - Month of JANUARY

	Date	Check #	Credit Card Code	Cash	Deposited	Reconciled	Accounting Code	Description	Amount		Check Balance Forward 1,560	
1	1/26				✓		4000A	INVOICES 1/22 - 1/24	47520			1
2							2080A	SALES TAX	3328			2
3							6900A	FREIGHT IN	1880			3
4									52728	208728		4
5												5
6	1/24						4000A	Invoices 1/22 - 1/24	4200			6
7							2080A	SALES TAX	294			7
8							6900A	FREIGHT IN	225			8
9									4719			9
10												10
11	1/25	100					6820A	ONE STOP SUPPLY	24000			11
12							5560A	FREIGHT PAID	750			12
13									24750	183978		13
14												14
15	1/25						5840A	BUCK'S OFFICE SUPPLY	2603			15
16	1/25	101					3020A	JOE, PERSONAL DRAW	5000	178978		16
17	1/25				✓		5480A	COFFEE w/JONES - DENNY'S				17
18								RE: CITY TAXI CO	550			18
19	1/25	102					6100A	BELL TELEPHONE	15000	163978		19
20	1/26						5160A	GULF OIL	1500			20
21	1/26						5640A	VISA INTEREST	81			21
22	1/26	103					7000A	VISA PAYMENT (CI)	4184	159794		21
23												22
24												23
25												24
26												25
27												26
28												27
29												28
30												29

End of Month
Posting

Step 4

At the end of the month total up all the amounts that have the same account number in the code column, for example all the 5000's or all the 5000A's if you have more than one business, all the 5020's, all the 5030's, etc.

Posting to
Reports

Step 5

These totals are then posted to the Profit and Loss Statement and Balance Sheet under the proper account code number and in the appropriate month column (see next page for examples). The bottom line is your profit or loss for the month. Now isn't that easy? There will be a separate Profit and Loss Statement and Balance Sheet for each business.

The Cash Account 1000 on the Balance Sheet can be obtained by subtracting the ending balance in the Check Balance Forward column on the Transaction Register from the balance at the beginning of the month on the Transaction Register. This is posted to the Balance Sheet under the proper period column.

You can check your figures by totaling all the expenses in the Amount column. Do not include the totals again when you add down. This figure should agree with the totals for the month from the year-to-date statements (Profit and Loss Statement and Balance Sheet) after taking out the Beginning and Ending Inventories if you have them.

Profit and Loss Statement Year

	Acct. Code	Description	January	Februa
1		Sales:		
2	4000	Retail Sales	51720	
3	4060	Sales - Services		
4		Total Sales	51720	
5				
6		Cost of Sales:		
7		Inventory at ____, 19 __		
8	6820	Merchandise Purchased	24000	
9	6900	Plus Freight In	2105	
10		Total	26105	
11		Less: Invent____,19		
12		Total Cost of Sales	26105	
13		Gross Profit	25615	
14				
15		Expenses:		
16	5000	Advertising		
17	5040	Auto	1500	
18	5360	Contract Labor		
19	5400	Depreciation		
20	5480	Entertainment	550	
21	5520	Family Labor		
22	5560	Freight Paid	750	
23	5640	Interest Paid	81	
24	5840	Office Supplies	2603	
25	5880	Payroll		
26	6100	Telephone	15000	
27		Total Expenses	20484	
28		NET INCOME	5131	
29				
30				
31	7000	Credit Card Payments	4184	
32	7020	Petty Cash		
33				

Balance Sheet Year To Date

	Acct. Code	Description	Beginning Balance	Period Covered
1		Current Assets:		
2	1000	Cash In Bank		
3	1040	Accounts Receivable		
4	1050	Less: Allow. for Bad Debts		
5	1070	Inventory		
6	1200	Prepaid Expenses		
7		Total Current Assets		
8		Fixed Assets:		
9	1250	Building		
10	1260	Less: Accumulated Depreciation		
11	1280	Office Furniture & Equipment		
12	1290	Less: Accumulated Depreciation		
13	1300	Auto		
14	1310	Less: Accumulated Depreciation		
15		Total Fixed Assets		
16		TOTAL ASSETS		
17				
18		Current Liabilities:		
19	2000	Accounts Payable		
20	2020	Notes Payable		
21	2080	Sales Tax Payable		3622
22	2100	Payroll Taxes Payable		
23		Total Current Liabilities		
24		Long Term Liabilities:		
25	2140	Mortgage Payable		
26		Total Long Term Liabilities		
27		Capital:		
28	3000	(Name of owner), Capital		
29	3020	JOE (Name of owner), Withdrawals		5000
30	3030	Accumulated Profit &j Loss		
31		Capital, End of Period		
32		TOTAL LIABILITIES & CAPITAL		
33				

There are two basic financial statements which, when both are used, reflect a clear picture of the status of the business.

One is the "Balance Sheet," the other a "Profit and Loss (or Income) Statement."

The balance sheet is a statement of your business' financial position at a particular point in time. At the top of the Balance Sheet it may say, "January 31, 19__."

The Profit and Loss statement is one of operation and shows profits or losses over a period of time. In the Profit and Loss statement heading it may say "For Period Ending January 31, 19____."

Let us analyze the Balance Sheet first. The line numbers on the left are only to aid in our analysis in this book.

Balance Sheet

1	**BALANCE SHEET**	
2	_____	
3	**As Of** _____	

4	ASSETS	
5	Current Assets:	
6	Cash In Bank	_____
7	Accounts Receivable	_____
8	Less: Allowance For Bad Debts	_____
9	Inventory	_____
10	Prepaid Expenses	_____
11	Total Current Assets	_____
12	Fixed Assets:	
13	Building	_____
14	Less: Accumulated Depreciation	_____
15	Office Furniture & Equipment	_____
16	Less: Accumulated Depreciation	_____
17	Auto	_____
18	Less: Accumulated Depreciation	_____
19	Total Fixed Assets	_____
20	Other Assets:	
21	Goodwill	_____
22	Total Other Assets	_____
23	TOTAL ASSETS	_____

24	LIABILITIES AND CAPITAL	
25	Current Liabilities:	
26	Accounts Payable	_____
27	Notes Payable	_____
28	Sales Tax Payable	_____
29	Payroll Taxes Payable	_____
30	Total Current Liabilities	_____
31	Long Term Liabilities:	
32	Mortgage Payable	_____
33	Total Long Term Liabilities	_____
34	Capital:	
35	(Name of owner), Capital	_____
36	(Name of owner), Withdrawals	_____
37	Accumulated Profit & Loss	_____
38	Capital, End of Period	_____
39	TOTAL LIABILITIES & CAPITAL	$ _____

Line 1:   The name _Balance Sheet_ means that the sum of the assets must equal the sum of the liabilities plus the capital (the owner's equity).

Line 2:   Name of the company

Line 3:   Date you want the statement to be current "as of."

Line 4:   *Assets* are items of benefit or value to the owner.

Line 5:   *Current Assets* are those assets that are cash or can easily and quickly be converted into cash within a year.

Line 6:   *Cash in Bank* includes cash on hand, bank deposits and/or short-term government securities.

Line 7:   *Accounts Receivable* are amounts owed to the business for merchandise sold on credit to its customers.

Line 8:   Less: *Allowance for Bad Debts*

Line 9:   *Inventory* is raw materials, work-in-progress, merchandise and supplies held for resale.

Line 10:   An example of *Prepaid Expenses* would be a three-year insurance policy paid this year but good for three years. You would expense only the portion for this year. The remainder would go on this line to be expensed over the next two years.

Line 11:   Total of lines 6 + 7 - 8 + 9 + 10

Line 12:   *Fixed Assets* would include buildings, furniture, equipment, land and leasehold improvements. These are assets that would be depreciated and used over a period of more than one year. They could not be turned into cash quickly.

Line 13:   *Cost* of the building

Line 14:   *Accumulated Depreciation* for the building is a running total of the amount of depreciation that has been expensed over the years. When you subtract the accumulated depreciation from the cost of the building you have the book value, not necessarily the market value.

Line 19: Total of lines 13 - 14 + 15 - 16 + 17 - 18

Line 20: *Other Assets* are intangibles such as research and development, copyrights and goodwill.

Line 22: Total of all Other Assets

Line 23: This is the total of lines 11, 19 and 22.

Line 24: *Liabilities* are items the business will have to pay.

Line 25: *Current Liabilities* are short-term loans or accounts that will usually be paid within 12 months or less.

Line 26: *Accounts Payable* are amounts you owe for merchandise bought on credit.

Line 28: *Sales Taxes* are put here after collected until they are paid to the government.

Line 29: *Payroll Taxes Payable* is where you book the payroll taxes on your employees until these taxes are deposited with a depository bank who will, in turn, forward them to IRS.

Line 30: Total of lines 26 + 27 + 28 + 29.

Line 31: *Long-Term Liabilities* are those that are due after the next 12 months.

Line 33: Total of long-term liabilities

Line 35: *Capital* is the owner's equity that includes the original amount invested in the business.

Line 36:   When you withdraw funds for personal use, this is where it is posted.

Line 37:   The profit or loss the business shows as of a particular date; that is, the difference between what is owned (assets) and what is owed (liabilities).

Line 38:   Total of lines 35 + 36 + 37

Line 39:   The total liabilities and capital have to equal the total assets.

*Profit and Loss
Statement*

PROFIT AND LOSS STATEMENT

1

2   _____

3   **For Period Ending** _____

4	INCOME

5   Sales:
6   Retail Sales   _____
7   Sales - Services   _____
8   Total Sales   _____
9   Cost of Sales:
10   Inventory at _____, 19__   _____
11   Merchandise Purchased   _____
12   Plus Freight In   _____
13   Total   _____
14   Less: Inventory at _____, 19__ _____
15   Total Cost of Sales   _____
16   Gross Profit   _____

17	EXPENSES

18   Expenses:
19   Advertising   _____
20   Auto   _____
21   Contract Labor   _____
22   Depreciation   _____
23   Entertainment   _____
24   Family Labor   _____
25   Freight Labor   _____
26   Interest Paid   _____
27   Office Supplies   _____
28   Payroll   _____
29   Telephone   _____
30   Total Expenses   _____

31   NET INCOME $ _____

Line 1:   The "Profit and Loss Statement" shows profit or loss over a particular period of time.

Line 2:   Name of the company

Line 3:   Shows final date of particular period

Line 5:   *Sales* is the amount received or receivable from customers.

Line 8:   Total of lines 6 + 7

Line 9:   *Cost of Sales* is the cost of materials necessary to produce a product; or cost of goods purchased to be resold.

Line 10:   Date for inventory and amount

Line 11:   *Merchandise Purchased* is made up of the following:
>   Goods you buy to resell
>   Goods you buy to resell, but return
>   Discounts you receive

Line 12:   *Freight In* is simply the freight charges you pay for freight on Merchandise Purchased.

Line 13:   Total of lines 10 + 11 + 12

Line 14:   Physical *inventory* taken on a particular date and amount

Line 15:   Total of lines 13 - 14

Line 16:   Total of lines 8 - 15

Line 22:   *Depreciation Expense* is a deduction from income that allows for the depreciation of equipment, buildings, and furnishings used in the business. (See Chapter 13 for detail.)

Line 30:   Total of all expenses

Line 31: Total of Lines 16 - 30. *Net Income* is the final earnings figure.

The following pages are provided for you to copy for use in the recordkeeping of your business.

A copy center can inexpensively print all the copies you need while you wait. For ease of use, ask them to print the copies on 3-hole prepunched paper so you can keep them neatly in a notebook.

Profit and Loss Statement Year To Date: Year _____

	Acct. Code	Description	January	February	March	April	May	
1		Sales:						1
2	4000	Retail Sales						2
3	4060	Sales - Services						3
4		Total Sales						4
5								5
6		Cost of Sales:						6
7		Inventory at _____, 19__						7
8	6820	Merchandise Purchased						8
9	6900	Plus Freight In						9
10		Total						10
11		Less: Invent_____,19__						11
12		Total Cost of Sales						12
13		Gross Profit						13
14								14
15		Expenses:						15
16	5000	Advertising						16
17	5040	Auto						17
18	5360	Contract Labor						18
19	5400	Depreciation						19
20	5480	Entertainment						20
21	5520	Family Labor						21
22	5560	Freight Paid						22
23	5640	Interest Paid						23
24	5840	Office Supplies						24
25	5880	Payroll						25
26	6100	Telephone						26
27		Total Expenses						27
28		NET INCOME						28
29								29
30								30
31	7000	Credit Card Payments						31
32	7020	Petty Cash						32
33								33

Profit and Loss Statement Year To Date: Year _____

	Acct. Code	Description	January	February	March	April	May	
1								1
2								2
3								3
4								4
5								5
6								6
7								7
8								8
9								9
10								10
11								11
12								12
13								13
14								14
15								15
16								16
17								17
18								18
19								19
20								20
21								21
22								22
23								23
24								24
25								25
26								26
27								27
28								28
29								29
30								30
31								31
32								32
33								33

Profit and Loss Statement Year To Date: Year _____

	June	July	August	September	October	November	December	Year Total	
1									1
2									2
3									3
4									4
5									5
6									6
7									7
8									8
9									9
10									10
11									11
12									12
13									13
14									14
15									15
16									16
17									17
18									18
19									19
20									20
21									21
22									22
23									23
24									24
25									25
26									26
27									27
28									28
29									29
30									30
31									31
32									32
33									33

PROFIT AND LOSS STATEMENT

1

2 _____

3 **For Period Ending** _____

	INCOME	
4		

5	Sales:		
6	Retail Sales	_____	
7	Sales - Services	_____	
8	Total Sales		_____
9	Cost of Sales:		
10	Inventory at _____, 19__	_____	
11	Merchandise Purchased	_____	
12	Plus Freight In	_____	
13	Total	_____	
14	Less: Inventory at _____, 19__	_____	
15	Total Cost of Sales		_____
16	Gross Profit		_____

	EXPENSES	
17		

18	Expenses:	
19	Advertising	_____
20	Auto	_____
21	Contract Labor	_____
22	Depreciation	_____
23	Entertainment	_____
24	Family Labor	_____
25	Freight Labor	_____
26	Interest Paid	_____
27	Office Supplies	_____
28	Payroll	_____
29	Telephone	_____
30	Total Expenses	_____

31 NET INCOME $ _____

PROFIT AND LOSS STATEMENT

1

2 _____

3 **For Period Ending** _____

4	INCOME

5
6 _____
7 _____
8 _____
9
10 _____
11 _____
12 _____
13 _____
14 _____
15 _____
16 _____

17	EXPENSES

18
19 _____
20 _____
21 _____
22 _____
23 _____
24 _____
25 _____
26 _____
27 _____
28 _____
29 _____
30 _____

31 $ _____

Inventory Control Card

Item _____

Cost _____ Supplier _____

Ordered		Received			
Quantity	Date	Quantity	Date	Sold	Balance

Balance Sheet Year To Date: Year _____

	Acct. Code	Description	Beginning Balance	Period Covered	Balance	Period Covered	Balance	
1		Current Assets:						1
2	1000	Cash In Bank						2
3	1040	Accounts Receivable						3
4	1050	Less: Allow. for Bad Debts						4
5	1070	Inventory						5
6	1200	Prepaid Expenses						6
7		Total Current Assets						7
8		Fixed Assets:						8
9	1250	Building						9
10	1260	Less: Accumulated Depreciation						10
11	1280	Office Furniture & Equipment						11
12	1290	Less: Accumulated Depreciation						12
13	1300	Auto						13
14	1310	Less: Accumulated Depreciation						14
15		Total Fixed Assets						15
16		TOTAL ASSETS						16
17								17
18		Current Liabilities:						18
19	2000	Accounts Payable						19
20	2020	Notes Payable						20
21	2080	Sales Tax Payable						21
22	2100	Payroll Taxes Payable						22
23		Total Current Liabilities						23
24		Long Term Liabilities:						24
25	2140	Mortgage Payable						25
26		Total Long Term Liabilities						26
27		Capital:						27
28	3000	(Name of owner), Capital						28
29	3020	(Name of owner), Withdrawals						29
30	3030	Accumulated Profit &j Loss						30
31		Capital, End of Period						31
32		TOTAL LIABILITIES & CAPITAL						32
33								33

Balance Sheet Year To Date: Year _____

	Acct. Code	Description	Beginning Balance	Period Covered	Balance	Period Covered	Balance	
1								1
2								2
3								3
4								4
5								5
6								6
7								7
8								8
9								9
10								10
11								11
12								12
13								13
14								14
15								15
16								16
17								17
18								18
19								19
20								20
21								21
22								22
23								23
24								24
25								25
26								26
27								27
28								28
29								29
30								30
31								31
32								32
33								33

Balance Sheet Year To Date: Year _____

	Period Covered	Balance	Period Covered	Balance	Period Covered	Balance	Period Covered	Balance	
1									1
2									2
3									3
4									4
5									5
6									6
7									7
8									8
9									9
10									10
11									11
12									12
13									13
14									14
15									15
16									16
17									17
18									18
19									19
20									20
21									21
22									22
23									23
24									24
25									25
26									26
27									27
28									28
29									29
30									30
31									31
32									32
33									33

BALANCE SHEET

_____

As Of _____

4	ASSETS	

5 Current Assets:
6   Cash In Bank _____
7   Accounts Receivable _____
8   Less: Allowance For Bad Debts _____
9   Inventory _____
10   Prepaid Expenses _____
11   Total Current Assets _____
12 Fixed Assets:
13   Building _____
14   Less: Accumulated Depreciation _____
15   Office Furniture & Equipment _____
16   Less: Accumulated Depreciation _____
17   Auto _____
18   Less: Accumulated Depreciation _____
19   Total Fixed Assets _____
20 Other Assets:
21   Goodwill _____
22   Total Other Assets _____
23 TOTAL ASSETS _____

24	LIABILITIES AND CAPITAL	

25 Current Liabilities:
26   Accounts Payable _____
27   Notes Payable _____
28   Sales Tax Payable _____
29   Payroll Taxes Payable _____
30   Total Current Liabilities _____
31 Long Term Liabilities:
32   Mortgage Payable _____
33 Total Long Term Liabilities _____
34 Capital:
35   (Name of owner), Capital _____
36   (Name of owner), Withdrawals _____
37   Accumulated Profit & Loss _____
38   Capital, End of Period _____
39 TOTAL LIABILITIES & CAPITAL $ _____

BALANCE SHEET

_____

	ASSETS

1

2

3

4

5

6 ———————

7 ———————

8 ———————

9 ———————

10 ———————

11 ———————

12

13 ———————

14 ———————

15 ———————

16 ———————

17 ———————

18 ———————

19 ———————

20

21 ———————

22 ———————

23 ———————

	LIABILITIES AND CAPITAL

24

25

26 ———————

27 ———————

28 ———————

29 ———————

30 ———————

31

32 ———————

33 ———————

34

35 ———————

36 ———————

37 ———————

38 ———————

39 $ ———————

Income Summary - Month of _____

Period Invoices Cover	Cash	Credit	Bank Deposit	Taxable Sales	Sales Tax	NON-TAXABLE SALES		TOTAL SALES
						FREIGHT	WHOLESALE	

INVOICE NUMBER: _____

SALESPERSON	DATE OF INVOICE

SHIP TO:

SOLD TO:

ACCOUNT NO.	DATE SHIPPED	SHIPPED VIA	TERMS	

QUANTITY	DESCRIPTION		
		Net Amount	_____
		Sales Tax	_____
		Freight &	_____
		TOTAL	_____

PLEASE PAY FROM THIS INVOICE.
NO STATEMENT WILL BE ISSUED.

THANK YOU

YOUR COMPANY NAME
ADDRESS
CITY, STATE, ZIP
TELEPHONE

INVOICE NUMBER: _____

SALESPERSON	DATE OF INVOICE

SHIP TO:

SOLD TO:

ACCOUNT NO.	DATE SHIPPED	SHIPPED VIA	TERMS

QUANTITY	DESCRIPTION		

Net Amount _____

Sales Tax _____

Freight & Handling _____

PLEASE PAY FROM THIS INVOICE.
NO STATEMENT WILL BE ISSUED.

TOTAL _____

THANK YOU

CASH RECEIPT NUMBER: _____

SALESPERSON	DATE OF INVOICE

SHIP TO:

SOLD TO:

ACCOUNT NO.	DATE SHIPPED	SHIPPED VIA	TERMS	

QUANTITY	DESCRIPTION		

Net Amount _____

Sales Tax _____

Freight & _____

TOTAL _____

THANK YOU

Transaction Register - Month of

	Date	Check #	Credit Card Code	Cash	Deposited	Reconciled	Accounting Code	Description	Amount	Check Balance Forward	
1											1
2											2
3											3
4											4
5											5
6											6
7											7
8											8
9											9
10											10
11											11
12											12
13											13
14											14
15											15
16											16
17											17
18											18
19											19
20											20
21											21
22											21
23											22
24											23
25											24
26											25
27											26
28											27
29											28
30											29
31											30

Credit Customer Summary

	Date	Customer	Invoice No.	Total Sales Amount	Date Paid	Memo	
1							1
2							2
3							3
4							4
5							5
6							6
7							7
8							8
9							9
10							10
11							11
12							12
13							13
14							14
15							15
16							16
17							17
18							18
19							19
20							20
21							21
22							21
23							22
24							23
25							24
26							25
27							26
28							27
29							28
30							29
31							30

CHART OF ACCOUNTS

ASSETS

1000 Cash In Bank
1040 Accounts Receivable
1050 Less: Allowance For Bad Debts
1070 Inventory

1200 Prepaid Expenses
1220 Utility Deposits
1240 Land
1250 Buildings

1260 Less: Accum. Depreciation-Bldg.
1280 Office Furniture and Equipment
1290 Less: Accum. Deprec. Furniture
1300 Auto
1310 Less: Accumulated Deprec.Auto

LIABILITIES

2000 Accounts Payable
2020 Notes Payable
2080 Sales Tax Payable

2100 Payroll Taxes Payable
(includes FICA and Withholding)

2120 Mortgages Payable
2140 Loans

CAPITAL

3000 (Name of proprietor), Capital
3020 (Name of proprietor), Withdrawals

3030 Accumulated Profit & Loss

INCOME

4000 Retail Sales
4080 Wholesale Sales

4120 Sales- Services
4160 Miscellaneous Income

4200 Commissions/Bonuses

EXPENSES

5000 Advertising
5040 Auto
5080   Insurance
5120   Fees & Licenses
5160   Gas or Diesel
5200   Repairs
5240   Tires
5280   Parking Fees & Tolls
5320 Bank Loan Interest
5360 Contract Labor
5400 Depreciation
5440 Dues & Subscriptions

5480 Entertainment
5520 Family Labor
5560 Freight Paid
5600 Insurance
5640 Interest
5680 Legal & Accounting
5720 Maintenance Expense
5760 Miscellaneous Expense
5800 Office Rental
5840 Office Supplies
5880 Payroll
5920   Payroll Taxes

5960 Taxes
6020 Postage
6060 Rent
6080 Sample Products
6100 Telephone
6140 Travel
6180 Utilities
        COST OF SALE ACCOUNTS
6820 Products Purchased For Resale
6860 Material And Supplies
6900 Freight In

NON-DEDUCTIBLE ITEMS:

7000 Credit Card Payments
7020 Petty Cash Checks
7030 Miscellaneous

CODE FOR BUSINESSES:
Example:
Business A — Profit Enterprises

Business A — _____
Business B — _____
Business C — _____
Business D — _____

CODE FOR CREDIT CARDS:
Example:
C1 — VISA

C1 — _____
C2 — _____
C3 — _____
C4 — _____
C5 — _____

CHAPTER 16 | SHELTERING YOUR PROFITS

By being in business, either as a sole proprietor, a partner, or an owner in a closely-held incorporated business, you have the advantage of being able to set up a retirement plan structured according to your ability to invest pre-tax income, free of current tax. In essence, such a plan permits you to "borrow" the taxes due interest-free and invest it. You'll only be taxed when you withdraw it. Before the Tax Reform Act of 1986, the retirement plans available to the unincorporated business person were not as advantageous as those available for the incorporated business person. Today this is not the case.

It is wise to systematically set aside money you have worked hard for so that later in life, when you may not be physically capable of hard work, the money can work hard for you.

Solomon points to the lowly ant as an example of saving for the future. He urges:

> Go to the ant, you sluggard, consider its way and be wise. It stores its provision in summer and gathers its food for harvest.
>
> Proverbs 6:6,8

This chapter offers ways you can take some of your present harvest for use later on in life and do so tax advantageously.

Keogh Plans

As an unincorporated business person, the IRS allows you to invest a portion of your business profits in special plans called Keoghs or a Simplified Employee Pension (SEP).

There are two types of Keogh plans. One is the *defined benefit* plan in which you decide what pension amount you would like to receive upon retirement. Your contributions are then based upon that pension amount. This is one for the late bloomers. It's for people with lots of surplus income they want to shelter from taxes. It is rather complicated and costly to set up this plan, and for that reason most small business people choose the more popular *defined contribution* plan in which you are allowed to invest up to 20% of your business profits up to a maximum of $30,000 every year.

Simplified Employee Pension (SEP)

SEPs (pronounced seps) are similar to Individual Retirement Accounts (IRAs). However, your maximum year's contribution to a SEP can be much larger than the $2,000 limit on IRAs, although not as large as in a Keogh plan. Refer to the table in this chapter for the limits.

You are required to include your employees in your retirement plans if your employees have worked for you for three years or more. Unfortunately, your employees cannot pay their own contribution. You must pay it for them. Any money invested for your employees is a tax-deductible business expense. Also if you have employees, the figuring of the amount of the contribution to the qualified plan is a rather complicated calculation. You may wish to consult with a qualified plan consultant and/or CPA. For more information you may refer to IRS Publication 560. For information on the forms that must be filed for your retirement plan get IRS Publication 1048.

Investing in a retirement plan will not reduce the amount of your self-employment (Social Security) tax since this tax is computed on the profits of your business before allowing for the retirement deduction. But it does reduce your taxable income so it allows you to pay less income taxes.

Self-Directed IRAs and Keoghs

To set up a retirement plan you may adopt your own plan that has been prepared by a qualified retirement plan consultant; or you may adopt one of a number of plans pre-approved by the IRS offered by banks, savings and loans and investment companies such as securities dealers.

My favorite is what is known as a "self-directed account." A self-directed account allows you to move your assets in your retirement account to the best investment in every economy.

Many mutual fund families offer such accounts that allow you to choose investments in their stock funds, bond funds and money market funds. You may prefer to choose their "no-load" funds where you pay no front-end sales commissions. You will find that most fund families provide these accounts. They generally charge a low annual trustee's fee.

In both IRA and Keogh accounts, the management fees are deductible as miscellaneous deductions subject to the 2% limitation of the adjusted gross income on Schedule A, but only if they are paid separately. So insist on paying the fee by check. Do not allow the trustee to simply deduct the fees from your account.

If you set up your self-directed account, choose one that gives you the flexibility of moving not only within that fund family but also provides the capability to buy from other fund families as well. This is important because some mutual fund families offer self-directed accounts only within their family of funds.

With a trustee like Charles Schwab, you may invest your retirement funds in mutual funds, stocks, options, bonds, government securities and money markets from various companies.

To get information on Charles Schwab & Company's self-directed retirement accounts, call 800-435-4000. Their annual trustee's fee is low.

Independent Trustee for Your IRA or Keogh

If you want the flexibility of investing in things other than securities, you may choose a truly "independent trustee" such as a few banks offer. Generally their fees are expensive and are based upon the size of your retirement fund. With such an account you can invest in almost any investment except precious metals (although certain gold and silver coins minted by the U.S. government are permissible), collectibles and investments in which your money is used as collateral. With a truly independent trustee you may also invest in discounted real estate mortgages.

My office has been informed that the following financial institutions can serve as an independent trustee. Since I have had no personal involvement with these companies, I cannot endorse them. You must do your own investigation.

First Trust
444 Sherman St.
Denver, Colorado 80203
800-525-2124

Retirement Accounts, Inc.
P. O. Box 3017
Winter Park, Florida 32790
800-325-4352

Resources

If you wish to take active control of your retirement account and see it experience maximum growth, you should consider subscribing to magazines such as *Money, Kiplinger's Personal Finance, Mutual Fund* magazine and/or a monthly newsletter such as *Mutual Fund Forecaster*. This newsletter makes recommendations that follow strategies designed to optimize your investment return. Call 800-442-9000 and ask for a sample copy.

IRA With a KEOGH

For even greater tax savings, depending upon the amount of your earned income, you can also open an Individual Retirement Account (IRA) in addition to your Keogh plan. The diagram at the end of this chapter is self explanatory and will help you determine if you qualify for a *deductible* IRA. Even if you determine that your IRA contribution itself is not deductible, each year you may still invest up to $2,000 of your earned income and have it grow within the IRA, sheltered from taxation until withdrawn.

Spousal IRA

Beginning in 1997, married couples with only one working spouse can make annual IRA contributions up to $2,000 each for a total of $4,000 as long as the working spouse's compensation at least equals the combined contributions and a joint return is filed. Be sure to study the charts on the various IRAs in this chapter.

IRA vs. Roth IRA

Deductible IRAs are best for older people who need the money soon. Roth IRAs are usually better for younger and wealthier investors.

Form 5500

Keogh plan owners with more than $25,000 in the plan or more than one participant, must file a special tax form with the IRS on or before July 31 each year. If you are the only participant, you must file Form 5500EZ. If your plan covers employees, use a tax professional to file Form 5500 for you.

For information on the different reporting forms required for different types of plans and when they must be filed, order the free report, *Reporting and Disclosure Guide for Employee Benefit Plans* from the IRS.

COMPARISON BETWEEN 1998 IRAS

	DEDUCTIBLE IRA	NONDEDUCTIBLE IRA	ROTH IRA	EDUCATIONAL IRA
AGI[1] limits for contributing in 1998	Single $30,000 to $40,000; Married filing jointly $50,000 to $60,000[2]	None	Single $95,000 to $110,000 Married filing jointly $150,000 to $160,000	Single $95,000 to $110,000 Married filing jointly $150,000 to $160,000
Annual contribution limit	$2,000 per person[3]	$2,000 per person	$2,000 per person[4]	$500 per child per year[9] until child reaches age 18[9]
Tax treatment of contributions	Deductible against taxable income	Not deductible	Not deductible	Not deductible
Tax treatment of monies in account	Monies grow tax-**deferred**	Monies grow tax-**deferred**	Monies grow tax-**free**	Monies grow tax **free** for education
Tax treatment of withdrawals	Taxable as ordinary income in year of withdrawal	Taxable as ordinary income in year of withdrawal[5]	Contributions are tax-free; earnings are tax-free if you've held your account at least five years and are older than 59½[6]	Tax free if for education; 10% penalty plus tax on balance
When you can withdraw money without penalty	Generally at age 59½; earlier for higher education expenses or first-time home purchase ($10,000 limit), medical expenses greater than 7.5% of AGI or disability	Generally at age 59½; earlier for higher education expenses or first-time home purchase ($10,000 limit), medical expenses greater than 7.5% of AGI or disability	Generally at age 59½; earlier for higher education expenses or first-time home purchase ($10,000 limit), medical expenses greater than 7.5% of AGI or disability; contributions may be withdrawn anytime w/o tax but with 10% penalty until 59½	Tax free for education
When withdrawals must begin	By age 70½[7]	By age 70½[7]	Not until after you die[8]	Age 30
IRA eligibility income phase-outs	Single $95,000 to $110,000; Married filing jointly $150,000 to $160,000	Single $95,000 to $110,000; Married filing jointly $150,000 to 160,000	Single $95,000 to $110,000 Married filing jointly $150,000 to $160,000	

[1] Adjusted Gross Income

[2] If a spouse is not an active participant in a retirement plan, he or she can contribute if combined AGI is less than $160,000. If neither is an active participant or if you're single and not a participant there is no AGI limit.

[3] For AGI less than $30,000 ($50,000 for married filing jointly), the limit is $2,000 per person or total earned income, whichever is lower. For an AGI between $30,000 and $40,000 ($50,000 to $60,000 for married couples), the contribution limit is prorated between $2,000 and zero per person.

[4] For AGI less than $95,000 ($150,000 for married filing jointly), the limit is $2,000 per person. For an AGI between $95,000 and $110,000 ($150,000 to $160,000 for married couples), the contribution limit is prorated between $2,000 and zero per person.

[5] If you have both deductible and nondeductible IRAs, the tax-free portion of withdrawals is the ratio of nondeductible contributions to your total IRA balance.

[6] Or if you die, become disabled or use the money for a first-time home purchase ($10,000 limit).

[7] If you die before then, your beneficiaries may have to start withdrawing the money as soon as the year after your death.

[8] Your beneficiaries have to start withdrawing the money as soon as one year after your death.

[9] Each child beneficiary can only have one educational IRA.

Adjusted Gross Income	1998 IRA BRACKETS: MARRIED FILING JOINTLY	
	Deductible IRA	Roth IRA
0		
$10,000	Contributions deductible for everyone	
20,000		
30,000		
40,000		
50,000	Deductibility Phase-Out Range	
60,000		
70,000		Eligible
80,000		
90,000		
100,000		
110,000	Contributions deductible only if taxpayer is not an active participant in an employer-sponsored pension plan	
120,000		
130,000		
140,000		
150,000	Deductibility Phase-Out Range	Deductibility Phase-Out Range
160,000		
170,000		
180,000	Contributions deductible only if taxpayer and spouse are not active participants in employer-sponsored pension plans.	Not Eligible
190,000		

1998 IRA Brackets for Single Taxpayers: For single taxpayers who are active participants in employer-sponsored pension plans, ordinary IRA deductibility phases out between AGI of $30,000 and $40,000. Both IRA eligibility phase-outs are between AGI of $95,000 and $110,000.

When Is An IRA Contribution Tax Deductible?

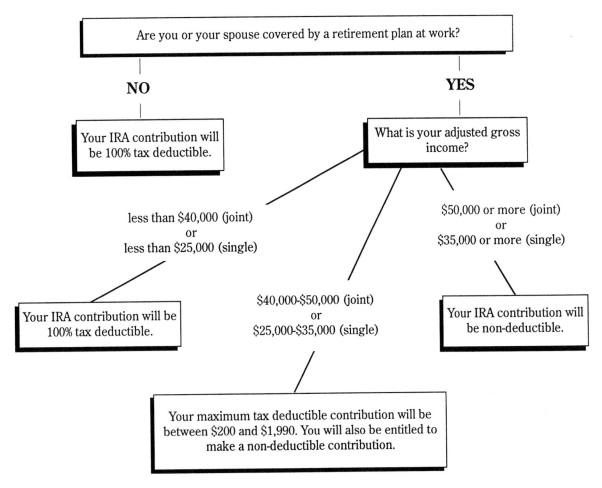

Are you or your spouse covered by a retirement plan at work?

NO

YES

Your IRA contribution will be 100% tax deductible.

What is your adjusted gross income?

less than $40,000 (joint)
or
less than $25,000 (single)

$50,000 or more (joint)
or
$35,000 or more (single)

Your IRA contribution will be 100% tax deductible.

$40,000-$50,000 (joint)
or
$25,000-$35,000 (single)

Your IRA contribution will be non-deductible.

Your maximum tax deductible contribution will be between $200 and $1,990. You will also be entitled to make a non-deductible contribution.

Example: A married couple, filing a joint return, has an adjusted gross income of $43,000. They both work and have IRAs. One spouse is an active participant in an employer-maintained retirement plan. Before 1987 each spouse could contribute and deduct $2,000 each or $4,000 but that is no longer the case. Now, because one spouse participates in a retirement plan, and their combined income falls within the $40,000 to $50,000 phaseout range, they cannot take a deduction for the full amount. They must apply the following formula:

1).	Regular deduction limit		$4,000
2).	Excess AGI amount		
	($43,000-$40,000)	$3,000	
3).	$10,000	10,000	
4).	Divide line 2 by line 3	0.3	
5).	Multiply line 1 by line 4 and round to		
	the next highest multiple of $10		1,200
6)	Allowable deduction—line 1 minus line 5		$2,800
	If this amount is between $0 and $200,		
	enter $200		

This $2,800 will then be allocated between husband and wife with neither one getting more than $2,000.

COMPARISON BETWEEN RETIREMENT PLANS
AVAILABLE FOR SMALL BUSINESSES

	SEP Self-Employed	SEP Employee	SIMPLE IRC Section	401(K)
Who qualifies and for how much?	Anyone with Schedule C (self employment) income; Contributions are treated same as IRA	Employee of a firm which offers a SEP; Employer makes SEP contributions to eligible employee's IRAs; An eligible employee is at least 21 who has worked 3 of the past 5 yrs and had wages greater than $400 in a calendar year	Employers with 100 or fewer employees; Self-employed individuals; Eligible employees must have received at least $5,000 in compensation in previous year	Any employee of company offering this plan is eligible; Contributions treated same as IRA; Must be age 21 with 1 yr of service and 1,000 hours to be eligible.
Maximum allowable contribution	13.0435% of net self-employment income, up to a maximum of $24,000. Self employment net income must first be reduced by 1/2 of self employment tax taken as an adjustment to income on page 1 of Form 1040.	15% of wages up to $24,000; SAR-SEP limits same as 401(k) plans	Employees can contribute up to $6,000 on a pre-tax basis; Exceptions for highly paid employees; details from IRC section 402(g), 404(a)(3), 404(a)(7), 415(c); Employer has to match up to lesser of 3% or $6,000.	Employees contributions up to $10,000 (1998); Employer deduction lesser of 15% of wage or $24,000. To 25% or $30,000 with other plans; Exceptions for highly paid employees; details from IRC section 402(g), 404(a)(3), 404(a)(7), 415(c).
Penalty for withdrawal before age 59 1/2	10% of distribution. Exceptions are shown in IRC section 72(t)	10% of distributions; Exceptions shown in IRC section 72(t)	10% of distribution or 25% if withdrawal made within 2 yrs of starting plan.	10% of distributions. Exceptions are detailed in IRC section 72(t)
Date to start contributions	Tax filing date with extensions	Tax filing date with extensions	December 31 to start plan; Employer contributions by tax filing date with extensions.	December 31 to start plan; Employer contributions by tax filing date with extensions.
Age when withdrawals must begin	Age 70 1/2 Contributions can continue if there is earned income	Age 70 1/2 Contribution can continue if there is earned income	Age 70 1/2	Age 70 1/2 or year of retirement.
Annual contributions required	No	No	Yes	Fixed amount can be changed twice per yr.
Borrowing allowed?	No	No	No	Yes, if plan permits
Excess contributions penalty	6% for both self-employed and employees	6% for both self-employed and employees	10%	Excess may be distributed within 2½ months of plan's year end; 10% thereafter.
Rollover allowed?	Yes	Yes	Yes	Yes

COMPARISON BETWEEN RETIREMENT PLANS AVAILABLE FOR SMALL BUSINESSES

KEOGH Defined Benefit	KEOGH Defined Contribution Money Purchase	KEOGH Defined Contribution Profit Sharing	KEOGH Defined Contribution Combination	TSA 403(b) Compensation	NONQUALIFIED Deferred
Sole proprietorships, partnership for themselves and their employees; Employees must be greater than age 21 and have at least 1 year of service;	Sole proprietorships, partnership for themselves and their employees; Employees must be greater than age 21 and have at least 1 year of service;	Sole proprietorships, partnership for themselves and their employees; Employees must be greater than age 21 and have at least 1 year of service;	Sole proprietorships, partnership for themselves and their employees Employees must be greater than age 21 and have at least 1 year of service	Employees of tax-exempt religious, charitable, educational organizations.	Company employees; Contributions deductible when included as taxable income; Can favor key employees
Employees can make nondeductible voluntary contributions; Lesser of $120,000 or 100% of average net income during 3 highest earning years	Employees can make nondeductible voluntary contributions. Lesser of $30,000 or 20% of net income. (25% for employee)	Employees can make nondeductible voluntary contributions. Lesser of $24,000 or 13.0435% of net income. Maximum contribution is less for some plans. 15% of $22,500 for employee	Employees can make nondeductible voluntary contributions. Lesser of $30,000 or 20% of net income. (25% for employee)	Employee contribution 20% of earned income times years of service - prior years tax-free.	No limits.
10% of distribution. Exceptions detailed in IRC section 72(t)	10% of distribution. Exceptions detailed in IRC section 72(t)	10% of distribution. Exceptions detailed in IRC section 72(t)	10% of distribution. Exceptions detailed in IRC section 72(t)	10% of distribution. Exceptions detailed in IRC section 72(t)	None
Establish by Dec 31	Establish by Dec 31	Establish by Dec 31	Establish by Dec 31	Establish by Dec. 31	December 31
Tax filing date for contributions plus extensions.	Tax filing date for contributions plus extensions.	Tax filing date for contributions plus extensions.	Tax filing date for contributions plus extensions.	Tax filing date for contributions plus extensions.	
Age 70½ for self-employed Retirement for employees.	70½ for self-employed: Retirement for employees.	70½ for self-employed; Retirement for employees.	70½ for self-employed: Retirement for employees.	70½ or year of retirement.	N/A
No	Yes; same %/year unless no income	No	Profit sharing + money purchase	Same as 401(k)	No
No	No	No	No	Yes	Depends on plan
10% penalty	10% penalty	10% penalty	10% penalty	Excess over limit taxable	None
Yes	Yes	Yes	Yes	Yes	No

NOTES

CHAPTER 17 | CHECKLIST FOR ACCOMPLISHMENTS

Success in business is no respecter of persons. If you do what other successful business people do, you too will be successful.

Building a business is not unlike constructing a building. Any building must be erected in a systematic order.

Paul noted:

> Everything should be done in a fitting and orderly way.
>
> I Corinthians 14:40

The remainder of this chapter consists of a checklist to help you accomplish the steps of starting your business in an "orderly way."

The first column asks for an accomplishment date. Take the time to set realistic target dates for each accomplishment. This is important because a goal without a target date remains nothing more than an idle daydream and is probably a waste of time.

Use the blank form at the end of the checklist to list any additional accomplishments needed for your particular business.

CHECKLIST FOR ACCOMPLISHMENTS

Date To Have This Accomplished	Check When Done	
_____	_____	1. Prayerfully determine if you are truly called to be in business for yourself.
_____	_____	2. Determine what business you are called to pursue.
_____	_____	3. Consult with other business operators in your chosen field.
_____	_____	4. Determine market feasibility.
_____	_____	5. Determine the legal form of ownership you need.
_____	_____	6. Settle upon a business name.
_____	_____	7. If a corporation is necessary, hire an attorney to file the articles of incorporation, adopt by-laws and observe necessary corporate formalities.
_____	_____	8. If you plan to operate as a sole proprietorship, file an assumed name (fictitious name) with the appropriate counties.
_____	_____	9. Open a business checking account.

CHECKLIST FOR ACCOMPLISHMENTS

	Check When Done	Date To Have This Accomplished
10. Establish contact with an attorney to prepare or review other documents pertaining to the start-up.	_____	_____
11. Begin a systematic reading program about your chosen field.	_____	_____
12. Order and read IRS Publication 334, *Tax Guide for the Small Business.*	_____	_____
13. Prepare a written business plan setting forth your short-range and long-range marketing and financial goals and objectives.	_____	_____
14. Determine the cash outlay required.	_____	_____
15. Determine if you must bring in money partners. If so, set forth the division of responsibilities, negotiate an equitable ownership split and have an attorney prepare the formal partnership documentation.	_____	_____
16. If institutional financing is necessary, prepare a loan package showing the amount requested, the desired terms and how your business can repay the loan. The banker will insist that everything be well documented.	_____	_____

CHECKLIST FOR ACCOMPLISHMENTS

Date To Have This Accomplished	Check When Done	
_____	_____	17. If needed, lease or purchase appropriate real estate but only after checking zoning requirements, traffic counts, economic trends of the area, etc.
_____	_____	18. Determine if a city business license is necessary. If so, make application.
_____	_____	19. Determine if your chosen business requires a state license. If so, make application.
_____	_____	20. Determine if your chosen business requires a federal permit or license. If so, make application.
_____	_____	21. Apply for a sales tax number if you will be selling tangible taxable goods.
_____	_____	22. Contact your bank and get set up to accept credit cards.
_____	_____	23. Arrange for telephones, fax machines, E-mail, web page and Yellow Page advertising.
_____	_____	24. Order business cards, stationery and printed promotional material.

CHECKLIST FOR ACCOMPLISHMENTS

	Check When Done	Date To Have This Accomplished
25. Purchase and become familiar with *QuickBooks.* Visit with a Certified Public Accountant if necessary.	___	_____
26. Establish Chart of Accounts and set up a set of books in *QuickBooks.*	___	_____
27. Retain a good insurance agent. Consult with agent regarding fire, accident, liability, theft and errors and omission coverage.	___	_____
28. Be prepared to make estimated income tax payments almost immediately after starting your business or incorporating.	___	_____
29. If you will have employees other than your immediate family members or if you form a corporation, apply for a Federal Employer Identification Number on Form SS-4.	___	_____
30. At year end, file appropriate W-2s and W-3s for all employees, Form 1099s to independent contractors receiving payments of $600 or more and Form 1096 to the IRS.	___	_____
31. At tax time, if a sole proprietorship, report the profit or loss of your business on Schedule C of Form 1040 and report any self-employment income on Schedule SE of Form 1040.	___	_____

CHECKLIST FOR ACCOMPLISHMENTS

Date To Have This Accomplished	Check When Done	
___	___	32. At tax time, if a partnership, file Form 1065 and give each partner a K-1. Each partner will report self-employment income on Schedule SE of Form 1040, and income or loss from the partnership on Schedule E of Form 1040.
___	___	33. At tax time, if a corporation, file Form 1120 or Form 1120-S for an "S" corporation.
___	___	34. At least quarterly, review the written goals in your business plan and make mid-course corrections as necessary.

CHECKLIST FOR ACCOMPLISHMENTS

	Check When Done	Date To Have This Accomplished

CHECKLIST FOR ACCOMPLISHMENTS

Date To Have This Accomplished	Check When Done	

CHAPTER 18 | *THE KEY TO MAKING IT HAPPEN*

There are people in business who are eager for big rewards but they offer as little as possible to get them. Needless to say, they seldom stay in business long. Planting always precedes harvesting. Fruit that remains doesn't just happen.

Greatness
Through Service

Without integrity—absolute integrity—you will never have enduring, positive results. You've heard it said before, "the customer is king" and "the customer is always right." A wise entrepreneur subscribes to the principles behind these maxims.

Customers or clients are looking for someone who will genuinely serve them and stand behind his or her word and product or service. No company has become great by cheating its customers.

Didn't Jesus teach the way to greatness lies in serving others?

> Whoever wants to become great among you must be your servant.
>
> Mark 10:43

The biblical way to fulfill your dream is to help others fulfill theirs. Paul taught that what you do for others, God will do for you.

> Whatever good thing any man doeth, the same shall he receive of the Lord.
>
> Ephesians 6:8 (KJV)

No matter what your business offers, it ultimately must be used by or at least please a human being. You are not merely manufacturing and/or distributing widgets or ideas. You are not merely selling investments or advice. In the final analysis, you are serving people and meeting human needs. You must always see yourself as being in the people business.

If you will treat every customer or client as if he or she is the most important person in the world, serve him or her with absolute integrity and give more and do more than is expected, then wonderful, profitable success is a foregone conclusion. Repeat business will be the norm. Referrals will abound. All because you have committed to do what very few do, i.e., to become a service and quality fanatic.

If you help your customers or clients grow, improve, profit and succeed, God will help you grow, improve, profit and succeed. Don't concentrate on being big or becoming wealthy. Rather, focus on offering quality and rendering service beyond your customers' expectations. With that as your focus, bigness and revenues will ultimately come.

Diligence Brings Success

If you are in business, then *be* in business. Some people

are so relieved to be free from the regimented demands of a nine-to-five job that they adopt a leisurely, haphazard style of doing business. With such behavior, how can they wonder why God is not blessing their business? "Busy" and "business" are from the same root word.

The Bible clearly teaches that diligence is a necessary ingredient of success.

> Lazy hands make a man poor, but diligent hands bring wealth.
>
> Proverbs 10:4

Solomon believed in diligence. He instructed:

> Whatever your hand finds to do, do it with all of your might.
>
> Ecclesiastes 9:10

Paul's instruction to the believers at Rome is relevant advice for any business person:

> Not slothful in business; fervent in spirit; serving the Lord.
>
> Romans 12:11 (KJV)

The Living Bible paraphrases "not slothful in business" as "never be lazy in your work." The word translated "slothful" is the same word Jesus uses in his Parable of the Talents to describe the servant who was given a deposit but who did not use diligence to make the master's investment grow. (See Matthew 25.) Not only does lack of diligence displease the Lord, it also brings dismal results and ultimate business failure.

**Recognize the
Real Boss**

Just because you no longer have a visible boss, be aware that as a self-employed person you still have the same boss you have always had, Jesus Christ.

Pertaining to a person's work, Paul said:

> Whatever you do, work at it with all your heart as working for the Lord, not for men, since you know that you will receive an inheritance from the Lord as a reward. It is the Lord Christ you are serving.
>
> Colossians 3:22-24

Some people are working for money. Others are working for the power, recognition or the satisfaction that comes with achievement. As a believer, first and foremost, you must be working for the Lord. If you are in business solely to make money, you are not serving God.

Jesus' remark left little room for misunderstanding when he bluntly said:

> You cannot serve both God and money.
>
> Luke 16:11

Get it indelibly imprinted in your thinking, your boss is

Jesus. The new company you are starting is owned by him. He has deferred the management of the business to you, but the business is his.

If by your actions you prove trustworthy, you will qualify for more. He will see that your diligent efforts as his manager are amply rewarded.

> Whoever can be trusted with very little can be trusted with much, and whoever is dishonest with very little will also be dishonest with much.
>
> So if you have not been trustworthy in handling worldly wealth, who will trust you with true riches?
>
> And if you have not been trustworthy with someone else's property, who will give you property of your own?
>
> Luke 16:10-12

Diligence in the Home Office

Especially if your new business is home-based, the temptation may be great to treat the business in a casual way. That can prove to be a costly mistake.

Clearly identify the place in your home that will be used regularly and exclusively for your business. Make every effort to ensure that family members, especially your small children, clearly understand and respect your diligence to business.

I know a man who wears a business suit during regular

business hours even though he works out of his home making calls and writing. He says, "Psychologically the suit and tie puts me in a business frame of mind. I do not make personal calls, watch television or read a novel with my suit on. While attired in my business suit I'm psychologically at work. At 5 p.m. I change into more casual attire and, psychologically, I'm home again." Perhaps this strategy may work for you.

A Time to Act

The title of this chapter is "The Key to Making it Happen." I hope by now you know what the key is—diligent action. Your greatest personal power is the ability to act on what you learn and to put into action all you feel and know. There are so-called professional students who learn for the sake of learning. What a waste. What will make you the success you deserve to be is the consistent application and implementation of what you learn. Many have ideas and dreams but few have the faith and fortitude to act upon them.

Excelling Financially

Sadly it never occurs to many Christians that they *can* excel financially, so they never decide to do anything about it. All achievement begins with a dream of something you believe you can be, have or do. Ultimately, it becomes reality when you take action against whatever stands between you and the fulfillment of that dream.

Time Perspective

Overnight success stories usually were preceded by years

of hard work and preparation. While working on your dream, remember that those who succeed in life are generally those who have the longest "time perspective" of the future. Many people can only see and think ahead one or two pay periods. On the other hand some super-wealthy individuals think ahead in terms of decades or even generations. Think big and think long term. Grow wealthy slowly.

We live in a society that demands instant gratification. However, there is no such thing as instant success. In life as well as in business you must *grow* into success. You must not just *go* through life; you must *grow* through life. Success is not revolutionary; it is evolutionary.

Someone lamented, "It is a shame that youth is wasted on the young. When the young get old enough to know what truly counts, they're too old to do much about it." Actually, all the time you have left is the time you have left. Get on with it!

Remember that:

- Dividends always follow the investment.

- Harvest always follows planting.

- Success is preceded by diligent dedication to a plan and hard work.

If you'll become one of those rare individuals with an ability to see into the future and an ability to anticipate the awesome rewards of his or her work, don't consider the long hours. Work is a privilege and fun. This can be true for you if you have a clear goal and if you focus your strengths on what you love to do. James pointed out that faith and positive thinking won't work without positive action.

> Faith without works is dead.
>
> James 2:20

A successful person is one who is willing to do those things other people are not willing to do. Successful people probably don't like to do these tasks either but they do them anyway. You've got to believe strongly and feel deeply that what you are doing is worth it. The strength of will to force yourself to do what others don't like to do—to go the extra mile—is called self-discipline and is an important key to excelling.

Never, Never Give Up!

Determined and consistent action is the only thing that translates dreams into reality. If you can discipline yourself to consistently produce the actions necessary, you will inevitably dominate the field of success.

Colonel Sanders

Consider Colonel Sanders, the famous founder of Kentucky Fried Chicken. At age 65 he received his first Social Security check. It was $99. He looked at the check and said, "I ain't living like this." He began to consider what resources he had. He had a recipe people liked. His idea was to take his recipe and give it to restaurant owners with the provision they would give him a percent of the profits from the increase of sales resulting from the use of his recipe.

Unlike most people, he followed through on his idea. He took action. He began contacting restaurant owners. He was turned down time after time. He kept on taking action, changing his method in search of an approach that worked. He traveled across the nation, sleeping in his car. It is reported he heard 1,009 "no's" before his first "yes." Would you say he had persistence? He kept on trying until he succeeded. He learned from each situation, adjusting and modifying his approach to get the desired results. Today there is a KFC in almost every city in the United States with a population of 30,000 or more. Each one stands as a tribute to his persistence.

Ideas themselves have little or no market value, but implementors of ideas are invaluable for they are rare indeed.

The things you have learned in this book will be either a waste of the money you have paid for it or it will be one of the highest yielding investments you will ever make. Application makes the difference.

Just because you *know* the biblical verses promising success doesn't ensure your success. All of the promises of God are conditional upon positive action.

> This Book of the Law shall not depart out of thy mouth; but thou shalt meditate therein day and night that thou mayest observe to do according to all that is written therein, for then thou shalt make thy way prosperous, and then thou shalt have good success.
>
> Joshua 1:8

Taking positive action upon God's word—doing what he says—is what he promises to bless. If you are not being blessed as bountifully as you want, then ask yourself if you are giving God actions he can bless.

The first Psalm reveals a powerful secret of success:

> Blessed is the man who does not walk in the counsel of the wicked or stand in the way of sinners or sit in the seat of mockers.
>
> But his delight is in the law of the Lord and on his law he meditates day and night.
>
> He is like a tree planted by streams of water, which yields its fruit in season and whose leaf does not wither. Whatever he _does_ prospers.
>
> Psalm 1:1-3

You cannot hibernate in a prayer closet and expect God to build a business for you. You must give the Lord some action to prosper. Deal a lethal blow to the destructive habit of laziness and procrastination. Become proactive. Resolve to do something today that will begin transforming your God-inspired dream of being in business into a reality.

Give God Something to Bless

Now that you have gone through the material, the next step is yours. In the real estate industry there is a phrase that describes a person who must always have all the facts before he or she makes a move. Every contingency must be planned for, every "i" dotted and every "t" crossed. The descriptive phrase for what that person does is "analysis to paralysis."

While this person is analyzing all the facts and gathering endless data, a nimble investor jumps on the opportunity, buys the property and profits wonderfully. Later when the "analysis-to-paralysis" person is ready to submit a contract, the deal is long gone.

We must not underestimate the necessity of proper planning; but there comes a point in time when action must be taken. There must be a time when research and talk gives way to action. Solomon observed:

> Whosoever watches the wind will not plant; whoever looks at the clouds will not reap.
>
> Ecclesiastes 11:4

The reality is that no one is going to do it for you. You must take charge of your future and not let circumstances, relatives, or any other outside force dim your vision or detour you.

It should be obvious by now that starting a small business is not a get-rich-quick scheme. It requires long-term resolve. It may require you to not allow yourself the luxury of late night TV, excessive socializing or simply doing what comes easy.

You've got to *make* things happen. It requires discipline. But if you want a successful business badly enough, you'll gladly make every sacrifice required.

The Price of Failure

People talk about the "price" of success. It is true, there is a price for success. But the greater price is the price of failure; the price of doing nothing; the dreadful price of working for someone else for a lifetime and reaching retirement years "used up," tired, broke and worse, never fulfilling your unique calling in life.

In one respect life is a self-fulfilling prophecy. Most psychologists recognize that people get what they sincerely expect to get out of life. Because of the many promises in God's Word you should expect good things. Expect the success God has promised you. You may be only one idea, one dream, one person, one customer, one client or one step of faith away from the miracle and success you deserve.

Perhaps the most powerful compilation of two-letter words in the English language is:

IF IT IS TO BE, IT IS UP TO ME!

These ten two-letter words speak a world of truth. It is up to you to take faith-filled action. Remember the promise of Psalm 1:

WHATEVER HE <u>DOES</u> PROSPERS.

ORDER FORM FOR RESOURCES

ORDERED BY

Name_____
          Please print clearly
Address_____

City _____ State ___ Zip _____

Telephone (___) _____

Daytime   (___) _____

SHIP-TO ADDRESS

If different from "Ordered By" Address

Name_____

Address_____

City _____ State ___Zip_____

Telephone (___) _____

ITEMS ORDERED

Note: Products purchased for professional purposes may be tax deductible.

		Quantity

Money & the Christian Syllabus—The basic textbook
for the seminar consisting of 9 sections and supporting material
for the audio or video editions of the seminar ....$20   ____   _____

Audio Tapes of Money & the Christian Seminar (expanded)—
16 audiocassettes of Caleb McAfee's seminar combining
timeless biblical principles with timely money strategies ....$79   ____   _____

Start Your Own Business—A Christian's step-by-step guide to
successfully starting and operating a profitable business ....$25   ____   _____

Home Free!—Includes a booklet and 2 audiocassettes on how you can
have a debt-free home for the glory of God; includes a coupon for a
free personalized mortgage analysis showing suggested rapid
debt reduction strategies ....$20   ____   _____

Video Edition—10 sessions of the Money and the Christian Seminar
with Caleb McAfee on 5 videos; suitable for group presentations; includes
one *Money & the Christian* syllabus...$195   ____   _____

SUBTOTAL FROM ABOVE ....   _____

Sales tax (Texas residents, please add 8.25%) ....   _____

Shipping and handling
($7 for first item, $2 for each additional item sent to same address) ......   _____

For shipments outside USA,
add $8 to above shipping/handling and pay in U.S. funds.....................   _____

Contribution to help Caleb McAfee Ministries advance the
kingdom worldwide (tax deductible) ....   _____

TOTAL ENCLOSED ....   _____

Thank you for your order!   *Prices subject to change.*

METHOD OF PAYMENT

☐   Enclosed is my check or money order made payable to
    Money and the Christian.

☐   Please charge to: ☐ MasterCard   ☐ Visa
    Credit card account number

Exp. Date ____/____ Signature _____

SEND OR FAX YOUR ORDER

Money and the Christian
P.O. Box 153989
Irving, Texas 75015-3989

Telephone (972) 438-1234
Fax (972) 438-1448

NOTES

ORDER FORM FOR RESOURCES

ORDERED BY

Name_____
Please print clearly

Address_____

City _____ State ___ Zip _____

Telephone (___) _____

Daytime   (___) _____

SHIP-TO ADDRESS

If different from "Ordered By" Address

Name_____

Address_____

City _____ State ___ Zip _____

Telephone (___) _____

ITEMS ORDERED

Note: Products purchased for professional purposes may be tax deductible.

	Quantity	
Money & the Christian Syllabus—The basic textbook for the seminar consisting of 9 sections and supporting material for the audio or video editions of the seminar $20	_____	_____
Audio Tapes of Money & the Christian Seminar (expanded)— 16 audiocassettes of Caleb McAfee's seminar combining timeless biblical principles with timely money strategies $79	_____	_____
Start Your Own Business—A Christian's step-by-step guide to successfully starting and operating a profitable business $25	_____	_____
Home Free!—Includes a booklet and 2 audiocassettes on how you can have a debt-free home for the glory of God; includes a coupon for a free personalized mortgage analysis showing suggested rapid debt reduction strategies $20	_____	_____
Video Edition—10 sessions of the Money and the Christian Seminar with Caleb McAfee on 5 videos; suitable for group presentations; includes one *Money & the Christian* syllabus $195	_____	_____
SUBTOTAL FROM ABOVE		_____
Sales tax (Texas residents, please add 8.25%)		_____
Shipping and handling ($7 for first item, $2 for each additional item sent to same address)		_____
For shipments outside USA, add $8 to above shipping/handling and pay in U.S. funds.....................		_____
Contribution to help Caleb McAfee Ministries advance the kingdom worldwide (tax deductible)		_____
TOTAL ENCLOSED		_____

Thank you for your order!   *Prices subject to change.*

METHOD OF PAYMENT

☐ Enclosed is my check or money order made payable to **Money and the Christian.**

☐ Please charge to: ☐ MasterCard   ☐ Visa
Credit card account number

Exp. Date ___/___ Signature _____

SEND OR FAX YOUR ORDER

Money and the Christian
P.O. Box 153989
Irving, Texas 75015-3989

Telephone (972) 438-1234
Fax (972) 438-1448

NOTES

NOTES

NOTES